BOLIVIA

Bolivia
Refounding the Nation

Kepa Artaraz

PlutoPress
www.plutobooks.com

First published 2012 by Pluto Press
345 Archway Road, London N6 5AA

www.plutobooks.com

Distributed in the United States of America exclusively by
Palgrave Macmillan, a division of St. Martin's Press LLC,
175 Fifth Avenue, New York, NY 10010

British Library Cataloguing in Publication Data
A catalogue record for this book is available from the British Library

ISBN 978 0 7453 3090 7   Hardback
ISBN 978 0 7453 3089 1   Paperback
ISBN 978 1 84964 661 1   PDF
ISBN 978 1 84964 663 5   Kindle
ISBN 978 1 84964 662 8   ePub

Library of Congress Cataloging in Publication Data applied for

This book is printed on paper suitable for recycling and made from fully managed and
sustained forest sources. Logging, pulping and manufacturing processes are expected to
conform to the environmental standards of the country of origin.

10 9 8 7 6 5 4 3 2 1

Designed and produced for Pluto Press by Curran Publishing Services, Norwich
Simultaneously printed digitally by CPI Group (UK) Ltd., Croydon, CR0 4YY and
Edwards Bros in the United States of America

CONTENTS

ACKNOWLEDGEMENTS

This book would not have been possible without the help, conscious or not, of many people both in Bolivia and elsewhere. In Bolivia, many people are unaware – as I was myself at the time – of just how much our conversations influenced my understanding of the historic events I was fortunate enough to witness on more than one occasion. Their names are many and I will not list them all, but they include, in no particular order, James (el Jimmy) Blackburn and Cecilia (la Ceci) Córdova, Iñigo Retolaza, Pablo Regalski and Maria Teresa Hosse. I am also most grateful to Ann Chaplin and José Pimentel, who fed both my body and my mind on a regular basis, as did Roxana Liendo and Héctor Córdova. All of them have privileged observation points for understanding Bolivia's current process of change, and were generous enough to informally share their views with me on many occasions.

The Fundación Xabier Albó (http://www.fxa.org.bo/) holds the largest social science library in Bolivia and fulfils a heroic role compiling and democratising access to research materials. I want to pay tribute to Lola Paredes and Marcelo in the library for the day-to-day struggle that goes into keeping alive the best source of Bolivian academic production. It was a privilege working with them, and I hope their efforts are soon repaid with the funds they need to keep this treasure illuminating our understanding of Bolivia.

This book aims to politically 'translate' Bolivia's social and political reality to a new, broader audience in the global north, in the hope that novel experiences in the global south can contribute to our questioning of key concepts like democracy, participation, well-being and development, as a small step towards achieving cognitive justice.[1]

Many people were instrumental in my getting close to the Bolivian climate change platform, a microcosm of the blurred relations between civil society and government institutions. I would like to thank the many people from the Bolivian indigenous social movements, national non-governmental organisations (NGOs) like the Centro de Investigación y Promoción del Campesinado (CIPCA), the Centro de Comunicación y Desarrollo Andino (CENDA), Agua Sustentable and Fundación Solón, and international NGOs Christian Aid, Cafod, Trocaire and Oxfam, for opening their doors to me and helping me glimpse at the pioneering work they are carrying out in Bolivia, warts and all.

Two of the 88 women elected as members of the constitutional assembly deserve special mention: Rosalía del Villar (MAS, El Alto), and Ana Maria Ruiz (MNR, Beni). I thank them for their time and for the honest commitment to their country that they demonstrated in their own ways. My thanks go also to Nila Heredia, a medically trained health minister who recognises that health policy is far too important to be left solely in the hands of doctors. Raquel Romero from Colectivo Cabildeo, Soledad Domínguez, Patricia Costas, Patrick Vanier and Julio Peñaloza Bretel were generous enough to give me copies of their own excellent documentaries on the constitutional assembly, which would otherwise have been difficult to access. Gaby Barriga and Marco were not only instrumental in gaining me access to the vice-minister of pensions and other key commentators, but remain close friends, as are Pablo and Yumy. I hope to see them all soon to put the world right over a caipicoca or two at Pablo's bar Etno in Calle Jaén.

Closer to home, the Bolivian Information Forum headed by Alex Tilley provided multiple analyses of Bolivia's critical junctures, and opportunities for visiting the presidential palace and ministries as an interpreter, which initially fed my appetite for trying to understand this fascinating country. In a similar way, regular dinners with Pierre Nouvellet and with Mei López-Trueba keep this hunger alive, especially through Mei's understanding of the micropolitics in Potosi and of the (short) life of the miner. A number of anonymous reviewers provided insightful comments in the early and final stages of this project. I would like to thank them all for their insights and generosity. Any merits in this book are in no small measure down to them. The limitations are however entirely my own.

Finally I would like to thank my family in Antwerp, Puy L'Evêque, Bilbao, and those who in Bolivia have become family, like Naty, Cielito and Kwenty. My most sincere thank you has to go to my wife Karen, who years ago took me to visit those Bolivian places (and people in Viloco, Urubichá, Puerto San Borja, Salvatierra and more) that were so formative in her youth and would shape her character and values. I hope I can repay her generosity of spirit by being able to understand and love her even more as a result.

ACRONYMS AND ABBREVIATIONS

ACLO   Acción Cultural Loyola (Loyola Cultural Action)
ADN   Acción Democrática Nacionalista (Democratic
            Nationalist Action)
ALBA   Alternativa Bolivariana para las Américas (Bolivarian
            Alternative for the Americas)
ATPDEA   Andean Trade Promotion and Drug Eradication Act
BONOSOL   Bono Solidario
BRICS   Brazil, Russia, India, China and South Africa
CAFOD   Catholic Agency for Overseas Development
CAN   Comunidad Andina de Naciones (Andean
            Community of Nations)
CAOI   Coordinadora Andina de Organizaciones Indígenas
            (Andean Network of Indigenous Organisations)
CEDIB   Centro de Documentación e Información de Bolivia
            (Bolivian Documentation and Information Centre)
CEJIS   Centro de Estudios Jurídicos e Investigación Social
            (Centre for Legal and Social Research)
CENDA   Centro de Comunicación y Desarrollo Andino
            (Andean Development and Communication Centre)
CEPS   Centro de Estudios Políticos y Sociales (Centre for
            Political and Social Studies)
CIDOB   Confederación Indígena del Oriente Boliviano
            (Indigenous Federation of Eastern Bolivia)
CIPCA   Centro de Investigación y Promoción del
            Campesinado (Peasant Research and Promotion
            Centre)
CNE   Corte Nacional Electoral (National Electoral Court)
CNMCIOB   Confederación Nacional de Mujeres Campesinas
  'BS'   Indígenas Originarias de Bolivia 'Bartolina Sisa'
            (Bartolina Sisa Federation of Indigenous Peasant
            Women of Bolivia)
COB   Central Obrera Boliviana (Trade Unions Federation)
COMCIPO   Comité Cívico de Potosí (Civic Committee of Potosi)

COMIBOL   Corporación Minera de Bolivia (Bolivian Mining
          Corporation)
CONALDE   Consejo Nacional de Defensa de la Democracia
          (National Council for the Defence of Democracy)
CONAMAQ Consejo Nacional de Ayllus y Markas del
          Qullasuyu (National Council of Ayllus and Markas
          of Qullasuyu)
CONDEPA   Conciencia de Patria (Conscience of the Fatherland)
CSCB   Confederación Sindical de Colonizadores de Bolivia
          (Federation of Bolivian Settlers' Union)
CSCIB   Confederación Sindical de Comunidades
          Interculturales de Bolivia (Federation of Bolivian
          Intercultural Communities)
CSUTCB   Confederación Sindical Única de Trabajadores
          Campesinos de Bolivia (Federation of Bolivian
          Peasant Workers)
DfID   (UK) Department for International Development
EBIH   Empresa Boliviana para la Industrialización de los
          Hidrocarburos (Bolivian Enterprise for the
          Industrialisation of Hydrocarbons)
ECLAC   Economic Commission for Latin America and the
          Caribbean
EGTK   Ejército Guerrillero Tupaj Katari (Tupaj Katari
          Guerrilla Army)
EMAPA   Empresa de Apoyo a la Producción de Alimentos
          (National Company for the Support of Food
          Production)
ENDE   Empresa Nacional de Electricidad (National
          Electricity Company)
ENFE   Empresa Nacional de Ferrocarriles (National Rail
          Company)
ENTEL   Empresa Nacional de Telecomunicaciones (National
          Telecommunications Company)
ESF   Emergency Social Fund
EU   European Union
FARC   Fuerzas Armadas Revolucionarias de Colombia
          (Colombian Revolutionary Armed Forces)
FEJUVE   Federación de Juntas Vecinales (Federation of
          Neighbourhood Committees)
FRUTCAS   Federación Regional Única de los Trabajadores
          Campesinos del Altiplano Sud (Regional Federation
          of South Highland Peasant Workers)

FSTMB	Federación Sindical Única de Trabajadores de la Minería Bolivianos (Federation of Bolivian Mining Workers)
FTAA	Free Trade Agreement of the Americas
HIPC	heavily indebted poor country
IDB	Interamerican Development Bank
IDH	Impuesto Directo a los Hidrocarburos (direct tax on hydrocarbons)
IFIs	international financial institutions
ILO	International Labour Organization
IMF	International Monetary Fund
INGO	international non-governmental organisation
INRA	Instituto Nacional de Reforma Agraria (National Institute of Agrarian Reform)
ISI	import substitution industrialisation
IU	Izquierda Unida (United Left)
LAB	Lloyd Aéreo Boliviano (Bolivian National Airline)
LASC	Latin American Security Council
LDCs	Less Developed Countries
LPP	Ley de Participación Popular (Law of Popular Participation)
MAS	Movimiento al Socialismo (Movement towards Socialism)
MBL	Movimiento Bolivia Libre (Free Bolivia Movement)
MDG	Millennium Development Goals
MDRI	Multilateral Debt Relief Initiative
MERCOSUR	Mercado del Sur (Market of the South)
MIP	Movimiento Indígena Pachakuti (Indigenous Pachakuti Movement)
MIR	Movimiento de Izquierda Revolucionario (Left Revolutionary Movement)
MNR	Movimiento Nacional Revolucionario (Revolutionary National Movement)
MRTKL	Movimiento Revolucionario Tupac Katari de Liberación (Tupac Katari Revolutionary Movement of Liberation)
MST	Movimiento Sin Tierra (Landless Movement)
NACLA	North American Congress on Latin America
NAFTA	North American Free Trade Agreement
NEP	new economic policy
NFR	Nueva Fuerza Republicana (New Republican Force)
NGO	non-governmental organisation

OAS   Organisation of American States
OPEC   Organisation of Petroleum Exporting Countries
OTB   Organizaciones Territoriales de Base (Territorial Base
           Organisations)
Oxfam   Oxford Committee for Famine Relief
PIIGS   Portugal, Ireland, Italy, Greece and Spain
PND   Plan Nacional de Desarrollo (National Development
           Plan)
PODEMOS   Poder Democrático y Social (Social and Democratic
           Power)
PP-CN   Plan Progreso-Convergencia Nacional (Progress and
           National Convergence Plan)
PRI   Partido Revolucionario Institucional (Institutional
           Revolutionary Party)
SAP   structural adjustment programme
SEDUCA   Servicio Departamental de Educación (Departmental
           Education Authority)
SMEs   small and medium-sized enterprises
SOA   School of the Americas
TIPNIS   Territorio Indígena Parque Nacional Isiboro-Sécure
           (Isiboro-Sécure Indigenous Territory and National
           Park)
TNCs   transnational corporations
UCS   Unidad Cívica Solidaridad (Solidarity Civic Union)
UDAPE   Unidad de Análisis de Políticas Económicas y Sociales
           (Centre for Social, Political and Economic Analysis)
UN-REDD   United Nations Reducing Emissions from
           Deforestation and Degradation in Developing
           Countries Programm
UNASUR   Unión de Naciones del Sur (Union of Southern
           Nations)
UNDP   United Nations Development Programme
UNESCO   United Nations Education, Scientific and Cultural
           Organization
UNFCCC   United Nations Framework Convention on Climate
           Change
UNITAR   United Nations Institute for Training and Research
WB   World Bank
WOLA   Washington Office on Latin America
WTO   World Trade Organization
YPFB   Yacimientos Petrolíferos Fiscales Bolivianos (Bolivian
           oil company)

Bolivia

INTRODUCTION
Bolivia: Refounding the nation

Long live motherland Bolivia,
a great nation,
for her I give my life
and also my heart.
    (Traditional Cueca song)

Aerial pictures on television showed the many columns of marchers, each of them thousands strong, approaching the city of La Paz. They had travelled from as far as the departments of Beni and Pando in the lowlands, from some of the major cities like Cochabamba and Sucre in the valleys, and from every corner of the Bolivian *altiplano*. It was October 20, 2008, and a historic day for La Paz, not only because that day marked the 460th anniversary of the city, but because this date will be remembered as the day when one of the biggest political marches in Bolivia's history descended on La Paz from every corner of the country. Organised and mobilised by grass-roots organisations and social movements, hundreds of thousands of indigenous and peasant Bolivians were making their way to the country's seat of government to demand from Congress a law that would give every citizen the opportunity to decide, through their vote in a referendum, whether or not they approved of the draft new constitution which had been finalised weeks earlier.

The threat of this massive march descending on La Paz had been hanging fire for a number of weeks, as politicians found it increasingly difficult to agree to call the referendum on the new constitution, something that required the support of the opposition as well as the government. Justifying the growing sense of disillusionment and cynicism with formal politics that pervades Bolivians, and increasingly citizens all over the world, opposition politicians had been using every trick in the book to delay the inevitable, hoping for some last-minute miracle to stop the radical process of change that began when Evo Morales was elected Bolivia's new president in the general elections of December 2005.

For their part, those well-to do-middle-class *paceños*, as residents from La Paz are known, who support the political opposition and live in the leafy lower parts of the city in the trendy *zona sur*, were terrified about the possibility of invasion by 'hordes' of 'indios', as they disparagingly refer to indigenous Bolivians. 'It is a disgrace that the government allows these dirty Indians to enter the city and hold Congress to ransom', went a typical rant from an otherwise respectable middle-class woman. Many are oblivious to the racist nature of such comments, since the fear of an indigenous uprising is deeply embedded in the national psyche of a nation born with the original sin of racist oppression.

This does not mean that indigenous uprisings have not taken place before in Bolivian history. On the contrary, during 1781 an army of indigenous Aymara people, led by Túpac Katari and his wife Bartolina Sisa, took over the area where the city of El Alto now sits overlooking La Paz, and laid siege to the city for 180 days, in what constituted the biggest challenge to the Spanish who then controlled Bolivia. They fed a sense of paranoia among certain sections of the population which lasts to this day, and which, in its modern guise, warned anyone who would listen of the violent confrontations and chaos that would befall the city with the arrival of these uninvited guests.

With these thoughts in my mind and sensing the historical significance of the images being shown on my television screen, I headed for the Plaza Murillo, walking, for lack of transport in a paralysed city, the 20-block distance from the popular neighbourhood of Sopocachi to the destination point of over half a million marchers.

CHANGE IS IN THE AIR

I had arrived in the country only a few months previously, and nothing had prepared me for what I would witness that night. The sheer size of the march was difficult to fathom. The first marchers had arrived at their destination at midday, but many more were still pouring in to the city nine hours later. Men, women and children, they came dressed in uniforms and national costume, each community, organisation or collective group headed by a banner announcing its affiliation, marching, chanting and in some cases dancing, to the tune of slogans and their own musical bands as well as to the applause of equally numerous bystanders. With *wiphalas* (an indigenous multicoloured flag) in their hands and their babies on their backs, women attired in every regional dress conceivable were being led by groups of men in red ponchos, carrying their symbols of community leadership status and power in the form of whips made of leather. In spite of their sandals – made of recycled car tyres, they betrayed real material poverty – a joyous dignity and sense of historic responsibility, unseen before in Bolivia, united all those who converged on Plaza Murillo that night.

I ended up barely 10 metres from the stage where the president stood, which was in the corner of the square between *el palacio quemado* (the name of the presidential palace is literally 'the burned palace', and somebody did indeed try to burn it down in 1875) and the Congress building. Crucially, he was positioned behind a front row of popular leaders representing the miners, the five main peasant and indigenous people's organisations, and all manner of grassroots movements, giving symbolic credence to the argument that the government was one of social movements. He only came to the front to take the microphone from time to time, as a succession of musical groups, community leaders and politicians converted the evening into a mixture of demonstration, political meeting and party all rolled into one. However, Evo Morales was clearly the hot ticket of the night, and when he came to the front to speak, conversations died down and thousands turned their attention to the stage.

The president told his people how they were making history that night because they had at last taken control of their own country and its destiny. He told them they were the new masters in a country that barely 50 years ago would not have permitted them, as indigenous people, to set foot in that square. And he told them that the will of the people would impose itself in spite of last-minute attempts by some 'snakes' inside Congress to derail the process of change and return Bolivia to a past that had always oppressed them. Every now and then he would stop his improvised speech – Morales rarely uses anything more than a few notes when addressing the masses at home – to welcome individual communities and thank them for coming. 'A big welcome to the community of Guaqui', he would say, and the square would erupt in cheers. 'Thank you to the miners from Huanuni for their presence here tonight', and a sea of miners' tin hats would rise above the crowd in salute.

The new constitution on which this multitude demanded the

right to express their view had taken two years to write, caused a number of deaths, and contributed to a politically explosive period of Bolivia's recent history. The president reminded his audience that the constitution marked several firsts for the country. For starters, it had been written by the people through a process of participation, to a level that few countries can boast of. More importantly, it was a constitution that would frame the process for Bolivia's refoundation, because it guaranteed the equality and participation of all Bolivians in society, including the historically marginalised indigenous majority. The constitution also recognised the many nations that made up the country of Bolivia, along with their cultures, languages and political traditions, creating a state structure that provided for high levels of decentralisation of resources, and crucially of power. The new constitutional text recognised a diversity of modes of economic activity (community-based, cooperative, private), various forms of autonomous government – including autonomies that would guarantee the cultural reproduction possibilities of indigenous groups – and a number of economic and social rights that would protect vulnerable groups in society and uphold the state ownership of key natural resources for the benefit of the people.[1] 'Hoooorahhhh!' went the cries of the congregated masses, who, as if choreographed, would break into spontaneous chanting of 'Cambio, cambio, cambio!' (change, change, change!).

As I was leaving the setting of this historic event to go to sleep at around 2 am, the sit-in continued in the stage area. I was amazed to find the back of the square full of marchers who had arranged themselves in circles and were preparing to set camp and sleep on the cold pavement. Lying on the blanket-covered ground, they were discussing what for many had been a ten-day-long march. Chewing coca leaves to fight hunger, tiredness and the bitter cold nights of La Paz, they struck me as a new breed of politically committed activists with a clarity of purpose and direction that has long since died in our own, older democracies in the global north.

The wait for the debate in Congress to end was long and painful, and by the early hours of the morning it had tested the patience of many, including the thousands of miners present at the vigil. Armed with dynamite, they threatened to storm the Congress building and take it by force. The president himself had to appeal to the civility of all those congregated to avoid deaths. He argued that since the indigenous people had been able to wait through 500 years of oppression, they could well show the patience needed to let Congress finish its task in a matter of hours or days.

I woke up seven hours later to learn from the television that the crowds were still in place, demonstrating their resolve to not leave until Congress agreed to their demand. The president was still on the stage where I had seen him the night before. He would remain there, with his people, keeping a vigil that lasted more than 30 hours, until he received the message that finally a referendum had been called for. The deal had been extracted from the opposition after last-minute concessions. One of the biggest concessions – and one that demonstrates Morales' political stature as president – was an agreement that a president could seek re-election only once, while the draft constitution had provided for a maximum of three terms of office. (Morales would seek re-election in December 2009.)

Around 2 pm on October 21, the vice-president Alvaro García Linera emerged from the debating chamber. He came to the stage in the square, escorted by thousands of cheering people, holding in his hands the text of the law calling for the referendum, which had been passed by Congress minutes earlier. And as befits a government of social movements, the president signed the document, making it law, in front of the cheering crowd of thousands. This ushered in a new political phase in Bolivia's turbulent history.[2] The possibility of change had come at last, in spite of the attempts to derail the process by the last remaining oligarchs with political representation.

POLITICS WITH A DIFFERENCE

It is difficult to imagine a more politically different Bolivia from the one that had persisted until recently. As the twentieth century drew to a close, there began to take shape a continent-wide shift to the left, which followed in the wake of failed neoliberal forms of economic development. It appeared that the instigators of this new Latin America were those historically voiceless majorities and marginal groups of the population who had finally constituted themselves as political agents. The masses of poor and the indigenous majority in Bolivia certainly fit this definition, creating a new plebeian political actor.[3] They were determined, as the episode from October 2008 shows, to make their newly found voice count. In Bolivia, this process of change is turning out to have a number of unique features, creating radical new forms of political commitment which this book aims to explain.

What should we make of this mass commitment to politics? It is certainly a kind of politics with a difference when, in the face of a major national demonstration, the president, instead of sending the army to suppress it and shoot at any demonstrators who refused to leave, as his predecessors would have done, joins his people, heading the march to La Paz to demand action from the country's lawmakers. We are witnessing a different kind of politics when the president sits behind the social movements' leaders and asks them to correct him if he ever loses direction, or speaks about his need to lead a radical process of change by obeying the voice of the people, by 'leading while obeying', as Morales is often quoted as saying in his speeches. For the millions around the world who have lost all faith in the practices that pass for politics in liberal democracies and actively 'hate politics',[4] this is little short of incredible. It is also refreshingly hopeful, as we see a strong link between those who govern and the governed. For me it brought flooding back images of the early days of the Cuban revolution, in which Fidel Castro would address large crowds for hours on end, developing a conversational tone to his speeches. Sympathetic foreign observers tried to describe this as a form of direct democracy.[5] Things are hardly ever so simple, but this book aims to follow, explain and assess this process of change in its painful complexity and its internal contradictions.

It is claimed that Evo Morales has cried in public twice during his political life. The first time was on January 21, 2006. A former llama herder turned coca grower, the son of indigenous Bolivians, he had just received from his running mate and vice-president the sash in the colours of the national flag that formally invested the presidency upon him. That such a man could ever become president in a country like Bolivia is a testament to the enormous degree of social and political change that has taken place in this country during the period of history covered by this book. The second time Morales cried was when he signed the referendum law, standing in front of thousands, tired and overwhelmed by the historic significance of the last day's events. The political tsunami of the poor that he represented had come out victorious. Nothing could seemingly stand on the way of a new Bolivia.

The process of writing the new Bolivian constitution has been likened to a very long pregnancy and painful delivery.[6] It featured two years of work by the 255 Constitutional Assembly members elected for the purpose, deliberate attempts to derail the entire process, provocations and violent deaths, calls for civil disobedience, and media manipulation: sections of the mass media attempted to delegitimise the debates taking place in Sucre. The government also made mistakes when, facing the possibility of civil war in September 2008, it negotiated with the regional leaders of the opposition and conceded many of their demands for specific changes to the draft text of the constitution. This process of last-minute tampering continued in Congress for a number of weeks. Violent and messy, the process of producing a new constitution for a new Bolivia had been imperfect in both its form and its content. However, the text was (and is) the closest thing achievable to a vision of Bolivia that includes every sector of society, just as all were represented in the drafting process. At last the constitution had been born, a baby constitution that would receive its birth certificate through the referendum that approved it on January 25, 2009.

A NEW ERA: ABOUT THIS BOOK

The reason why the particular episode recounted in these pages is important is that the approval of the new Bolivian constitution closes a political era and opens a new one. This book is about the transition to this new era, concentrating on the political process that has taken the country to this point, and on the content and form taken by this new vision of Bolivia as it is specified in the country's new constitution. Besides explaining the meaning of what is a coherent set of discursive narratives and a unique set of ideological principles, the book is also about separating these aspirations from their realisation, in the form of policies and the changes they are delivering to the daily lives of Bolivians. Indeed, if there is a constant element that has been maintained in the process of national rebirth that the Movimiento al Socialismo (MAS) government claims to be constructing, it is precisely the gap that remains between lofty political aspirations on the one hand and the unchanging nature of people's everyday lives.

The starting point for this book is the return of democracy in 1982 after the long interlude of military rule that frustrated the hopes generated by the 1952 revolution. 1982 proved to be a false dawn. It was hoped that freedom and political participation for all would usher in a new era of well-being for Bolivians. Yet it seems clear now that although 1982 did not immediately lead to this, it was the start of a new political path, in search of a definition of the type of society most Bolivians wanted to see in their country. Two main promises had implicitly been part of the democratic dream that officially began in 1982.

The first, explored in Chapter 1, follows the economic ups and downs of a country that for the two decades following the return of democracy was dominated, along with the rest of Latin America, by neoliberal economic policies. In the 1980s a serious economic downturn led to a process of hyperinflation, lack of economic growth, budgetary deficits and a mountain of debt. The economic recipe for solving these problems came from North American academic circles in the form of monetarist policies. Bolivia was in this respect a testing ground for the idea that economic stabilisation could be achieved by means of structural adjustment policies imposed from the outside. This economic model fed on the neoliberal thinking that had been inaugurated in Chile back in the 1970s during the Pinochet dictatorship. It was then extended in the 1990s with the wholesale privatisation of companies and public assets, as part of a trend followed in much of Latin America, with disastrous socioeconomic consequences for the vast majority of the population, who at the end of this period were more likely to be poor and jobless than they had been at the beginning of it.

The second promise implicit in the 1982 return to democracy was contained precisely in the term 'democracy'. An imported element of the democratisation process, the model of liberal democracy and management that had generated so much hope in the population after years of dictatorship failed during the next two decades to live up to its promise. Not only did the system not generate participation from the population, it produced a corrupt elite bent on sharing the spoils of office, and a generalised public disenchantment with politics. It appeared that little had been achieved to liberate Bolivia from the politically corrosive elements of illegitimate military governments, which had for years acted with impunity, repressing the population. Had the political victims of dictatorship, those illegally incarcerated, the tortured and disappeared, the tens of thousands in exile, died in vain?

This double crisis of legitimacy led to a fundamental questioning of the model of society and its management that had been bequeathed to Bolivia. The political questioning and the proposed alternatives did not come from traditional forces and actors from the left, such as trade unions, as they had been decimated by the neoliberal attack. It came instead from those excluded by the previous system, political actors who incorporated a coalition of peasants, the indigenous movement emerging in the 1980s and 1990s, the coca growers' trade unions where the current president's political origins can be located, and the poor urban masses. The result is a radically new form of politics led by non-traditional actors, who in 2005 were tasked by the electorate with recreating society in new and original ways.

This book also explores the extent to which the crisis of the old political and economic model has resulted in progress towards the type of society envisaged by the current political leadership. Taking the new Bolivian constitution as its central theme, we explore the nature of the political process in Bolivia. In particular, we concentrate on a discussion of the process by which the new constitution was written, a process that permits us to analyse the quintessential characteristics of Bolivia's new participatory forms of politics and their limitations in practice.

A central section of the book is devoted to assessing the real changes that have taken place in Bolivia since the election of Evo Morales, and the extent to which these reflect the aspirations contained in the new constitutional text. First, we concentrate on the increasingly blurred relationship between the state and civil society, with an emphasis on the way in which the institutions of the state have been taken over by social movements and the new role of 'social control' that has been assigned to them, effectively overseeing government activities and performance. In relation to the constitution, the book also explores the new Bolivian state structure, which includes many layers of devolution and decentralisation, posing a number of questions about the likely scenarios and possibilities for conflict that are created by this.

Another key theme running through the heart of Bolivia's current process of change is that of indigenous politics and citizenship. The book follows the development of a strong indigenous movement, and maps out how the formation of this new political actor has resulted in the incorporation into Bolivian society of what had been an excluded majority. Specific elements of this incorporation that stand out can be seen in the new description of Bolivia as a country of many nations that incorporates new social rights at both individual and collective levels. Does the new constitution at last mark the end of an unapologetically racist country, or will its ambitions be curtailed by a society less prone to radical change that might have been assumed at first sight?

An area of significance in the constitution for which the multinational vision of the state is highly relevant is that of Bolivia's new model of development. Like most of Latin America, Bolivia had periods of dominant state-led forms of development followed by a textbook case of neoliberal reform that did not deliver in economic or social terms. Part of this book's aims is to assess the model of development that is now being followed by the country and is specified in the new constitutional text. It is a development model that emphasises a strong state which plays a role in the exploitation and management of natural resources, aided by indigenous communities, but without compromising the role of markets and private property. Does this halfway position deliver in its aims or, as its critics of the right claim, will it create a new Cuba in the Andes? Alternatively, does the economic model being proposed fail to respect the fundamental principles of respect for Mother Earth, and irreparably damage relations between the government and the social movements whose support keeps it in power?

Moving beyond Bolivia's borders, the book takes a look at the regional and international implications of the country's process of change in two further chapters. Given the importance of the United States to Latin America's development and politics since the Monroe Doctrine, it is not surprising that the election of Morales to the Bolivian presidency caused ripples in this relationship. Picking on familiar themes such as the historic US domination of Bolivia and the war on drugs, this part of the book ends with an assessment of current relations with Obama's US administration, much changed from the Bush era.

The international implications of Bolivia's current process of change are also explored in a consideration of the regional expansion of some of the ideological principles that dominate in Bolivia. These principles are the legacy of twentieth-century revolutionary movements which unashamedly took their cue from Cuba, and they extend to the entire region through Bolivia's participation in the Bolivarian Alternative for the Americas (ALBA), together with Venezuela, Ecuador, Paraguay and other countries. Chapter 8 explores the role of ALBA in regional politics but pays particular attention to the role it is playing in the development of a coherent social policy inside Bolivia, examining the specific interventions of Cuban solidarity in this regard.

I write six years after Evo Morales stood outside the Tiwanaku ruins close to Lake Titikaka in January 2006, and was invested as president of Bolivia in an indigenous ceremony. During that period much has changed in the country. A particular change of mentality appears to provide a new opportunity to take control of the vast natural riches, which should be a blessing to the country, but which have in fact been more of a curse since the times of the Spanish Conquest. Will the new era that began with new constitution deliver the vision of a fairer and more equitable society demanded by the majority, or will the many unresolved tensions of the past return to haunt Bolivia's future?[7]

In spite of the increasing political violence of 2007–8, the resounding victory of MAS in the first elections to take place under the new constitution in December 2009 gave the party of government the green light to deepen the process of change and put this process on a more solid footing than ever before. This book tries to understand both the path to this point and the likely future scenarios. Bolivia constitutes an interesting case study because, as with Cuba before it, the country represents an example of what is possible in societies that do not follow the liberal western model. Instead they bring into question our culturally specific forms of understanding, often taken for granted, about what is (and should be) the best way to conduct politics and develop democracy, what is the best model for economic activity, and the values that should inform our daily relationships.

In earlier writings I discussed the dominant interpretations of the Cuban Revolution that emerged from New Left circles in Europe and North America during the 1960s. I argued that a hierarchy of relations developed during the intellectual exchanges between Cuba and its northern supporters, who expected Cuba to follow the path prescribed by their own theoretical models.[8] These exchanges were in this sense an extension of 'colonial' north–south relations. This book attempts to make the opposite journey. It describes some of the political, social and economic events in Bolivia's current process of change, and attempts to make sense of them for readers of the global north by politically 'translating' them, taking as its starting point what has been termed as a 'southern epistemology' to build a bridge of understanding with northern audiences.[9]

The current Bolivian process of change challenges our thinking on citizenship, political participation, development and more. It challenges existing hierarchies of knowledge in an act of resistance built on the audacity to think differently. It is in the spirit of cognitive justice as an ethical framework on which to build knowledge systems that do not result in forms of oppression that this book has been written.

1 THE ECONOMIC BIRTH PAINS OF POOR COUNTRIES

'Refounding the nation' is an expression commonly used by the current Movimiento al Socialismo (MAS) (Movement towards Socialism) government of Bolivia to describe its political project. Refounding the nation is the national project for a government whose official political discourse mixes traditional Marxist language, indigenous liberationist concepts and anti-imperialist rhetoric to describe the situation of a country that suffered 500 years of colonialism and plunder. This plundering, the discourse goes, was carried out first by the Spanish conquerors, then in the twentieth century by the United States and the transnational corporations that represent the economic interests of a global capitalist elite.

This long night of oppression and Bolivia's marginal position in the family of nations are often blamed for the appalling socioeconomic inequalities that continue to dominate Bolivian society, the marginalisation and exclusion of large sectors of society, the country's historic chronic political instability and its lack of progress towards delivering minimum levels of well-being to the population at large. Only in recent times have we seen Bolivia emerging from this situation through a process often described as a 'revolution in democracy'. This political process is quite different from previous revolutionary situations in twentieth-century Latin America, including the 1952 Bolivian revolution. In addition, the current process of change can be seen as part of a much wider continental political turn to the left and contestation of dominant political and economic models.

This book attempts to make sense of the current process of change, which has been brought about by the MAS government since the historic election of Evo Morales as president of Bolivia on 18 December 2005. In his first speech as president, Morales hailed the 'end of the colonial and neoliberal era'.[1] This book explores the meaning of this statement, and follows the country's social, political

13

and economic changes in all their vicissitudes since the accession of MAS to power. In the first part of the book, Chapters 1 and 2 outline the origins of this process of change, origins that have to be found in the double failure, economic and political, to fulfil the promises that the formal return to democracy offered in 1982. The history of plunder of the country's resources and the poverty that followed is the history of Bolivia.

FIVE HUNDRED YEARS OF PLUNDER?

What was once called the 'imperial city' of Potosí sits in the Bolivian *altiplano* at over 14,000 feet. It is one of the poorest cities in the poorest department of Bolivia, itself one of the poorest countries of Latin America. One single economic activity, which began in the 1500s shortly after the arrival of Spanish conquerors, continues to dominate to this day: mining. The income gained through the exploitation of tin from the unnaturally perfect cone that is the Cerro Rico barely feeds a population of around 130,000 people today. But things were not always like this. At its height in the mid-seventeenth century, Potosí was one of the biggest cities in the world, with a population as large as London. The reason for this was the rich silver deposits that lay beneath the mountain, extracted in such quantities that some say it would have been enough to build a bridge of silver between the city and the centre of the Spanish empire that Bolivian silver fed for centuries. This is how Eduardo Galeano describes the city of Potosí in one of his best-known books:

> The sword and the cross marched together in the conquest and plunder of Latin America, and captains and ascetics, knights and evangelists, soldiers and monks, came together in Potosí to help themselves to its silver. Moulded into cones and ingots, the viscera of the Cerro Rico – the rich hill – substantially fed the development of Europe.[2]

If we believe Galeano, the history of Bolivia is very like the history of the rest of Latin America, and indeed of much of the poor Global South. In *Open Veins of Latin America,* Galeano effectively popularised the case made by the development of underdevelopment school, applying it to the Latin American continent. He described Potosí as the first link in the chain of exploitation imposed by the colonial masters in the sixteenth century, which would fund much of Europe's development for the next two centuries. Theories of development might be open to debate, but it is clear that Bolivia is a good example of a resource-rich country whose resources have made countless others rich, but have rarely benefited the population of the country as a whole.

The reasons for Bolivia's peculiar economic development (or underdevelopment) must be found in the country's history, and in the relations with other countries that have characterised it. The colonial experience of plunder vividly described by Galeano brought Bolivia to high levels of involvement in the global economy. When the country became independent in the nineteenth century, its role in the global economy was already well established, and subsequently Bolivia continued to pursue a model of development based on the export of raw materials, mostly mineral resources, as part of an enclave economy. In other words, its national economy played a role in a larger system which meant that although its activities were highly profitable, they did not deliver prosperity to the country as a whole, or even to rural communities geographically close to the mines.[3]

This is apparent for example in the history of Bolivian rail transport. High levels of investment were made in building railways, including much private investment by mining companies themselves. The rail system that emerged effectively brought the mines closer to the seaports, and made mineral exports easier and cheaper. Bolivia's first railway line, completed in 1892, linked Oruro and Uyuni with the Chilean seaport of Antofagasta.[4] The system was much less well suited to internal passenger transport. It did not provide effective links between Bolivia's cities, or constitute a good base on which to build a national rail network.

The large-scale mechanised exploitation of silver and tin deposits in mines like those near Potosí, and Siglo XX in the town of Llallagua, brought enormous wealth to a small class of capitalists. Simón Patiño, for example, was a Bolivian tin baron who became one of the world's richest men in the early part of the 1900s. But the country as a whole failed to benefit from this bonanza. Millions were squandered in the conspicuous consumption of imported luxury goods by a tiny elite. In the early 1900s imports included Oregon pine, German mining equipment, caviar, fine lace, cashmere wool, and basic foodstuffs. These used the transportation network that had been established to export minerals, and in the process they hindered the local production of agricultural and manufactured goods and the emergence of local markets.[5] Following the neoliberal economic ravages of the mid-1980s, 'cooperativist' miners at Siglo XX have reverted to back-breaking manual methods for the extraction and refinement of minerals. Poverty reigns today, and the era of rich imports is long gone.

In these respects, the Bolivian economy was much like many others in Latin America. From the late nineteenth century onwards, these economies achieved a high level of integration into international markets which delivered an export model of growth. It was typically based on single type of commodity – in Bolivia's case, minerals – and as a result was prone to boom and bust cycles in response to fluctuations in international prices. In parallel with this export-led economic activity, most of Bolivia's rural majority at the time of independence and until the 1952 revolution was engaged in agricultural production, in the form of either subsistence agriculture or small-scale production in haciendas.[6] In this Bolivia differed from most of Latin America, where the expansion of the hacienda system responded to the increasing demand for agricultural products from Europe and the growing value of land. Bolivia was very slow to insert agriculture into the export model of economic development, and 90 per cent of the country's exports in the 1960s continued to be in the form of minerals.[7] However it shared with the rest of Latin America the phenomenon of indigenous communities continuing to suffer from the expropriation of the most valuable lands during the neocolonial period. Foreign domination and control of assets increased throughout the continent, making the United States the largest foreign influence in the region.

It would appear therefore that the accusation of plunder made by Morales at the beginning of this chapter has held true for a large part of Bolivian history. Plunder, by a small capitalist elite and the transnational corporations through which raw materials flowed and assets were controlled, was the characteristic note of an economic model that was based on the export of raw materials. Dependency theories grew in the 1960s to explain this process. Two clear strands can be detected in this body of literature. The first is a Latin American thesis, originated by authors like Raúl Prebisch, economist at the Economic Commission for Latin America and the Caribbean (ECLAC), who first noticed in 1950 a deterioration in the terms of trade between poor and rich countries. They argued that a measure of protectionism was necessary for poor countries to be able to make inroads into their next stage of development, which would entail a policy of import substitution industrialisation (ISI) to replace the trade and export model that had been dominant up to that point.[8] Many other Latin American writers contributed in the following two decades to the dependency school, particularly with empirical evidence drawn from a number of case studies.[9]

A second strand of dependency theory consists of Marxist analyses closely linked to the US journal, the *Monthly Review*. The contributors included Paul Baran, Andre Gunder Frank, and more recently authors associated with world systems theory, such as Samir Amin and Immanuel Wallerstein.[10] Dependency theorists have long argued that wealth and resources tend to flow from poor countries in the periphery of the global economic system, to rich countries that constitute a core capitalist group. According to this body of theories, this global system of exploitation is responsible for the misery and poverty (exacerbated by underdevelopment) that accumulates in those countries with the largest natural resources at their disposal, Latin America being a prime example.[11] Some commentators have gone beyond a purely economic argument. Frank, for example, influenced by the Cuban revolution of 1959, argued that the only possible way for poor dependent countries to reclaim national sovereignty and assert their independence was through armed revolutionary struggle, which could lead them out of this global system of domination. Arguably they could then develop a 'third way', an alternative that was not based on either the capitalist or the socialist models.

It would be difficult to claim that Bolivia's 1952 revolution delivered industrialisation in its broadest sense. In the case of mining, the debate about how best to industrialise this sector – introducing mineral refinement processes or creating smelting plants for example – continues to rage in Bolivian government circles today. A similar concern characterises debates about oil and gas processing. There was however some economic diversification and import substitution from the 1950s onwards. There was also a development in agricultural policy and production in this period, which involved the large-scale development of vast areas of the Bolivian lowlands, which until then had comprised forest and wilderness that official land policy makers perceived as uninhabited. (In fact, this territory was home to a sizeable population of indigenous people.) The aim was to develop agriculture on a more efficient medium and large scale.[12] This policy of expansion had a mixed success, delivering greater levels of production but at a cost which included the displacement of the existing population and large-scale deforestation.

What is not in doubt is that the economic model during the three decades between 1952 and the return to democracy in the 1980s was based on the development of state capitalism. Essentially, this form of state capitalism represented an attempt to overhaul the pre-modern and pre-capitalist forms of production.[13] The strategy included the wholesale nationalisation of mines and railroads. In addition, the 1952 government of the National Revolutionary Movement (MNR), led by Victor Paz Estenssoro, introduced radical land reform in the highlands. This affected the haciendas, which had operated using indigenous labourers who were effectively tied to the land.

The creation of joint labour–government management committees for the running of the nationalised mines, the enfranchisement of the indigenous population, and the land reform, made the 1952 government truly revolutionary in the eyes of the population. However, pressure from the United States soon made itself felt. It affected the role of workers in government, and the amount of compensation the government was forced to pay owners of those mines that had been expropriated. The United States also trained the Bolivian military, so it played a hand in the military takeover of power in 1964. The military did not relinquish their control until the 1980s.[14]

In economic terms, the results of the nationalisation of mines and of the land reform were mixed. Informal economic activity increased in the cities, but there was stagnation in rural production in the highlands. In part this was because the land reform led to unproductive small landholdings (*minifundios*), which received little in the way of credit or technical assistance, and individual land titles which were unsuited to areas of the country where communal agricultural practices had traditionally provided better insurance against the possibility of crop failures. This had been a part of the basic principles of community life in Bolivia, which emphasised the values of solidarity and reciprocity.[15] A process of semi-industrialisation did take place in the eastern lowlands. Finally, this period of state capitalism led to the creation of a large, salaried working class. There were high levels of unionisation, and some of today's indigenous social movements – such as the Confederation of Bolivia's Peasant Workers' Trade Union (CSUTCB), founded in 1979 – claim to have originated as part of the trade union movement. These levels of unionisation contributed to the expansion of insurance-based forms of social security such as pensions, and of workers' rights for a small percentage of the population in the cities and for a smaller percentage in rural zones. In summary, the period of state capitalism delivered a dual economy, comprising a small export-driven sector, and a majority of poor people with no cohesion and without social and employment rights.

ECONOMIC LIBERALISM REBORN

By the 1980s, ISI had run its course, and had delivered only to a modest extent against the long-term objectives of economic modernisation and increased well-being for the majority of the Latin American population. The formal return to democracy in Bolivia would be marked by the resurrection of some of the fundamental economic beliefs that had dominated the continent until the middle of the twentieth century. As with previous paradigm shifts in the continent, the new orthodoxy imposed itself rapidly in the corridors of power in Latin America, and its consequences changed the continent beyond recognition. Neoliberalism, it seemed, would finally deliver where previous approaches to economic development had failed. The reasons for this dramatic shift of economic policy direction are explored below.

There are many reasons why ISI never succeeded in Latin America. First, domestic demand for Latin American products was limited because of the small consumer base in many countries. The products were also relatively low in quality and expensive compared with the output of major established international producers. However, the first major reason for a change in economic policy must be found in the enormous debt that most Latin American countries were running. As no private investors were forthcoming, during the dominant period of ISI, Latin American states borrowed heavily in order to invest in infrastructure and the desired process of industrialisation. This heavy borrowing was fostered by the availability of cheap credit from international banks that were lending money from the Organisation of Petroleum Exporting Countries (OPEC), which were awash with petrodollars. An oil crisis in 1973 had led to an enormous increase in the price of oil and fuelled this credit source. As the second oil crisis in 1979 increased prices again, the response from rich countries was to raise interest rates to subdue their own runaway inflation, dampening consumption in their own societies. This had a double-whammy effect on Latin American countries: their export markets were unable to absorb their products, at a time when their debt repayments increased sharply as a result of higher interest rates. By 1982, Mexico was unable to service its international debt. The problems were not dissimilar in Brazil and Argentina, and a wave of near-defaults affected most of Latin America. Bolivian had a foreign debt of US$5 billion by 1984. The country could no longer afford to service it, and as in most of Latin America, this sparked a serious economic crisis with severe social consequences.[16] The 1980s would be known in the region as the 'lost decade' because GDP per capita in many countries was no better at the end of the decade than it had been at the beginning.

The second reason for the dramatic gain of ground for neoliberal thinking was a radical change of economic ideology and thinking in western countries and in the international financial institutions (IFIs) they support, such as the International Monetary Fund (IMF) and the World Bank (WB). It seemed that the great consensus of the 1950s and 1960s. built on Keynesian economics, which had delivered welfare states in European countries, was ditched in favour of the monetarist economic policies advocated by the Chicago school of economics fronted by Milton Friedman. This economic thinking was adopted by the powerful coalition of UK prime minister Margaret Thatcher and US President Ronald Reagan. Both their domestic economic policies reflected a determined effort to implement monetarism in order to control inflation. This priority supplanted the previous Keynesian focus on full employment and a strong welfare state. At its heart lay strong philosophical beliefs in freedom, individual choice, market mechanisms for the delivery of goods and services, and a reduced role for the state, which was seen as interfering, bureaucratic and inefficient.

Neoliberal thinking spread throughout Latin America like wildfire. What Duncan Green described in 1995 as a 'silent revolution' became the accepted consensus among politicians and the small thriving middle class. These were broadly the individuals who benefited from the new economic policies.[17] Critics from the left, however, have argued that a second, perhaps more important reason why the new economic policy was implemented throughout the continent was because of the leverage that creditors were able to exert through the IMF and other IFIs on countries facing serious debt problems. Neoliberalism was sold as the solution to the debt crisis, and the export of this particular brand of policy to Latin American countries was swift. It began with Chile in 1973, but Bolivia would become its most fervent believer and pupil.

A HEAVY DOSE OF SHOCK THERAPY AND THE BITTER PILL OF STRUCTURAL ADJUSTMENT

The return to democracy in Bolivia was painful and protracted. Popular hopes however were raised when the corrupt and brutal narco-state of General García Meza finally transferred power to Hernán Siles Zuazo. Two years after he had won an election, Zuazo took office as president of Bolivia in October 1982. The new president attempted to deal with the calamitous state of the economy by reverting to some of the leftist and nationalist policies from the 1952 era. For example, he brought communists into the cabinet to deal with labour relations. However the economic slide continued unabated, weighed down by a continuing fall of the price of tin in the international markets. By 1984, inflation had risen to over 1,000 per cent and the national debt was such that Bolivia had to stop repayments in March of that year, signalling the end of the line for the first democratically elected Bolivian president for many years.[18] The result of the subsequent elections was that it fell to Paz Estenssoro, the leader of the Movimiento Nacional Revolucionario (MNR) and the hero of the 1952 revolution, to deal with the acute problems of hyperinflation and unserviceable debt. He won after a lacklustre campaign against former dictator Hugo Banzer on a vague promise to deliver well-being for Bolivians, yet he implemented the exact opposite of what the electorate expected. Enter the new economic policy (NEP).

NEP is the euphemistic name that was given to the imposition of neoliberal economic policies in Bolivia. The overall objective of these policies was to foster export-led growth, returning the country to its original economic model and categorically consigning to history the period dominated by ISI. The premise of NEP was that export-led growth required the country to attract foreign investment and technology, and that this could be achieved by making state assets available for foreign takeover through privatisation. Before the anticipated economic recovery could take place, however, two steps were seen as necessary. The first was stabilisation of the runaway inflation, a key objective in neoliberal economic thinking, which neoliberals argue can only be achieved through a reduction of the money supply, slashing public spending and letting the market decide the value of wages. This is normally followed by a large devaluation of the national currency, in this case the Boliviano, and the unification of both official and street-level exchange rates against the US dollar. This last measure is supposed to make national production competitive in international markets. All of these policies amount to a cold shower that paralyses economic activity inside the country, but is followed by a process of 'structural adjustment'. This shock therapy has been described as akin to pressing the reset button on the entire economy.[19]

In the textbook shock therapy that was followed by Bolivia in the mid-1980s, structural adjustment was basically designed to put centre stage the unregulated market as arbiter and allocator of goods, services and resources. It included measures to reduce the size of the state and public sector deficit, as well as the liberalisation of trade and capital markets. This effectively involved removing all structural barriers to the free functioning of markets, including regulation and legislation, workers' rights, minimum salaries, subsidised prices of staple goods and so on. It also included the elimination of all import restrictions, remnants of the ISI period when protectionist measures had been taken to encourage local production rather than imports, and the liberalisation of interest rates.[20] Subsidised or regulated prices for basic goods had delivered some degree of protection to the most financially vulnerable sections of society, ensuring they could afford basics such as bread, milk and cooking fuel. Liberalisation effectively left pricing entirely to the market, which in the context of hyperinflation quickly put basic foodstuffs beyond the reach of many.

In short, the entire process consisted of doing away with government decision making and transferring control to the 'self-regulating' market. One of the mechanisms was the privatisation or decentralisation of public enterprises.[21] This was backed up by a new legislative framework that permitted employers to hire and fire at will, reduce labour costs, opt out of welfare contributions for their employees, introduce short-term and precarious contracts, stop recognition for trade unions, and generally remove all measures that contribute to the security of workers. Another immediate measure that formed part of the structural adjustment programme (SAP) in Bolivia was a four-month freeze on all public sector wages.

The Bolivian process of SAP hit the state mining monopoly, the Bolivian Mining Corporation (COMIBOL) in a particularly harsh way. It could not have been otherwise, since mining constituted, and continues to constitute, one of the biggest sources of national income. The reduction in the state bureaucracy effectively meant that the country's mining industry was handed over for minimal return to private foreign companies. These were able to pick and choose the most profitable mines and those that had received the greatest levels of investment. The remainder (most of the operating mines) were simply closed. This resulted in between 23,000 and 30,000 miners being made redundant in 1985, around two-thirds of the total.[22] In a typically euphemistic way, Bolivia's policy makers referred to this unemployment catastrophe as the great *relocalización* (relocation). Showing a greater sense of humour still, Luis Rico, a Bolivian singing legend, refers in his songs to the way in which miners were 'relocated' all right – from the mines to the streets. The reform was devastating for the mining industry in Bolivia, which had already been reeling from the collapse in international tin prices a few years earlier.[23]

Initially, the reforms were met by a lot of popular protest, especially from those sectors that stood to lose the most, such as miners and public sector workers, who were also at the receiving end of a wave of redundancies. However, the almost immediate effect of eliminating exchange rate controls was that the runaway inflation that had afflicted the country in 1985 – as much as 23,000 per cent a year – was halted and brought back down to 14 per cent by 1987. The economy, in free fall since 1980, began to grow again in the same year, and the government understandably felt vindicated. It was enabled to press on, having mustered enough support to remain inflexible regarding the pace of reforms.

As a result, Bolivia's stabilisation of its economy through shock therapy plus the process of SAP that followed became a template for the kind of neoliberal policy packages promoted internationally by IFIs such as the IMF and the WB. Officially at least, Jeffrey Sachs, the architect of Bolivia's economic resuscitation, was heralded as a hero of troubled economies, and he was dispatched to other parts of the world where he could work his magic. The fall of the Berlin Wall shortly afterwards offered new opportunities to administer the same medicine in countries like Poland and Russia.[24]

The positive early economic results of the initial stabilisation package in Bolivia were welcomed by IFIs. The IMF made more loans to the country – it even announced the creation of an emergency social fund (ESF) of US$200 million to create jobs – as did the WB, and other countries were prepared to accept the judgement of these institutions and reschedule Bolivia's debt.[25] Bolivia was presented by mainstream economists and senior officials in the international financial sector as a shining example of how to deal with inflation, deliver (some) economic growth and continue to repay international debt. It was no wonder, then, that in the 1990s the government would build on some of the reforms begun in the 1980s.

THE DEEPENING OF THE NEOLIBERAL PROJECT

President Jaime Paz Zamora (1989–93) continued the process of privatisation began by his predecessor, but the president that most Bolivians associate with the neoliberal economic period is Gonzalo Sánchez de Lozada. There are a number of reasons for this. First, Sánchez de Lozada, a former student at the University of Chicago where Friedman formulated his thinking, is strongly associated with the United States. His nickname in Bolivia is *el gringo*, on account of his heavy accent and the length of time he lived in that country. In addition, he had effectively been the architect of decree 21060 in 1985 – still recognised by its number in Bolivia – which translated the principles for stabilisation and SAP prescribed by Sachs into the Bolivian legislative framework. As senator, he had been chosen by Paz Estenssoro to lead the secret bipartisan team that would draw up this piece of legislation that inaugurated the neoliberal period in the record period of barely three weeks. He also represented the interests of the new economic elite that stood to win from the process of privatisation heralded by 21060. As the owner of a successful privatised mine, he was following in the footsteps of tin barons of yesteryear like Patiño. However, unlike Patiño, Sánchez de Lozada symbolised the new fusion between big business and political power that would characterise Bolivia's neoliberal era.

Finally, Sánchez de Lozada used his first four-year term as president of Bolivia (1993–97) to take the privatisation agenda to a new level. In essence, his master plan was to privatise all the major national companies and to use some of the proceeds to fund social benefits.[26] He called this process (with no sense of irony) *Plan de todos* (everyone's plan). The claim was that the privatisation process – referred to as 'capitalisation' in Bolivia – would benefit all Bolivians, because 50 per cent of the shares of some of the newly privatised companies would be retained by the state, and the dividends would fund social programmes such as a universal pension.[27] As Chapter 5 explores, commentators have criticised this privatisation spree by arguing that it amounted to the bribery of the population. People were led to believe that this process would put social welfare on a secure financial footing, something that was not the case at the time.[28] This period saw the sale of state companies like ENDE (the national electricity company), LAB (Bolivia's state airline), ENFE (the national railway company) and the biggest asset of them all, YPFB, the national oil and gas company, as well as a number of water companies.

In sum, neoliberalism in Bolivia was inaugurated in 1985 with the introduction of decree 21060 as part of an emergency series of policies to stem an economic crisis that was characterised by hyperinflation and negative growth. Control of the inflation was swift, following a strong devaluation and the removal of exchange controls.[29] The longer-term neoliberal economic policies pursued throughout the 1980s and 1990s included a dramatic transfer of public monopolies into private hands, through a series of steps: privatisation of all major national companies, including the gas and oil industries; market liberalisation and the introduction of flat tariffs; and deregulation, including increasing levels of labour flexibility.[30] The introduction of these policies brought Bolivia into the world of respectability in the international community of nations and among mainstream economists in IFIs.[31] Indeed, a new long-term relationship with the IMF and the WB was inaugurated from 1986 onwards in recognition of the 'correct economic path' taken by Bolivia, resulting in new loans to the country and increasing levels of debt.

An alternative view is taken by critics who have explored the Bolivian case study as part of the wider debate on the possibilities and limitations of the neoliberal economic model. They have generally been less than flattering regarding the country's achievements. The criticisms are many and varied, and they can only be briefly summarised here.

First, although the country moved to an export-led model and there was a degree of inward investment, particularly in the key gas and oil industries, and also to a moderate extent in telecommunications, there was hardly any inward investment in many other areas of the economy.

The loss of state control led to a shrinkage in many economic sectors. The control of the state was significantly reduced in some companies and lost altogether in others. As a result, the majority of railways in the country were closed. The case of the country's airline is typical of the predatory practices that took place. Buyers often found it more profitable to asset-strip newly privatised companies than to invest in making them work effectively.[32] LAB went bankrupt within ten years and was closed down.

There were also major environmental and social costs. Soya production provides a good example. Exports of soya increased enormously, and from 1996 to 2000 soya became almost as important in terms of the revenue generated as gas and oil, fostering rapid economic growth in the country's eastern lowlands.

It required the clearing of large forested areas to create the large plantations required for industrial-scale production. There was increasing conflict over land ownership in the Eastern lowlands between indigenous groups and the new agribusinesses.[33] Soya also pushed out a more mixed agricultural base, and this had an impact on the satisfaction of basic needs. Bolivia, a vast country in which a large percentage of the population lives from agricultural work, which has the climate and ecosystems required to produce all food types and be self-sufficient, began to import basic foodstuffs like fruit.

If we consider economic performance as a proxy indicator of well-being and needs satisfaction in a society, then we can say without any doubt that the Bolivian economic performance during the neoliberal period left a lot to be desired. During the period between 1985 and 2005 the economy grew on average by 3 per cent per year. However, when we take into account a population growth of 2.4 per cent a year on average, growth in real terms, though positive, was less than satisfactory. The theory of the invisible hand, or of the rising tide of economic growth that benefits all, certainly did not work in Bolivia. Inflation had been dealt with by the late 1980s but the country did not recover from the severe economic contraction that had begun in 1981. As a result, GDP per capita in 2000 was effectively the same as it had been in 1980. Students of Latin American economics refer to the 1980s as the 'lost decade',[34] but in Bolivia, this lost decade was 20 years long.

Bolivia emerged from the neoliberal economic period with a minimally growing economy that was able to satisfy neither the needs nor the aspirations of the majority of the population.[35] Poverty increased during this period in a country that had been the poorest in South America to start with. More than two-thirds of the population were living in poverty in 2005, and 40 per cent were living in extreme poverty. Inequality increased even more during that period, making Bolivia one of the most unequal of Latin American countries.[36] Much of the new accumulation of wealth in the hands of a few was connected with the growth of *latifundia* and the speculative management of land. This benefited a small coterie of cattle ranchers and soya producers who in many cases had appropriated their large estates illegally. On the flipside of these small stories of rural success, a large percentage of Bolivia's population, around 40 per cent, continued to live in rural areas and practise community-based subsistence agriculture.

Many of those who decided to join the great migration that

took ex-miners and landless peasants to the cities, typically to La Paz, ended up joining the hundreds of thousands of unemployed or underemployed citizens of the burgeoning slum city of El Alto. There they could look forward to joining the informal economy of street-sellers that still employs up to two-thirds of all those in the city. These people have for decades now been engaged in a hand-to-mouth existence.[37] This class includes not just people of working age but increasing numbers of children as young as eight years old. It is still common to see small children working as shoe-shiners in El Prado for a couple of pesos per client, and there are increasing numbers who, from the middle of the 1980s onwards, joined the armies of street beggars.

Data on the effects of poverty are not hard to come by in Bolivia. United Nations Development Programme (UNDP) figures confirm that extreme poverty affected around 40 per cent of the population between 1985 and 2005. In the department of Potosi, the great original source of European wealth, the figure was 66 per cent.[38] In 2005, infant mortality rates in Bolivia were around 60 per 1000 live births, with an obstinately high figure of up to 99 in places like Potosí; this in a continent where the average is 25 per 1000. The number of children who abandoned their schooling during the worst years of the SAP increased enormously. Primary school completion figures in 2005 continued to be as low as 72 per cent, with even lower figures for the poorest parts of the country.[39]

Bolivia had some of the worst percentages in Latin America for maternal death and chronic malnutrition at the end of the neoliberal economic period. These problems particularly affected women and children, indigenous and rural populations.[40] For example, in 2002, more than a quarter of all children in Bolivia suffered from chronic malnutrition, although this figure does not reflect the enormous inequality between rural areas – where severe malnutrition was more prevalent – and urban areas, or the inequalities between indigenous and non-indigenous peoples.[41]

Apologists for neoliberalism point to successes in the creation of universal welfare provision, such as the Bonosol, predecessor to the current universal pension. But this was very limited, and it was accompanied by a number of other measures that effectively privatised the existing pensions system, transforming a 'pay as you go' system that included elements of intergenerational solidarity into one that individualised risk and relieved the state and employers from contributions. As a result, although Bolivia became one of the most open economies in Latin America, the academic judgement of that period is that trade liberalisation was not particularly success-ful.[42] Some commentators argued as early as 1996 that 'there are some criticisms of the SAP that cannot be easily ignored ... some of the reforms have not resulted in vigorous and sustained economic growth, and the SAP has produced no significant progress in social development'.[43]

Another major criticism of the neoliberal economic period is the loss of sovereign power it entailed. This point is intimately linked to the previous one because, at the same time as the Bolivian popula-tion suffered the consequences of increasing inequality and poverty, it became intensely conscious of the fact that the country's natural resources, the source of Bolivia's wealth, were increasingly in the hands of foreign companies and transnational corporations (TNCs). A serious externalisation of profits from gas and oil exploitation took place during the neoliberal period: as much as 73 per cent of all profits was exported.[44] This period was also characterised by extremely low levels of taxation on these companies. For ordinary Bolivians who struggled to buy gas for their cooking, the sight of foreign companies enriching themselves through the exploitation of the country's vast natural resources brought back memories of the country's colonial economic relations with Spain. The times of plunder were apparently back, and the new masters of Bolivia, these foreign-owned TNCs, had imposed themselves thanks to the role played by IFIs and organisations like the IMF and the WB. Many saw these bodies as hell-bent on perpetuating a new era of neocolonial relations, as TNCs made the most of the opportunities created by the hyperinflation crisis of 1984/5 to regain control of the country's natural resources.[45] This is certainly the conclusion of none other than Joseph Stiglitz, who argues that the neoliberal era inaugurated by Reagan and Thatcher in the 1980s aimed at increasing the relative power of corporations over governments. The IMF became the main institutional vehicle for exporting this thinking around the world, and the economic leverage provided by the its ability to approve or deny loans acted to impose these policies on poor countries.[46] The social consequences that these IMF-designed policies had on the Bolivian population have been best portrayed by witnesses on the ground.[47]

Finally, for critics of the Bolivian neoliberal period, it represented a shocking lack of democratic accountability. The people who voted for Paz Estenssoro in 1985 did certainly not vote for decree 21060 and for the social and economic hardships that followed, and yet the plan was implemented regardless. There was simply no public debate on the relative merits of the NEP, and no information. Even the cabinet was kept in the dark about the existence of decree 21060, and its implementation was not open to debate in either Parliament or the cabinet. The original package was forced through in spite of initial opposition from the organised labour movement, students and the popular classes. Indeed, the government of Estenssoro had to resort to repression, including the imposition of a state of siege for the three months that it took to implement decree 21060, and the collective kidnapping of the entire leadership of the trade union movement. These individuals were kept confined in internment camps in the lowlands, with no access to information or freedom of movement, until 21060 became a reality.[48]

Given the failings of the neoliberal economic period, it is no wonder that neoliberalism in Bolivia has become a term of abuse. It is regularly used by President Morales to define opposition politicians. One of the main consequences of this period was particularly ironic: the penury brought about by the economic policies forced tens of thousands of the newly dispossessed to find an alternative income in the production of coca. The coca leaf is a perfectly natural product that meets important nutritional and symbolic roles in Andean societies, but what the 1980s economic crisis produced was an enormous increase in the number of people growing coca leaf to feed the illegal international sale of cocaine. For many – including the family of the same Evo Morales who would one day become president – it offered the only possibility of survival. Some sources go further, and suggest that the 'cocainisation' of the Bolivian economy was the only factor that cushioned the worst effects of the economic policies introduced in the 1980s, preventing total economic collapse.[49]

If the economic and social consequences of the neoliberal period in Bolivia were as disastrous as this chapter suggests, is there still an argument in favour of neoliberalism? One of the original arguments of neoliberals was that it would usher in a new period of political freedom. However, I shall argue in Chapter 2 that Bolivia's democracy also failed in this period. Indeed, the political consequences of the neoliberal period were many. Because of the serious reduction in public sector jobs during this period, the organised labour movement and the traditional left opposition politics lost a great deal of bargaining power. And yet the election in 2005 of Evo Morales constituted nothing short of a political revolution, and it surely represents the best opportunity for a new type of politics and societal model. It is now accepted that the collapse of the traditional left in Bolivia opened new spaces for resistance from civil society, in the form of indigenous and agrarian peoples.[50] The resistance began in the Chapare, the area of the country that was most militarised in reaction to the US-imposed *cero coca* policy. But for many indigenous peoples, the impetus for becoming political actors came because of the large-scale deforestation to facilitate industrial-scale agriculture, and because the ever-increasing land requirements for these projects threatened their own survival.[51] By 2000, Bolivia showed a generalised resistance to the neoliberal model of development, and the demands from the radicalised indigenous sector spreads to other social groups, including the urban middle classes. Chapter 2 traces this piece of history.

THE LATIN AMERICAN TURN TO THE LEFT

The Latin American 'lost decade', a region-wide economic debacle caused by the debt crisis and subsequent SAPs, resulted in economic stagnation and growing levels of social suffering in many of the region's countries. In addition, decades of IMF prescriptions have resulted in a crisis of legitimacy for global financial institutions. This is compounded by the failures of an economic model that did not deliver significant poverty reduction and economic growth, to the extent that a quarter of the population in the region continues to live on less than US$2 per day.[52]

The return to democracy in the 1980s and 1990s was quickly followed by a turn to the left in many of the countries of Latin America, a political wave that represents a common critique of the neoliberal models of development that have been unable to stem high levels of poverty and social need.[53] This critique of neoliberal models of development was in some cases led by civil society and grassroots organisations working to create alternative models of development to those inspired by the United States and the Washington Consensus. The new political conviction in the region is that state-sponsored social protection and development have to go hand in hand.[54] Thus, in Latin America, the socially regressive results of neoliberalism have brought about a rejection of economic globalisation, not only from the social movements and civil society that have spearheaded political protests, but from the governments themselves which have, as in Bolivia, come under the strong influence of social movements.[55]

Bolivia exemplifies perfectly this Latin American context, and provides a good case study of a country forging a path towards a new kind of political and developmental practice. With a traditionally weak state, the country has been ruled by small elites for much of its history. The majority indigenous and rural population was excluded socially, politically and economically.[56] Economically, structural adjustment and monetarist policies were adopted to stop runaway inflation in 1985, often following policy demands inspired by the IMF. In the 1990s, the neoliberal economic project included a wave of privatisations – of water, electricity, the oil industry and so on – that characterised the governments of Sánchez de Lozada in 1993–97 and 2002–03, and of Banzer-Quiroga in 1997–2002. The social dislocation caused by the neoliberal experiment and the high levels of repression that followed the US-inspired coca eradication programme acted as the catalyst for popular uprisings that led to a mass rejection of these economic policies and of the neoliberal model of economic development.[57] Chapter 6 picks up this thread to explore and assess Bolivia's current 'post-neoliberal' economic model.

On the other hand, Bolivia's road towards a new kind of politics has been inspired by the catastrophic failure of the formal liberal democratic system that returned to the country in 1982 after almost two decades of military rule. Although mainstream political parties brought democracy to the country, deep levels of corruption and an inability to deliver democratic decision making put the system on a collision course with the Bolivian mass of increasingly dispossessed citizens, now looking for alternative forms of association and political activism. Two moments of deep crisis in the system were the water wars in Cochabamba in 2000 and the 2003 popular uprising in the city of El Alto, which was motivated by a combination of higher property taxes and the sale of gas to Chile. These events represent the pinnacles of a long-drawn-out process that has seen the rise of a new kind of politics since the mid-1990s. Led by the Movement towards Socialism (MAS), an umbrella term that brings together what were throughout the 1990s disparate popular uprisings, this political movement/party represents the entry of social movements and alternative political actors into the formal political system. The process culminated in the election of Evo Morales to the presidency in 2005 and the occupation of the institutions of the state by social movements and representatives of grassroots-level political organisations. We turn to this part of the story in the next chapter.

2 POLITICAL FAILURES AND POLITICAL REVIVAL

For the clenched teeth
For the knot in the throat
For the contained rage
For the mouths that do not sing
For the censored verse
For the clandestine kiss
For the young exile
For the forbidden names
I call your name, freedom.
                    Jean Franco Pagliano

The verses above, inspired by Second World War French resist-ance poet Paul Eluard, became the anthem of the Latin American protest movement, confronting the dictatorships that took hold of the region in the second half of the twentieth century. In Bolivia, the lyrics inspired a version of banned song *Yo te nombro* (I name you) by Savia Nueva, a band formed in 1976 by the Junaro brothers. Their music would force them into exile like many other singers of their generation. Once the particularly brutal dictatorship of García Meza was over, the return to democracy seemed to promise the renewal of the hopes generated by the 1952 revolution that had been frustrated by the long interlude of military rule.

However, as we have seen, the 1980s in Bolivia were dominated by a serious economic downturn that converted the country into a testing ground for structural adjustment policies. It is fair to say that, although the arrest of hyperinflation was necessary at the time, the economic policies implemented throughout much of the 1980s and 1990s did not deliver for the vast majority of Bolivians because they failed to reduce socioeconomic inequalities, and led to a reduction of social protection and a vast increase of poverty, spreading social insecurity through a dramatic reduction in the reach of the state.

At least, some would say, Bolivia had abandoned the dictatorships of the past, and the democratisation process that began in the 1980s brought an imported model of liberal democracy and management that generated much hope in the population. If democracy is the expression of the popular will, the expectation was that the people would be able to determine the economic path of the country. Yet in spite of the increasing levels of popular unrest, Bolivia failed to change economic direction in the 1980s and 1990s. Not only did the democratic system not generate participation from the population, it produced a corrupt elite and a generalised disenchantment with politics itself, which translated into an increasing critical stance towards politicians and the symbols of party politics. At the same time, a growing feeling emerged in the population at large that the formal political system lacked legitimacy.

Bolivia's political history is one of struggle and rebellion, something that even a cursory glance at the academic literature evidences.[1] The democratic period which commenced in 1982 and the subsequent advent of neoliberal reforms with decree 21060 did much to reinvigorate popular struggle and opposition, which reached a zenith of sorts during the years leading up to the 2005 elections. What did away with the political system that the return to democracy in 1982 had brought to Bolivia was the sense of frustration and disempowerment in the general population. Bolivians felt unrepresented by a political system that was corrupt. They felt disempowered in the face of the role played by transnational corporations (TNCs), which wielded more power than their elected politicians and effectively took natural resources, in a new phase of predatory extraction that did not benefit Bolivians. They felt disempowered in the face of international financial institutions (IFIs) that were able to dictate the terms of reform in ways that poured all the pain over the Bolivian population and increased Bolivia's international debt. People felt disempowered by the inability of politicians to stand firm against the domination of the United States and the US-backed plan to tackle coca leaf production in the Chapare region. It would be here that the resistance began, first to the US coca eradication programme, and later to the entire model of development. Along the way, this process would profoundly affect Bolivia's politics, society, economics and the country's international standing in the region and beyond, spearheading what some authors have referred to as 'the new cycle of resistance' in which indigenous struggle across Latin America has played a central role.[2]

Bolivia's double crisis of legitimacy led to a fundamental questioning of the political, social and economic model of society and its management. The process of change that began with widespread resistance and culminated with the overthrow of the country's political structures was not led by the traditional forces and political actors from the left, for example the Trade Unions Federation (COB), but by those who had been excluded by the previous system, one that the Movimiento al Socialismo (MAS) has referred to as a neocolonial society. These political actors included a coalition of peasants, the emerging indigenous movement, the coca growers' trade unions where the current president's political origins can be located, and the poor urban masses. The result is a radically new form of politics led by non-traditional political actors who have been tasked by the population with recreating society in new and original ways.

This chapter traces the origins of Bolivia's political volte face in the 1990s and beyond until the MAS electoral victory of 2005, explaining the significance of this new political formation and its promise for the refoundation of Bolivia in ways that that were meant to significantly improve the quality of democratic practice in order to steer the country in a new economic direction, reposition the well-being of the Bolivian population as the central objective of the state, and establish a new role for the country in the region.

THE FRUSTRATED EXPECTATIONS OF THE TRANSITION TO DEMOCRATIC RULE: THE VIEW FROM BELOW

As Chapter 1 discussed, the 1952 revolution, with its government management committees for the running of the nationalised mines, the enfranchisement of the indigenous population, and land reform, made the government led by the Movimiento Nacional Revolucionario (MNR) truly revolutionary in the eyes of the population. However, pressure from the United States soon made itself felt, affecting the role of workers in government and the amount of compensation the government was forced to pay owners of those mines that had been expropriated. The Bolivian military were trained by US personnel, including officer training in the now infamous School of the Americas (SOA) in Fort Benning.[3] The military, led by General Barrientos, took power in 1964 and did not relinquish it until the 1980s. And even if a number of the military governments did not challenge the orthodoxy of import substitution industrialisation (ISI) that prevailed after the 1952 revolution – General Ovando nationalised the oil companies and allowed an important political role to the newly created COB and to the miners' trade union (FSTMB) – their rule was inevitably undemocratic. It has been characterised as clientelist, authoritarian and bureaucratic.[4] With this coming after the MNR experience of the 1950s that had – following the experience of the Institutional Revolutionary Party in Mexico – rejected pluralist democracy in favour of a single party system dressed as democratic by institutional and electoral mechanisms, the odds for the future were against a smooth transition to democracy.[5]

Bolivia's return to democracy was indeed fraught with serious difficulties from the beginning. The short period between 1978 and 1982 alone delivered seven military governments, among them the fascist regime of García Meza (1980–81). Taking its cue and advice from the infamous Argentinian dictatorship, he banned all political parties, jailed and tortured thousands of citizens and converted Bolivia into a narco-state. After this period, however, a more stable party-political system emerged in Bolivia, in the sense that regular elections have taken place with guarantees that they will be free and fair. However, there are some peculiar characteristics in the Bolivian political system that have for a long time occupied commentators and put into question its ability to deliver political stability. The problems began as soon as democracy returned. Siles Zuazo, the first elected president in Bolivia's current democratic era, struggled for three years to keep control of both the economy and the multiparty coalition in his government. In the process he appointed and fired dozens of ministers. As discussed in the preceding chapter, his period in government delivered high levels of social unrest and a seriously deteriorated economy, and this paved the way for the neoliberal era.

One of the problems of Bolivian politics that contributes to its instability is the tendency for political parties to appear and disappear regularly, making it difficult for the uninitiated to keep track of who is who in the political system. The MAS is not immune to this since, as we shall see later in this chapter, there have been numerous names and acronyms over time for the political orientation it represents. The instability of political formations is closely linked to the role played by established power groups and the way in which parties are often built around charismatic figures, without

whom they cannot survive. For example, Acción Democrática
Nacionalista (ADN) was virtually wiped out in the 2002 presi-
dential elections following the death of its leader Hugo Banzer.
The same happened to the Unidad Cívica Solidaridad (UCS) and
Conciencia de Patria (CONDEPA). The Nueva Fuerza Republicana
(NFR) emerged in those elections, led by another charismatic
individual, Manfred Reyes Villa, but it did not run in the 2005
elections. Instead, Reyes Villa provided support for former president
Jorge 'Tuto' Quiroga to run for president under yet another party
that was virtually identical to the disappeared ADN, the Poder
Democrático y Social (PODEMOS).

Traditional forces of the left like the trade unions have always
played an important political role in Bolivia. Although their voice
was heard mainly from the streets, they constituted the key political
force of opposition to the dictatorships. However, after the return of
democracy, the 1980s neoliberal attack on state companies and the
large job losses than ensued affected the political force of the trade
unions, especially the miners' union. The damage done to them was
such that they played a relatively low-key role in the relaunch of
the resistance to the neoliberal order that began in the 1990s. The
weakness of the mining trade unions was reflected in the capacity
of action of the COB. Other established power groups, like the
Catholic Church – a large landowner in its own right – continue
to exercise their influence from outside the formal political system.
The Church allied itself entirely with the anti-MAS opposition
during the first administration, playing a particularly strong role
in the opposition to the new constitution, through Cardinal Julio
Terrazas, archbishop of the archdiocese of Santa Cruz.

The power groups that were most closely associated with
political parties during the neoliberal period were the civic committees, representing (mostly) separatist sentiments in the east of
the country, which grew in force in the first MAS administration
(2006–10), and the confederation of businesses.[6] The latter – representing the interest of cattle ranchers and agribusinesses such as
soya producers – replaced the Bolivian tin barons at the top of
Bolivia's socioeconomic structure and began to dominate Bolivian
politics in the Eastern Lowlands. Both of these groups made
important inroads into the political system from 1985 onwards,
especially in Santa Cruz and in Beni. They were over-represented
in established political parties, particularly in the Movimiento de
Izquierda Revolucionario (MIR), ADN and MNR.[7] Increasing
levels of clientelism in the Bolivian politics of the 1980s and 1990s,

with candidates promising to provide favours to groups or communities of supporters in return for their electoral support, have also been seen as an obstacle to democracy, although some commentators have focused on the extent to which clientelism can be seen as a form of citizenship practice that brings groups of the electorate in contact with the state.[8]

Perhaps one of the biggest problems in Bolivian politics that developed in the 1980s, which led to a profound crisis of confidence and legitimacy in the political system, was its unusual hybrid nature, a mix of presidential and parliamentary forms.[9] The presidential selection process consisted of a first public vote followed by a further round of voting in Congress, with no public participation. The president then selected the executive.

Between 1985 and 2005, no presidential candidate reached the 50 per cent mark in the first round, and each time, a candidate who had not topped the popular vote in the first round was eventually voted in as president. The MNR's Victor Paz Estenssoro became president in 1985 with the support of MIR, even though he had been second as the popular choice. In 1989 the candidate who had come third in the first round, Jaime Paz Zamora from MIR (the third-largest party in Congress), became president because he was also supported by the second party, ADN (under a deal which entailed its acquiring the majority of cabinet positions), leaving the individual who had gained most votes in the first round, Gonzalo Sánchez de Lozada, or 'Goni', to lead the opposition.[10]

Unsurprisingly, this system led to a feeling that the public did not actually choose the president at all, and that their preference was not properly taken into consideration. Other complaints were that all the major candidates were tainted by the failings of a party-political system that was focused more on making deals to obtain power and privileges than on serving the public, and that the United States exerted undue influence on the process. Opportunistic coalitions to elect a president continued well into the 1990s, including the controversial choice by Sánchez de Lozada of Hugo Cárdenas, an Aymara and previously presidential candidate for the Movimiento Revolucionario Tupac Katari de Liberación (MRTKL), as his vice-president in 1993. In essence, the criticism is that established political parties lost the confidence of the Bolivian population in the two decades following the return to democracy.

Coalition governments, what Bolivians refer to as *democracia pactada* (a democracy of pacts),[11] were disliked not because coalitions are perceived as always flawed, but because in Bolivia the groupings of parties were typically based on pragmatism rather than principles. Political power increasingly came to be seen as a corrupt merry-go-round of influence, in which a small elite of 'professional' politicians effectively took turns in power. The candidates were able to offer each other what Bolivians call *pegas* – which involves sharing the spoils of office, access to public funds, influence over other public bodies, and so on – to such an extent that it is said that during this period cabinet posts were effectively being sold to the highest bidder. The growing sense of distance between politicians and voters, the hypocritical manoeuvring and broken promises, reached a zenith between 1997 and 2003. In this the period a mega-coalition brought to government ADN, MIR, NFR, CONDEPA and UCS.[12] Opinion polls conducted at the time show that the country's political parties had the confidence of less than 4 per cent of the population, trailing all other institutions of the state, including the police, and showing much greater levels of disaffection with the formal democratic system than anywhere else in Latin America.[13]

Beyond the specific problems created by the Bolivian political system and the double limitation of permanent instability and lack of trust it generated in the electorate during the failed period of *democracia pactada*,[14] the post-dictatorship period exhibited a broader set of problems that put in doubt the country's governability more generally. It could be argued (and has been, by the renascent Bolivian political class), that the political problems of Bolivia were not entirely new and self-imposed, but rather reflected a wider set of parameters and sources deeply rooted in the country's history of dependency. For a country to maintain a relative sense of political stability, economic stability is also necessary. It must produce not only economic growth, but also a minimum and improving level of social well-being and living standards. As we saw in Chapter 1, these basic objectives were not achieved in Bolivia during the neoliberal period. The economy began to grow in the late 1980s, but very slowly, only to stagnate again between 1998 and 1999.[15] The period of neoliberal revolution delivered increasing levels of inequality in what was already one of the most unequal countries in the world, and as the state retrenched ever further, there was a growing degree of labour insecurity and poverty. An increasing percentage of the population were unable to meet their basic needs.

The effects of this crisis were worst felt among those sectors of the population who lost out as a result of decree 21060: the unemployed miners, and also the rural and indigenous population, who in the 1980s began a process of rapid migration to the cities in search of employment, increasing the size of shanty towns like El Alto on the outskirts of La Paz. A core issue when a growing mass of the population, effectively the casualties of the process of economic globalisation, become surplus to economic requirements in a society that creates a small numbers of winners, is that they are not able to exercise their basic civil, political and social rights, and feel effectively disenfranchised.[16] The inability of a large percentage of the population to exercise their social citizenship was based on the economic and political failures of the neoliberal era, and also, crucially, on the failures of a deeply unequal and divided society that marginalised and excluded a majority of its members.[17] This marginalisation can be traced to the origins of the colonial and racist state in the nineteenth century, which 150 years of independence had not been able to challenge. This realisation began to dawn on critics during the early part of the twentieth century, and the national humiliation that was the Chaco War (1932–35) would come to inform the ideology of the 1952 revolution, which enfranchised the indigenous majority.[18] However, by the mid-1980s, it seemed that for a majority of the population, political citizenship in the form of the right to vote was not, by itself, sufficient for them to enjoy full citizenship.

A final characteristic that finds its roots in the country's history and partly explains its difficulties of governability is the profound institutional weakness of the Bolivian state. The state has not, at any point in its independent history, exercised control over the entire territory within its borders. This has implications for Bolivia's land mass and for the exercise of citizenship discussed above. This lack of control has resulted in myriad instances of territorial loss throughout the country's history. Bolivia lost land to Brazil at the turn of the twentieth century (1903), and more famously, it lost access to the sea and the biggest reserves of copper in the world after the War of the Pacific with Chile (1879–83).[19] There was a major loss of territory to Paraguay following defeat during the Chaco War. Bolivia's institutional weakness has been likened to a state that, like a Swiss cheese, is full of holes.[20]

Part of the problem here is the normative assumption in dominant theories of the state that boundaries between nations and states are coterminous. This does not reflect the reality in highly diverse societies marked by cleavages of a cultural, ethnic, linguistic and regional nature.[21] Add to this the extreme economic inequalities between cities and rural areas observed in Bolivia, and it is apparent that these lacunae in the institutional presence throughout the national territory are very much linked to the problem highlighted above of large sections of Bolivian society not being able to exercise their full citizenship rights. How can rural populations without access to electricity, telephones or roads, legal ownership for their land and territories, identity cards or formal provision of services like health and education, feel entirely part of their own country? And yet, as the chapter explores further on, it is here, among the rural and indigenous populations, that Bolivia's contribution to a Latin American-wide 'new cycle of resistance' would begin.

THE FRUSTRATED EXPECTATIONS OF THE TRANSITION TO DEMOCRATIC RULE: THE VIEW FROM ABOVE

The last section considered the political and historical specificities of Bolivia and the limitations to the particular form that liberal democracy took in the country after decades of military rule.[22] They constitute the background to the country's endogenous political failings, and explain to some extent the domestic discontent that fuelled the revolutionary period that led to the electoral victory of MAS in 2005. After years of a democracy of pacts that changed the names at the helm but did not change the political and economic directions of the country, or the corruption at the centre of politics, the crisis of political parties slowly became a profound crisis of democracy, where the term itself lost all legitimacy in the eyes of the population. At some level, the origins and responsibility for this loss of legitimacy could be considered endogenous, with failings including poor representation, electoral illegitimacy, a weak state, and even a culture of protest that has traditionally contributed to the country's politics as much from the streets as from inside Congress.[23] In offering an understanding of the political tsunami that took place in Bolivia in 2005, some have emphasised the transformation of electoral rules during this period.[24] I have already outlined the broader set of factors that, by the end of the 1990s, put into question the political and democratic viability of Bolivia.[25] The argument can therefore be made that, during the two decades following the transition to democratisation, the Bolivian party-political system failed to deliver and adapt to popular demand, sowing the seeds for popular discontent and the eventual overthrow of the entire political system and its established actors.

What a vision from below does not provide, however, is an understanding of the pressures exerted by the neoliberal globalisation project and the way in which, in the context of Bolivia's historical specificity, many of the country's economic and political directions have throughout its history been patterned by its role in the global economic system. These factors are also common to other peripheral countries. In the case of Bolivia, the impact of international economic factors runs deep, and has shaped every aspect of the country through its colonial history. It has shaped issues as varied as economic patterns of development focused on mineral extraction and the prevalent racist attitudes towards the indigenous population, which are still evident today.[26] A view from above explains the national frustrations that followed the return to democracy in relation to the two main crises of legitimacy that provide the explanatory framework for this book.

So, for example, as Chapter 1 explored, Bolivia's economy has historically responded to the global need for mineral resources and has grown to accommodate this. It would be mistaken to argue that Bolivia is unique in harnessing social discontent and proposing a political, social and economic alternative to neoliberalism. As was discussed in Chapter 1, during the neoliberal revolution, Latin American countries, and particularly Bolivia, became the testing ground of economic and development policies designed in the west. Indeed, Bolivia is one of a number of countries around the world where the neoliberal economic experiment that began in Pinochet's Chile, what Naomi Klein has dubbed 'disaster capitalism', was most determinedly imposed in spite of popular opposition.[27]

What is interesting about this period, however, is the way in which the new period of Bolivian struggle that began in the 1980s as a resistance movement to neoliberalism has interpreted this economic pattern. It has described decree 21060 as the perfect example of how austerity packages and other economic measures that were effectively imposed by IFIs acting in the interests of countries of the north had detrimental effects on societal well-being and led to an increase in poverty. In addition, these new commentators have interpreted Bolivia's role in the global economy as one dictated by the desire of a small global capitalist class to bring about a modern-day pillage of natural resources, from minerals to gas, forests and even water.[28] Thus it is not surprising that the defence of natural resources became a key objective of the popular resistance movement during the highest moments of crisis in 2000 and 2003, and have driven subsequent political processes during the MAS era.[29]

From this perspective, in which the global context largely determined the course of events, and global interests cannot be

overridden by national determination, we can also find explanations for Bolivia's failings at the political level during the period
immediately following the return to democracy. Many commentators of the 1980s and 1990s marvelled at Bolivia's achievement in
emerging from the long night of dictatorship, only to despair at the
flawed quality of the democracy that resulted.[30] We have already
considered the endogenous explanations for these failings, including
poor representation, limited legitimacy, a weak state and a culture
of protest. Others take a global-structural approach that links the
country to the processes of globalisation within a framework of
world systems theory.[31] These analyses have argued instead that the
process of 'democratisation' in Latin America, and other peripheral and semi-peripheral areas of the world economic system, in
fact reflects a broader US agenda. Although the United States has
claimed to promote democracy, its real aim has been to rearrange
the political systems in these countries in a way that continues to
support the unjust international order. By definition, the result
cannot be a democracy that serves the real interests of the mass of
the population.

This feature of the emerging global society is referred to as
'polyarchy', and is characterised by the imposition of what William
Robinson describes as 'low-intensity democracies'.[32] According to
this view, this was the strategy the United States essentially pursued
following the end of the cold war period, in which US domination had been exerted through the imposition of, and support for,
right-wing dictatorships.[33] Robinson has more recently returned
to this theme, arguing that the 1980s democratic transition in
Latin America was predicated on a minimalist understanding of
democracy, which effectively limited it to a narrow choice between
quasi-identical elites that were unquestioning of their role as
implementers of a globally hegemonic capitalist project.[34]

As Chapter 7 explores, one of the ways in which this theory of
hegemonic domination took form in Bolivia was through the implementation of the US-sponsored coca eradication programme, called
plan dignidad (dignity plan). Critics have interpreted this as part of
a neoimperial strategy for securing the control of distant economies
through military means.[35]

Whether we see the frustrated expectations of Bolivia's transition
to democratic rule as the result of flaws inherent to the country's
politics and political class, or as the result of external impositions
driven by a neoimperial project aiming to further integrate Latin
America into the global neoliberal system, there is no doubt of

the popular response. There was increasing restlessness inside the country, particularly among non-traditional political players such as the indigenous population. These actors were able to challenge the failed political system that had grown with the return to democracy and the economic model of development that supported it, at least discursively, making the link between their country's situation and the global capitalist system. The chapter now turns to Bolivia's reaction and resistance to the various forms of impositions on the country, by exploring the birth of the MAS and the way in which the 'process of change' became a reality.

MAS: AN ALTERNATIVE POLITICAL MOVEMENT

The book so far has explored how in two areas that are crucial to the effective working of any society, there was a sustained period of crisis following the return of democracy to Bolivia. The first, discussed in Chapter 1, concerns the economic system and its wider social implications. The model of neoliberal economic development generated large profits for TNCs and for a small national elite, including individuals close to or at the top of the political structure. (For example, Sánchez de Lozada and his brother were millionaires many times over by the time the president had to flee to Miami in 2003.) For the majority of Bolivians, the neoliberal revolution delivered unremitting social and economic pain, unemployment, higher levels of socioeconomic inequality, and greater precariousness even for those lucky enough to have kept their jobs. For the country, what passed for a privatisation of assets, including mines, the national airline and water companies, could better be described as a wholesale giveaway, since these assets were sold at minimal prices and have delivered little income through taxation since their privatisation. There was a close and collaborative relationship between Bolivia's government and the IFIs and northern governments that prescribed or imposed these economic policies. They delivered a growing deficit in public finances and increasing levels of debt, which have saddled Bolivia with an uncertain long-term economic future. In the late 1980s Bolivia would have been unable to pay civil servants their Christmas bonus had it not received international loans via the IMF, in a situation that, the time of writing in the summer of 2011, is not dissimilar to that of Greece.

The second crisis discussed in this chapter was the crisis of the party political system and the institutions of the state, which led to the term 'democracy' losing all legitimacy in the eyes of the Bolivian population. This was because of the way in which Bolivia's experiment with democracy in the context of dependency brought to the surface the Latin American legacy of *caudillismo*, clientelism, increasing levels of corruption and weak links between political parties and the electorate they claimed to represent.

This fundamental dual crisis sets the explanatory framework for this book. It explains to some extent the emergence of a popular rebellion, a bottom-up mobilisation of citizens through the channels of organised civil society, which would deliver the MAS movement. However, two other key circumstances are fundamental to understanding the recent process of mobilisation and to explaining the rise of MAS as an alternative political movement that has become hegemonic: the urban/rural divide and the municipalisation of Bolivian politics since 1994.

The deep cleavages that exist in Bolivia between cities and rural areas are obvious to any visitor, as are the profound socioeconomic differences between these two constituencies. What these divisions have emphasised throughout the history of Bolivia is an equally deep division in the identities of the peoples of these areas. Against a *mestizo* culture that dominated the city and the political institutions of a republican Bolivia, the rural area claimed a series of strong indigenous identities with their own cultures, languages and territories. Whether the disparate groups were focused around a lowland or highland indigenous identity, or a rural peasant identity, an important element of MAS is their unifying rural nature. This integrated them in their opposition to a state that was seen to represent conceptions of democracy belonging to a *mestizo* republican Bolivia. This explains why in the early 1990s, during the official celebrations of 500 years since the 'discovery' of Latin America, just as the Spanish king paraded through the continent's cities and had audiences with presidents in front of television cameras, an indigenous-led continental campaign of resistance to 500 years of domination began its march. The MAS is the Bolivian political expression of that demand for recognition and integration into the mainstream of their own version of history, cultures, new visions of democracy, and more importantly, new political institutions that could make these demands a reality.[36]

Therefore MAS became a new political actor which, in its origins, represented rural popular sentiment against an ill-fitting democracy. This is why it emerged from civil society, outside the formal political system and in rural areas, before, led by the coca growers, it was adopted by the urban poor and part of the middle classes during the revolutionary period of 2000–03. If it has a date of birth, this can be located in the Sixth congress of the peasant workers' federation, the Confederación Sindical Única de Trabajadores Campesinos de Bolivia (CSUTCB). Meeting in 1994, CSUTCB resolved to create a 'political instrument' in order to 'create our own state, with our own constitution, in which indigenous nations can produce their own state'.[37] It was in the following year, during a congress that brought together four of the five main indigenous social movements (CSUTCB, Confederación Nacional de Mujeres Campesinas Indígenas Originarias de Bolivia 'Bartolina Sisa' (CNMCIOB-'BS'), Confederación Sindical de Colonizadores de Bolivia (CSCB), and Confederación Indígena del Oriente Boliviano (CIDOB)) that the Political Instrument for the Sovereignty of the Peoples (originally referred to as IPSP, later as MAS-IPSP) was created under the acronym ASP (Assembly of the Nations). This marked the beginning of the political unity of indigenous peoples in Bolivia.[38] It is interesting to note that the origins of the MAS took the form of a 'political instrument', a term deliberately chosen by the social movements to distinguish them from political parties, which were then considered to be the biggest obstacle to Bolivia's democracy because of their loss of legitimacy.

The formal union of indigenous peoples under this political instrument was followed by a period of consolidation of the various member groups under the leadership of Evo Morales. Morales' leadership began to become established during the period of criminalisation of the coca growers in the Chapare region. A state of emergency was established, which was characterised by militarisation of the area, the violation of basic human rights and repression.[39] At this juncture, the demand for recognition and for the creation of alternative political institutions that characterised the entry of the indigenous populations into Bolivian politics as independent political actors who identified the Bolivian state and its institutions as alien to them, became complemented by a new reading of the country's political reality, which emerged from the militarisation of the Chapare and the role played by the United States in this policy. This reading added to the demand for political sovereignty made by the indigenous populations a new anti-imperialist, anti-US discourse that stemmed from the federation of the coca growers' trade unions. This ideological contribution to the MAS saw Morales eventually wrest control of the political instrument from Alejo Véliz, its first leader during the period when it had gone under the acronym ASP.

The anti-imperialist discourse is also a crucial difference between the MAS led by Morales and one that could have been led by Felipe Quispe, an indigenous leader and member of the Tupaj Katari guerrilla group (EGTK), who after a period of imprisonment in the 1990s would go on to create the alternative Pachakuti Indigenous Movement (MIP), a more radical *indigenista* party which would challenge MAS in future elections.[40]

Finally, the municipalisation of Bolivian politics in the 1990s was another factor that helps explain the rise of MAS as a representative of subaltern, hitherto voiceless, rural political actors. The municipalisation began in 1994 with the enactment of Law 1551, or the Law of Popular Participation (LPP). It increased the powers of municipal governments and promoted the participation of community organisations in municipal-level politics. The LPP established new municipalities in the country as the base of power and administration, transferring around 20 per cent of the national budget to the municipal level in proportion to the local population. In order to obtain these funds, communities had to develop spending and management plans in a participatory manner which included all local political players. As a result, these new municipal authorities became responsible for the planning of services such as health and education at the local level, as well as the planning of new infrastructure such as access roads and canals for irrigation, all a part of five-year local development plans.

The LLP also created 'vigilance committees' with veto powers to ensure that municipalities could deliver the plans proposed and corruption did not set in. Many of these committees were staffed, advised or trained by non-governmental organisations (NGOs) funded by the World Bank, USAID and other governmental partners that brought a neoliberal logic to the administration of public policy. This process that has been described as a 'construction of neoliberal hegemony'.[41] In contrast, the MAS was accompanied by a growing global citizens' movement in the form of NGOs. These contributed to and supported the process of empowerment and capacity building that had to take place for rural communities to take their place in Bolivian politics.

The LPP was introduced as part of a wider process of decentralisation, and Sánchez de Lozada's neoliberal *plan de todos*, which included a wholesale 'modernisation' agenda. This could be understood as a way for the Bolivian state to increase the participation and involvement of local communities in the decision-making process, improving the quality of local democracy.[42] The LPP certainly increased the political and economic autonomy of municipalities by means of a transfer of both responsibilities and some, though not all, of the economic means to meet those responsibilities. In addition, the law contributed to the creation of local forms of administration in rural areas where there had been none before. Thus, although critics have pointed that in some cases LPP led to a 'decentralisation of corruption', it is credited with establishing a working mechanism for the participation of a previously excluded majority of the population, in both rural and urban areas.[43] It did so by giving recognition to territorially-based organisations: that is, community organisations that included indigenous communities, rural and peasant communities, and neighbourhood committees such as those from El Alto which would play an important role in 2003. The inclusion in formal local politics of a civil society that had normally only played a political role through protest from the 'outside' was not without problems. For example, trade unions were excluded from formal recognition as legitimate participants. However, the system did bring about a new political culture of grassroots-level forms of organisation and participation.

The LPP could also be understood as a way for the state to extend its reach to rural locations and parts of the country where it had not traditionally managed to achieve a presence. In the process it could clamp down on possibilities of rebellion and exercise some form of hegemonic control, including facilitating the extraction of natural resources.[44] The process of administrative decentralisation introduced by LPP has been explored in tandem with the economic reform (that is, privatisation) process introduced by the Law of Capitalisation. It has been argued that this was designed to provide TNCs with the access and political stability to exploit Bolivia's vast natural resources.[45] So, for example, the LPP was limited in reach because participation did not extend further than the offer of consultation on predefined choices and preferences. To apply the original model of citizen participation devised by Sherry Arnstein in 1969 to LPP, it amounted to a form of state-introduced consultation and not full participation in the form of a community-initiated decision-making process.[46] This is because the communities had no route for challenging the structural conditions of inequality in the country, such as the urban/rural divide, the extreme inequalities stemming from an obscene land distribution, and the non-existence at the time of a minimum wage. As a result, the LPP has been dubbed the result of a politics of recognition without the politics of redistribution.[47]

The municipalisation of Bolivian politics delivered ambiguous results.[48] Because of the inherent limitations of the LPP, it led to higher levels of dissatisfaction within civil society and a wholesale rejection of the neoliberal agenda being delivered by the mainstream political parties. At the same time, the LPP permitted non-traditional political actors to enter formal politics, albeit at the local level. This level had until then been ignored by political parties, whose lists for proportional elections were created centrally. By the time the 1996 electoral reform established the need to elect some representatives in both chambers through a constituency system, these new actors were ready to enter the frame. The LPP was therefore instrumental in bringing about, not only a new and revitalised civil society,[49] but one prepared to vent its frustrations through the formal political system. It was a coalition of grassroots-level organisations representing the views of local political actors, which would eventually overturn the Bolivian political system. It led to the election of MAS in 2005, and set under way the process of peaceful revolution, challenging the entire model of development and politics as it had been known in Bolivia.

The story of MAS since then is relatively well known. Under the name of Izquierda Unida (the United Left, IU), a coalition of civil society forces took part in the 1996 local elections and was successful in winning ten mayoral contests and seeing a number of councillors elected. They were most successful in the Chapare region, where Morales was already leader of the coca growers' federation, and this electoral success would catapult him to the leadership of the political instrument ASP-IPSP. By 1997, IU took part in the national elections and achieved 3.7 per cent of the vote, gaining four members of Congress, including Morales. This cemented his position as both leader of the ASP-IPSP and leader of the *cocalero* movement which had become the public face of the political instrument, significantly raising his appeal and image at the national level. The acronym MAS (Movimiento al Socialismo, Movement towards Socialism) was finally adopted in 1999 as a pragmatic response to the legal difficulties of adopting other names. MAS was the name of a registered but defunct party, and Morales was permitted to effectively take over this shell and apply it to the movement he led.[50] The name has not changed since, and it is under this acronym that what was originally a coalition of indigenous and rural/peasant social movements that fell under the leadership of the coca growers eventually found support among the urban poor and part of the middle classes during the revolutionary period of 2000–03.

A REVOLUTIONARY PERIOD: THREE KEY MOMENTS

The period between 1997 and 2002 has been described as the worst political period in recent Bolivian history. This is because of a combination of factors that set the conditions for a 'perfect storm'. In addition to a mega-coalition government headed by the Banzer-Quiroga led right-wing ADN, the economic crisis that ensued in 1999 led to a growing realisation by the population that governments did not represent the interests of the people, and were prepared to use repressive tactics in order to push through unpalatable policies. The coca eradication plan was one such policy. Observers at the time made clear that the poor legitimacy of the governing coalition was made all the poorer by its inability or unwillingness to pay closer attention to the everyday concerns of the population.[51] As a result, regular confrontations with the police turned increasingly violent from 1999 onwards. One of the causes that caught the public's imagination in Bolivia and that of the global solidarity movement was the Cochabamba 'water war' in 2000, the first major revolt of the period of transition to a new politics that is represented by the MAS government.

This was in essence a struggle by the city's residents against the privatisation of their water supply. Law 2029, or the 'law of drinking water and sanitary sewer systems' was introduced by the Banzer-Quiroga administration in 1999 to privatise water provision. Nobody denied at the time of the privatisation that the city of Cochabamba had a chronic problem in the supply of clean drinking water. Of its population of over 1 million, about half had no access to safe piped water, and had to rely on obtaining supplies at the extortionate rates charged by water carriers and sellers. In a move that was promoted by the World Bank and replicated in other parts of the developing world with similar consequences, President Banzer sold the infrastructure and the rights to supply water in Cochabamba to Aguas del Tunari, a subsidiary of the Bechtel-owned International Water.[52] Aguas del Tunari obtained ownership of all water in the city, including well-water and collected rainwater. As with other privatisations in the country since 1985, this legislation was passed through Congress with a minimum of discussion, debate and information. Nor was this lack of transparency limited to Congress: it seems that politicians expected to privatise the water supply without informing their own citizens. For example, the mayor of Cochabamba and future presidential candidate Manfred Reyes Villa did not once mention the issue in his electoral campaign at the time.

Shortly after winning the concession, Aguas del Tunari announced that it was increasing water rates by between 100 and 300 per cent. Protests began in November 1999, led by an organically grown social movement called Platform for the Defence of Life and Water. (The events of this a period are vividly recounted by Olivera and Lewis in *Cochabamba! Water war in Bolivia*.[53]) There were many objections to the policy of privatisation, but one that caught the public's imagination, and convinced protesters that neoliberal privatisation policies went contrary to their well-being, was that Law 2029 made it impossible to avoid becoming a customer of Aguas del Tunari. The price rises introduced by the company put piped water out of reach for the city's poor, but it was the way in which the collection of rainwater was policed and penalised that brought the city to the streets. The wave of strikes, roadblocks and protests was so intense that the city seemed to be doomed to paralysis for the foreseeable future.[54] Eventually Bechtel had to abandon its plans in Bolivia.

The implications of the water war were many. Not least, it was seen as a model for resisting other attempts at privatisation of the water supply. For example, in La Paz a contract had been signed with Aguas del Illimani and its parent company Suez Lyonnais in 2005, but after public protests and demonstrations in El Alto, President Mesa was forced to break the contract. More important, however, was the new understanding that a united and organised civil society could challenge the imposition of neoliberal policies and demand a different decision-making process. This demand for a different politics was a prelude of the larger revolutionary upheaval that would envelop Bolivia in 2003.

The connection made by the electorate between these street victories and the new political challenge presented by MAS and the indigenist movement was accentuated as a result of the water war, to such an extent that, in the 2002 presidential elections, the combined vote of MAS and Felipe Quispe's MIP was 27 per cent.[55]

The second key series of moments of crisis in Bolivia's recent political history took place in 2003. February of the year began with a presidential attempt to increase taxes. This decision led to shooting incidents between members of the police and the military in the presidential square, and a mass uprising that took hold of La Paz, creating a vacuum of power that lasted a couple of days. This was followed by the best-known popular uprising of 2003, which took place in October, following the passing of Law 3058 (the Hydrocarbons Law), which paved the way for the privatisation of gas exploitation by TNCs. This led to plans to export gas via Chile. The victory against the privatisation of water in Cochabamba prompted a similar movement for the 'recovery' (in other words, the renationalisation) of gas and natural resources. Demonstrations in the satellite city of El Alto effectively created a siege of La Paz. There had recently been an unrelated massacre of indigenous peoples in Warisata which had caused much anger, and when the military tried to break the siege, tensions boiled over. The violence that erupted in the days following 12 October resulted in the deaths of over 70 people and hundreds of injuries. At this point, the entire country erupted in demands for the resignation of Sánchez de Lozada. He left the presidential palace for Miami the following week.[56] In the wake of this, the plan to export gas via Chile was abandoned.

At this point, the writing was on the wall for the doomed MNR-led government and for the unstable version of democracy, based on behind-the-scenes pacts, that had dominated Bolivian politics between 1983 and 2003. The 2002 election results had signalled the death knell for parties like MIR, the Bolivia Free Movement (MBL), ADN, CONDEPA, UCS and Nueva Fuerza Republicana (NFR) and the 2003 Gas War reinforced this development.[57] Vice president Carlos Mesa took over from Sánchez de Lozada and placated the populace, lowering the level of outrage for a time. However, he eventually proved unable to stem the outpouring of popular protests.

The third key period of national crisis occurred in May and June 2005, when the social movements demanded the renationalisation of natural resources.[58] Mesa was unable or unwilling to deliver this, and the level of mass protest forced him to resign, making him the second president to do so in the space of two years. A caretaker president, Eduardo Rodríguez Veltzé, set the scene for early elections in December. These were won by MAS in the first round with 53.7 per cent of the vote, inaugurating the political era explored in the reminder of this book.

The role of MAS in this period is not entirely clear. The official version of events would like to portray the 2005 electoral victory as the organic expression of the will of the rural and indigenous people, who were joined in their struggle by the urban social movements, creating the type of plebeian uprising that has been extolled by vice-president García Linera. However, the MAS underwent a very clear transformation from social movement to party in the period between 1999 and 2005. Arguably it became just the type of less than democratic party it had originally been supposed to challenge.[59] The electoral results then and since suggest that MAS has become a new hegemonic party, much as MNR once was. In addition, several commentators have noted how, instead of spearheading the social revolt of 2000, 2003 or 2005, MAS in fact followed behind these historic events. It only supported the protests once their success had become inevitable, in order to prevent its own marginalisation.[60]

What is not in doubt about the course of political events is that at some point after June 2004, a confrontation took place in the country between what were effectively two Bolivias. The first grouping was supported by the Bolivian masses, and emerged from the events of 'black October' in 2003. They demanded the nationalisation of gas and Bolivia's natural resources, and the creation of a new constitution through an inclusive participatory process. The second focused on the June agenda of 2004. It aggregated the interests of the landowning elites of Santa Cruz with those in Tarija, Beni and Pando, and came to be known as the Media Luna. This grouping formed an opposition to the future government of Morales, and was built on a desire to maintain the social and economic privileges of this class, although it was dressed up as a demand for autonomous government.[61] This national division between the two Bolivias would cast a long shadow over the early years of the Morales era, and would come close to derailing the process of change during the period of the Constitutional Assembly.

TOWARDS THE 2005 VICTORY

I began this book with Morales' first speech as president, in which he hailed the 'end of the colonial and neoliberal era'. Chapter 1 explored the neoliberal economic reforms that dominated Bolivia after the hyperinflation crisis of 1985, and the structural adjustment programme (SAP) that was implemented to deal with it, as well as the period of economic liberalisation and privatisation that followed in the 1990s. In the 1980s a serious economic downturn led to a process of hyperinflation, lack of economic growth, budgetary deficits and a mountain of debt. The economic recipe for solving these problems came from North American academic circles in the form of monetarist economic policies. Bolivia was in this respect a testing ground for ideas of economic stabilisation by means of SAPs imposed from the outside. This economic model was fed by the neoliberal thinking that had been inaugurated in Chile back in the 1970s during the Pinochet dictatorship. It was then extended in the 1990s with the wholesale privatization of companies and public assets, as part of a trend followed in much of Latin America, with disastrous socioeconomic consequences for the vast majority of the population, who were more likely to be poor and jobless at the end of this period that at the beginning.

The second promise implicit in the 1982 return to democracy was contained precisely in the term 'democracy'. An imported element of the democratisation process, the model of liberal democracy and management that had generated so much hope in the population after years of dictatorship, failed during the following two decades to live up to its promise. This was also true of the decentralisation reforms that went hand in hand with some of the economic policies discussed in Chapter 1. Not only did the system not generate participation from the population, it produced a corrupt elite and a generalised disenchantment with politics, which translated into low political participation. It appeared that little had been achieved to liberate Bolivia from the politically corrosive elements of illegitimate military governments, which had for years acted with impunity, repressing the population. In addition to this, the neoliberal model imposed by a New Right distanced the state even further from its citizens. The result was not a positive one on the whole, certainly not in terms of the social suffering caused by these policies on the people of Bolivia. Both can be seen as an expression of what the president then called colonialism and neoliberalism: in other words, of models of economic development and of government that had been created elsewhere. These were problematic in their application in Bolivia, and were often imposed from the outside.

By 2005, the political momentum that had been gathering from outside the formal political system began to pay off. This momentum came from civil society, dating from the first demonstrations against decree 21060; through the political opposition of *cocaleros* to the militarisation of the Chapare region at the behest of the United States; and from the struggle commenced by indigenous organisations demanding dignity and natural resources. In addition, there were neighbourhood associations, from Cochabamba to Potosi to El Alto, organised in defence of basic social rights like housing, access to water and employment. All this led to the creation of a broad coalition of movements that supported MAS and Morales' bid for the presidency. The successive crises of 2000, 2003 and 2005 set the scene for the challenges to Bolivia's process of change: one economic, changing the neoliberal economic order; the other political, reinventing a new form of inclusive and participatory democracy.[62] Both are considered in the next few chapters through the prism of the new constitution, which is explored in Chapter 3.

3 REVOLUTION IN DEMOCRACY?

On January 25, 2009, the people of Bolivia went to the polls for the fourth time in three years. The first of these four elections delivered a historic victory for Evo Morales in December 2005. In June of 2006 Bolivians chose the assembly members who would write a new constitution. This demand of the Bolivian people for change was followed by the only and most consistent show of support for a president in the republican history of the country, when he received a 67 per cent endorsement in a recall referendum celebrated in August 2008. The final vote in January 2009 was to either approve or reject the new constitutional text, which had been heralded as the basis on which to re-found Bolivia and 'decolonise' a country that had been a victim of five centuries of oppression.

As expected, the new constitution received the broad support of the people, with 61 per cent of the votes. Bolivia would now begin a process of implementation of the new constitutional text, which includes, amongst other things, proposals to end centuries of oppression and exclusion of the indigenous majority. Indeed, this referendum can be seen as the end of a process of political mobilisation began by lowland indigenous Bolivians as far back as 1990 to demand their recognition and inclusion in a society traditionally led by urbanites of European extraction. But the path to recognition of this forgotten majority was not easy. First, it required their political participation en masse, followed by their takeover of the institutions of government to deliver the 2005 presidential seat to one of their own. Second, it required a strong dose of patience and *sang froid* during the myriad violent attempts to destabilise the country led by reactionary opposition parties. Along the way lay scattered the ingenuity of those who three years before had thought the process of writing a new constitution would be easy, the lost support of key social groups, and the bodies of dozens of Bolivian citizens.

If the referendum symbolises the end of a chapter in Bolivia's process of change, a new chapter began soon after. For this constitution has to be understood as the road map towards the new type of society the Bolivian majority has come to demand, even if it is not entirely clear what form this society will take or what the end point might look like. Uncharted territory it might be, but it requires that tomorrow's Bolivia becomes more equal, fair, democratic and prosperous within the confines of a new model of development that does not replicate the political, economic and environmental contradictions that afflict us elsewhere and that led Bolivians to search for alternatives in the first place.

The second part of this book takes as its central theme this new Bolivian constitution. This chapter focuses on two areas related to the constitution. The first is a discussion of the process by which it was written, a process that permits us to analyse the quintessential characteristics of Bolivia's new participatory forms of politics and its limitations. The second is the discussion of some of the fundamental elements of this constitutional text in the form of the structure of the state, rights and citizenship, and new models of development that it presages for Bolivia. These elements constitute the backbone of the second part of this book, and set the scene for the themes that are developed in Chapters 4, 5 and 6.

DEMANDING RECOGNITION: THE MARCHES FOR TERRITORY AND DIGNITY

In Venezuela and Ecuador too, new constitutions have come into force of late. It has been said that Bolivia shares a number of similar characteristics and common experiences with these countries.[1] The first two of these characteristics constitute the backbone of the argument presented in the first part of the book: both refer to fundamental failures that took place during the period immediately after the end of military rule. First came the crisis of the neoliberal economic order in the region and its failure to deliver great rates of economic growth and the eradication of poverty. Second, the political systems that replaced military rule failed to deliver meaningful democracy by providing avenues for either the representation or participation of citizens. Instead, corruption tainted the workings of the political systems and fuelled the high levels of apathy and cynicism that dominated the electorate in the region.

The next two characteristics find their own unique expression in this country above all. One was the way in which, by the 1990s, the project of national identity forged with the 1952 revolution, which negated that which was indigenous, had finally come to an end. The new Bolivia would have to define itself in plural cultural, ethnic and national terms for the first time in its history, finally bestowing recognition on the forgotten majorities. (It had actually done so in an amendment to the constitution in the mid-1990s, but, as with many other laws, its meaning was drowned in platitudes that had little to do with the daily life of a majority of the population.) This new plurinational identity would not have come to be fully realised had it not been for the rise of civil society, which took over from the failed political parties as an actor in response to the first two crises described above. The rise of civil society took the form of indigenous and rural social movements, in association with women's movements and civic associations generally.[2] It was the return of what vice-president García Linera has referred to as the plebeian Bolivia.[3]

This part of the book explores the alternative vision of nationhood, taking the political framework represented in the new constitution as the basis from which to explore and build explanations for the current process of change. However, consideration needs to be given to the fact that, beyond the political process of change that brought the MAS to power, Bolivia's new 2009 constitution was the result of political demands that were started originally by indigenous peoples of the vast areas of the lowlands on a number of historic marches to La Paz.[4] At this point, it is important to emphasise that, for indigenous peoples whose livelihoods are based on subsistence agriculture and the exploitation of natural resources, marching on foot from their distant communities to parliament is the only type of action that gives them voice and a common political identity. This type of political action, which could be considered equivalent to a strike by a salaried worker, carries a significant symbolic meaning in Bolivian politics, and originates largely in the 1990s, constituting a fundamental piece of the political jigsaw that occupies us in this book.

The first of these marches took place in 1990 under the banner of 'territory and dignity'. This march is key to the recent emergence of Bolivia's indigenous people's emancipation and their becoming the strongest national political actor, and also achieved a great deal on its own terms. First, along with the marches that followed, it made a whole range of indigenous peoples from the lowlands of Bolivia visible for the first time. The awareness of highland indigenous groups had been guaranteed by the physical presence of more than 4 million Quechua and Aymara speakers and by a history of rebellion that goes back to Túpac Katari and his wife Bartolina Sisa. In a manner that betrays the underlying fear of the indigenous on which modern Bolivia has been built, these two historic actors laid siege to La Paz for six months in 1781 in the greatest ever rebellion of indigenous peoples against Spanish rule.[5] Their legacy is without question today. Not only do their mobilisation tactics hold validity, as the 2003 events in El Alto show, their memory has been rescued for the first time by the new Bolivia being forged by an indigenous president. They have joined the ranks of would-be liberation and revolutionary leaders whose names are frequently remembered by President Morales in his speeches. Indeed, the hold that Túpac Katari and Bartolina Sisa have on indigenous history and identity politics is such that they inspired *katarismo*, the first indigenous movement in Bolivia since the 1952 revolution, which fed on the highland Aymara tradition of rebellion and played an important role in the country's transition to democracy in 1982. Sisa's name has been adopted by the biggest women's indigenous social movement, whose members refer to themselves as *Bartolinas*.[6]

The case of the lowland indigenous peoples is different indeed. There is, to be sure, a history of resistance – either passive resistance or direct confrontation – in this part of the country to Spanish rule and to the Jesuit and other orders that arrived early in the colonial era to evangelise and control the indigenous populations from their missions.[7] And yet successive governments since the 1950s have regarded the Bolivian lowlands as 'empty' of both populations and cultures, at the same time as seeing what constitutes three-quarters of Bolivia's land mass as a boundless source of natural resources and land for others to acquire. This was the view impressed on successive waves of new colonisers who were encouraged by governments keen to populate and exploit the vast natural resources of the Amazonian part of the country. The first lowland indigenous march therefore served to bring a forgotten part of the population to the forefront of an incipient political process of change. In this, they were aided by a growing international indigenous movement, which from 1992 onwards was becoming an effective transnational political actor.[8]

Thus, the growing indigenous movement in Bolivia has both internal and external influences. Internally, it responds to a history of rebellion in the Bolivian highlands, whereas in the lowlands it reflects the growing threat to land and natural resources brought about by the arrival of numerous waves of new migrants. Many of these new migrant groups were simply trying to make a living after the economic crisis of the 1980s and decree 21060 (discussed in Chapter I) had taken their mining jobs and livelihoods. In addition, during the second half of the twentieth century, the increasingly intensive exploitation of land for commercial crops like soya and for raising cattle, as well as logging, mining and oil exploration activities in the lowlands, encroached on the traditional lands of indigenous groups and forced them to be militant in defence of their way of life.[9]

Externally, the Bolivian indigenous movement responded to an increasing international preoccupation with the well-being of indigenous groups around the world, which was led by the United Nations and by a growing number of advocacy and support organisations from the 1970s onwards. The United Nations took particular leadership on indigenous issues after the 1992 demonstrations against the 500th anniversary of the 'discovery' of the Americas, declaring 1995–2004 the decade of indigenous peoples and creating in 2002 the Permanent Forum on Indigenous Issues, a new body that reports directly to the Economic and Social Council of the United Nations.[10] This body is testament of how far the transnational indigenous movement, which consists of indigenous organisations, international non-governmental organisations (NGOs) and advocacy groups, and individual supporters around the world, has travelled, and how effectively it has mobilised in support of recognition and participation of indigenous peoples in their societies and in the international system of governance.[11]

In Bolivia, indigenous demands for recognition from the 1990s were the main element that fuelled the rise of indigenous social movements and their emergence as key political actors in the current process of change. From the original march for territory and dignity in 1990, the indigenous movements came to be seen as associated with the demand for a new constitution to be drawn up with high levels of public participation. The Confederación Indígena del Oriente Boliviano (CIDOB) takes credit for making this demand as far back as 1996, and the demand grew in strength in subsequent years. The major indigenous demands regarding the new constitution were based on specific proposals to bring about the recognition of the indigenous majority in Bolivian society. This is reminiscent of what Nancy Fraser has described as 'transformative change', a change that encompasses both the political and economic dimensions of inequality based on ethnicity, redistribution, and the cultural-valuation dimensions, what she refers to as the recognition element.[12]

The specific proposals were to increase social equality, the repre-sentation of indigenous peoples in the higher echelons of power, and policies destined to defend and increase indigenous produc-tive processes, culture and world-views. In particular, CIDOB demanded a new legislative system, the end of the dominant role of political parties in favour of more direct and participative types of association, a new politico-administrative division of the country that recognised the ancestral lands of many indigenous groups, the recognition and promotion of indigenous languages, including the introduction of bilingual education, an expansion of the economic role of the state, and policies for the protection of the natural envi-ronment as well as the defence of Bolivia's vast natural resources under the authority of a strong state.

For its part, the highlands-based Consejo Nacional de Ayllus y Markas del Qullasuyu (CONAMAQ) proposed as early as 2000 the creation of a constitutional assembly that was truly participa-tive and that operated on the principles of the *ayllu: ama sua, ama llulla, ama qhella*.[13] These terms summarise the basic Andean moral principles, which can be roughly translated as 'do not steal, do not lie, do not be lazy'. They were immortalised for the world outside Bolivia by Luzmila Carpio's 1970s song of the same title, and have become included in the new constitution as the moral-ethical principles of the new Bolivia.[14]

Others argue that in fact it was the fourth march to La Paz, begun in May 2002 and formally organised under the slogan 'in favour of popular sovereignty, territory and natural resources' that constituted the clearest demand for a constitutional assembly.[15] As the march advanced towards the seat of government, it became increasingly associated with this demand, something that went much further than the constitutional reform demanded in 2000 by a broad base of civil society organisations that emerged in the shadow of the Cochabamba water war that year. In 2002 CIDOB and lowland indigenous organisations were the key participants, but starting in Oruro and Potosí, their highland indigenous coun-terparts organised as part of CONAMAQ led a second branch of the march to La Paz. And then a third strand emerged, and others that incorporated the *Bartolinas*, the Movimiento Sin Tierra, the landless peasants' movement (MST), and peasant organisations of indigenous peoples who have colonised vast areas of the Bolivian lowlands in search of land and livelihoods, and are often referred to as the *colonizadores* or *interculturales* (settlers and intercultural groups).[16] Missing in all of this were the coca growers of the

Chapare region, who were organisationally closer to the MAS and were working hard on the campaign for the elections that were due to take place that June.

The marchers arrived together in La Paz on June 19, 2002, when less than two weeks remained before the elections. Parliament responded to their demands by passing a law that recognised the need for a future constitutional assembly, an enormous victory for the indigenous movement and one that would have the most profound influence for the future of the country.

The constitutional assembly debate did not return to the political agenda until after the collapse of Gonzalo Sánchez de Lozada's 15-month-long government in 2003. The demand for a constitutional assembly charged with the writing of a new constitution was part of the October Agenda, a series of demands made by the social movements that included the repeal of decree 21060 and the nationalisation of Bolivia's natural resources. Even then Lozada's vice president and successor, the renowned historian Carlos Mesa, failed to convene the assembly, and the issue was parked until a solution could be found to the problems of the increasingly crisis-ridden political system. Out of this emerged the political hegemony of the MAS after the electoral victory of December 2005.

In the meantime, the same indigenous political actors that had led the calls for a new constitution and for new forms of recognition continued to strengthen their organisations and their political role by creating the Pacto de Unidad (Unity Pact). This bloc of civil society organisations brought together all main indigenous organisations, the landless movement and other civil society organisations such as Bolivian NGOs Centro de Estudios Jurídicos e Investigación Social (CEJIS), Centro de Comunicación y Desarrollo Andino (CENDA) and Centro de Documentación e Información de Bolivia (CEDIB).[17] The pact's purpose was in fact to produce, through consensus, deliberation and a broad representation of the wishes of their grassroots membership, a draft constitution that could be presented to the future constitutional assembly for discussion and consideration.

Thus the Pacto de Unidad represented the coming together of civil society, led by the indigenous social movements, and their emergence as key political actors driving the process of change like never before in Bolivian history.[18] Indeed, if the birth of the republic in 1826 had represented the desire for independence of the *criollo* elite from the Spanish crown, the newly independent country replicated a strict social hierarchy that ignored the existence of the indigenous majority.[19] It would take more than 100 years (until 1952) for the indigenous peoples to be enfranchised, but even then they were not recognised as indigenous. Instead, indigenous peoples, divested of cultural recognition, were described as peasants by the revolution, an identity not of their choosing which made them Bolivians in theory while perpetuating their lack of recognition and marginalisation in all areas of society. It would not be until the 1994 constitutional reform that the multicultural nature of Bolivia was finally recognised, and yet by that time it was already too late for symbolic gestures, as Bolivia's indigenous peoples were already engaged in the political struggle that lies at the heart of the country's current process of change.[20]

From opposition politics and mobilisation, these movements that incorporated the very poorest and marginalised found a political voice that demanded recognition and soon made the government of Paz Zamora ratify the International Labour Organization (ILO) Convention 169 on the Rights of Indigenous Peoples in 1991.[21] By the middle of the 1990s the dignified 'uprising' of the lowland indigenous peoples had achieved a great deal, including rights over their ancestral territories. However, their political struggle went much further. Not stopping at achieving indigenous rights, they came together with the remnants of the trade union movement and other organisations to create the political instrument that, under the name of Izquierda Unida (United Left), would contest the municipal and presidential elections of 1997. These elections took Evo Morales to Congress for the first time. Having begun a process of change that could no longer be stopped, the indigenous movement and civil society organisations became the backbone of the political representation that would eventually occupy the institutions of the state in the 2005 elections as part of MAS.[22] Further, the indigenous movement took the leadership in the process of change by articulating the demands of the population through the Pacto de Unidad which, in the case of the constitutional project, included the production of a complete new draft constitution, the only one presented to assembly members when the inauguration of the Constitutional Assembly took place, on August 6, 2006 in the capital city of Sucre. This draft was 'adopted' by MAS and became the basis for building the new constitution. Because August 6 is a bank holiday that celebrates the country's independence in 1825, it was a fitting day to commence the process of writing the new constitution, which would set the process of decolonisation finally in motion, even if it came almost two centuries late. This was the sentiment that inspired some of the participants in this historic process that we explore in the next section.

A REVOLUTION IN DEMOCRACY OR A REVOLUTIONARY FORM OF DEMOCRACY?

If the new politics inaugurated in January 2006 with the swearing in of President Morales was the result of social movement demands mobilised to take control of state institutions that had repeatedly failed the country throughout its history, the biggest challenge that lay ahead at that point was to rewrite the basic societal rules for the re-foundation of a country with chronic problems, including weak institutions mired in political corruption, the political and economic domination of a small oligarchic groups, and an excluded and poor indigenous majority.

The response from the new government was to deepen the process that had already begun to empower a traditionally disempowered majority and help it take ownership of the major national debates, building democracy through bottom-up participation in order to deliver sorely needed structural changes rather than purely cosmetic ones. This type of process of democratic practice has been studied by the literature in terms of 'deep' forms of democracy where citizens have opportunities for their voice to be heard and taken into account.[23] The argument that feeds theoretical debates on deep forms of democracy in their participative or deliberative guises is that dominant models of democracy where our participation is limited to taking part in elections every few years are insufficiently democratic and therefore deficient in delivering a minimum of participation and representation. Mature democracies around the world contend with the related problems caused by the overbearing influence of special interest groups and markets on party policies that leave citizens out of the decision-making equation. As a result, these systems call into question the legitimacy of the entire political process that claims to organise our societies. This problem is compounded when citizens, feeling left out, refuse to take part in the electoral process, as is shown by the increasingly high abstention rates that characterise elections in European countries.

Thus the process of writing a new constitution in Bolivia included far-reaching participation levels and the provision of deliberative spaces for every section of society. It could not have been otherwise, for if the ultimate aim was to achieve a democratic society, the means to achieve this goal had to be as democratic as possible in terms of the participation it afforded to those excluded sections of society. Furthermore, MAS itself represented the power of civil society to challenge formal political structures and parties. After bubbling under the political radar for over a decade, the original demands of the indigenous communities had, through MAS, risen to represent the October Agenda in 2003, and they were joined now by Bolivia's masses to demand the nationalisation of the country's natural resources and the creation of a new constitution through a participatory process of deliberation.[24]

The history of that process, however, demonstrates the limits to participative democracy in highly unequal societies.[25] Indeed, Bolivia is more than just divided. Bolivia's best-known twentieth-century social scientist, René Zabaleta Mercado, is famous for coining the term *sociedad abigarrada* (it has been translated as motley society), by which he meant that Bolivia was a heterogeneous society with extreme social diversity and multiple overlapping histories, forms of economic practice and consequently power.[26] If shortly after Black October the rise of MAS, representing the popular demand for a new covenant between the state and its citizens, took place, the June agenda of 2004 that saw a growing demand for autonomic government in the regions would become the other side of the coin, the side of the 'other Bolivia' who, aggregating the interests of those with most to lose from the Bolivia demanded by the majority, sought to recreate the past in their own regions. The former is the expression of inclusion, democracy, equality; in short, of a revolution in democracy. The latter is the expression of a desire to defend class and ethnic interests by raising the spectre of fear and doom. The *empate catastrófico* (catastrophic draw) – as vice-president Linera would dub it – between these two Bolivias was played out for the following five years. It came closest to derailing the country's profound process of social change during and immediately after the end of the work carried out by the Constitutional Assembly.[27]

Difficult beginnings

The process of producing the new constitution started well enough. Having understood the groundswell of Bolivia's demand for a new constitution, President Morales convened the Constitutional Assembly in March 2006, soon after his own election. During the process of negotiation and debate that established the rules of election and powers of future assembly members, Congress became

the scene of the kind of political war and crisis that had delegitimised party politics in the eyes of the Bolivian electorate and made
possible the recent election of MAS.[28] More than 20 proposals
were debated until a compromise was found on a model of election
of assembly members. MAS had to give in to opposition demands
that over-represented their interests and limited those of the indigenous peoples. The agreed basis was that three *asambleistas* would
be chosen in each of the country's 70 constituencies, two for the
winning party and one for the runner-up, making 210. In addition,
five more members would be chosen in each of the nine *departa-
mentos* (regions), according to a formula that gave two seats to the
winning party and one for each of the next three according to their
share of the vote, bringing the total to 255.[29] In addition to this,
the electoral law established that the constitutional draft produced
by the Assembly would have to be ratified by two-thirds of its
members.

As a result of this system, the plurality of voices in Sucre, the
country's capital and venue of the constitution-writing process,
was widely broadened, yet it still remained unrepresentative of the
country as a whole. Given the enormous population density differences between the highlands, in the west of the country, and the
lowlands in the east, an *asambleista* required up to ten times more
votes in La Paz for example than in rural Beni. Indigenous peoples,
the main instigators of demands for recognition in the framework
of a new constitution, who had mobilised for over a decade to reach
this point, did not achieve their proposals for special indigenous
constituencies or direct representation to the *asamblea*, and the vast
majority of those elected were MAS candidates. In addition, the
electoral formula applied permitted the presence in the *asamblea* of
a wide range of minority interest groups that had little interest in
its success and denied the MAS the two-thirds of the votes needed
to control the process that was about to begin. Where four main
parties dominated Congress, the constituent assembly had 16 such
groups.[30]

The justification for agreeing to this formula of election, which
was detrimental to the interests and demands of the Bolivian population as a whole, was that the new constitutional text had to be the
result of consensus building through a process of deliberation, and
represent a multiplicity of views in the country. It would be fair to
say at this stage that, having recognised the historic importance of
this process, MAS took the view that without as broad a spectrum of
voices as possible in Sucre, the result of the process of constitutional

creation could be accused of having been imposed by the majority rather than being the result of true deliberation, an accusation that would weaken the constitutional outcome in future. In retrospect, it is perhaps clear also that there was a certain naivety to this view, based as it was on the belief that opposition parties would be prepared to play an active role in the assembly and not to try to derail the process, taking advantage of the opportunity handed to them.

In spite of this, the final composition of *asambleistas* was something never seen before in terms of the access it gave to new and hitherto discriminated-against voices in Bolivian society. For starters, the July 2006 referendum gave MAS almost exactly the same percentage of the vote (54 per cent) that it had received in the presidential elections the year before, and 137 assembly members, with Poder democrático y social (PODEMOS), the main opposition, dropping from 28 per cent to around 15 per cent. In addition, more than 55 per cent of those who became *asambleistas* in 2006 classified themselves as belonging to one of the 36 indigenous nations of Bolivia.[31] This is nothing short of remarkable in a country where barely 50 years previously indigenous people were barred from walking in the Plaza Murillo, the seat of government in La Paz, or where they would still subject to the humiliations of May 2008 in Sucre and the massacre of September in Porvenir.[32] In addition, 88 out of the 255 *asambleistas* were women, including the president of the assembly, indigenous leader Silvia Lazarte, a prelude of things to come in the future MAS governments.[33] These larger than expected levels of representation of historically silenced voices were made possible by the parity rule that, where two candidates for the same party were chosen in a constituency, one had to be a woman.

The result was a kaleidoscopic representation of Bolivia from every sector of society, who gathered in Sucre between August 2006 and December 2007 to put into practice an idea of deliberative democracy and to reach a consensus on the vision of society they dreamed of. This included men and women, city dwellers and peasants, poor and middle classes, professionals and workers, whites and representatives of the indigenous majority, educated and semi-literate individuals. Professionals and legal experts complained about the prevalence of poor, rural indigenous people without the necessary 'education' to carry out this historic task. Others reflect on this as the highest expression of democratic participation in the history of Bolivia.[34] The result of their discussions was, in spite of a small intransigent right's every attempt to boycott and derail the process, a collective vision of the future Bolivia that included everyone.

The limits of deliberation

After the Constitutional Assembly was inaugurated, problems soon became evident.[35] The Constitutional Assembly had been envisaged by Bolivians as the basis on which to build a new country that would bring about a social pact of reconciliation between polarised and confronted sectors of society. However, that this would be difficult was evident from the very beginning, and was first expressed in the inability of the assembly to agree on the basic negotiating rules. The Assembly was originally created for a period of 12 months, and was due to be wound up in August 2007. It became bogged down on a debate about whether the draft constitution needed to be approved by a simple majority, or by two-thirds of the votes. MAS was in favour of the former whereas PODEMOS and other small parties demanded the latter.[36] The debate went on for months, and was manipulated by an opposition-inspired media which presented itself as a defender of democracy in opposition to a 'MAS dictatorship'.[37]

Besides making the process difficult, these basic disagreements reflected very real differences in the understanding of the purposes of the assembly. For MAS, it was the basis of nothing less that the refoundation of Bolivia, whereas for the opposition parties, dragged unwillingly to this process, its purpose was to reform the existing constitution in as cosmetic a way as possible. The strategy of putting obstacles in the path of the constitution-writing process worked. The work of writing the actual constitution, divided into 21 commissions or teams, only started in the early part of 2007 after months of delays over the rules governing the process, making it evident that an extension to the original deadline of August 2007 would be necessary.

At this point, thousands of individual proposals had already been made to the assembly. Most of them represented the desires and expectations of specific interest groups, although one proposal included a full constitutional draft presented to the constituent assembly on the day of its inauguration by the Pacto de Unidad. This proposal represented the vision of a coalition of indigenous social movements and sections of civil society who were largely behind the process of change. It was the only full draft proposal (not even MAS had a proposal of the type of document it wanted to see produced), and one that would be the basis for many discussions in the 21 thematic teams in which *asambleistas* were divided to work through the basic skeleton of the future constitution.[38] Before starting to debate the proposals, the commissions and their members were sent on a tour of the country to explain the purpose of the constitution to as wide an audience as possible, listening to and collecting their demands in workshops that took place in churches, town halls and squares up and down the country.[39] Only after this process had taken place did the commissions begin to debate in teams the main articles they wanted to see included in the constitution.[40]

The return to Sucre at the end of April 2007 did not offer much relief to those who believed in the process of change gestating in the country's capital. The subject-specific commissions were supposed to put into practice and demonstrate the possibility of building consensus through a deliberative process. Unfortunately, with very limited exceptions, they proved the opposite, demonstrating that each of the two main groupings in Bolivia was far from ready to offer 'the other' those levels of recognition of manners of speech, language, and narrative that authors have identified as key for the successful outcome of deliberative processes.[41] Yet, as some authors have argued, the existence of deliberation does not preclude conflict,[42] which is almost certain to be an inevitable part of the process of change if this change is based on a substantial redistribution of power, as Bolivia's new constitution attempted to achieve. Conflict was indeed the main characteristic of the work of most of the commissions. However, what Sucre saw in the following months were less disagreements than repeated attempts to paralyse altogether the workings of the assembly, both inside and outside the debating theatre. As Ana María Ruiz, assembly member for the MNR from the region of Beni, acknowledged, her own attempts to work constructively towards a consensus in the commission on land and territory out of a historic sense of duty towards the refoundation of Bolivia led to her being ostracised by her own party under the argument that 'she was not there to make the process work but to help derail it'.[43]

Outside the assembly hall, Sucre became mired in daily protests aimed at paralysing the constitutional process. The main issue of contention was a local demand to bring to Sucre the seat of government, which had been in La Paz since the end of the nineteenth century. This demand was backed by the regional opposition based in the lowlands.[44] When the assembly refused to debate the issue in July and August 2007, the daily demonstrations turned violent and openly racist against indigenous assembly members. Levels of violence reached such a point that the assembly venue had to be closed, and there was no further session in the city. Instead, a military school outside the city was the venue for one session in November, followed by a final extended session in December in the city of Oruro, which delivered the approval of the constitutional draft. It was an ignominious end to a demonstration of deep democracy about which the rest of the world could learn valuable lessons, particularly in relation to mechanisms for the inclusion of all strata in a society that is extremely diverse culturally and deeply divided socioeconomically.

For 18 months, Bolivians from every part of the country, socioeconomic and ethnic group came together to establish the basic principles on which their country is to function in future, leaving no stone unturned. The Constitutional Assembly debated and changed the very definition of Bolivia; it modified the architecture of the state and its relationship to the Bolivian people; it altered dominant definitions of citizenship and citizens' rights and duties; it opened, finally, the possibility of challenging the dominant model of development and starting the search for a new one that will deliver well-being to the population in synchrony with the need to protect the environment. It was, as the president is fond of repeating, a revolution in democracy. To what extent this new document reflects and embodies a revolutionary process is something we explore in the rest of the book. That also needs to be judged in relation to the progress (or not) that the post-constitutional legislative process takes towards the achievement of the ideals and aspirations embedded in the new constitutional text during Morales' last term as president, which began in January 2010. This is particularly important because Bolivia has a tradition of implementation gaps: that is, a practice of adopting progressive legislation that makes no practical difference or does not deal with the root cause of inequality.

Stepping back from the brink

The process of the Constitutional Assembly was limited and manipulated by all sides. The opposition parties in the Assembly used every strategy at their disposal to block and paralyse proceedings for as long as possible, eventually resorting to organised violence outside the building, based around the demand that the seat of government be transferred to Sucre. Some in the MAS have argued that, for all the rhetoric about a constitutional assembly that did not derive its powers from Congress or the government, the government went beyond its formal remit, especially in the final stages.[45] Worse was yet to come. As 2008 went on, regional opposition to the MAS government increased to the point of forcing a recall referendum on the presidential team and prefects in the nine regions of the country. This was scheduled for August of that year. In the meantime, the constitutional draft lay untouched and the government was unable to call a referendum to ask the Bolivian people whether they approved or rejected the new text. Bolivia was effectively divided in two: the western highlands where people were mostly in favour of the process of change, and the eastern lowlands where a semi-feudal society with high levels of inequality in land distribution emphasised the economic and political interests of a small agribusiness and cattle-ranching minority. The impasse between these two Bolivias would eventually be resolved, but not before violence compromised the integrity of the country, and political negotiation the integrity of the constitutional text.

The first element that helped turn the tide in favour of MAS was the result of the recall referendum which the president had been forced to call. On the night of August 10, 2008, as the referendum's results were being announced, it became clear that, in spite of the increasingly radicalised diatribes against them, both the president and the process of change had the overwhelming support of Bolivians. After an increasingly difficult two and a half years at the helm, the 67 per cent of support gained by Morales was a significantly better result than expected and a real shot in the arm for MAS. It also revived the process of constitutional change. In addition, the opposition leadership lost two of their prefects in La Paz and in Cochabamba – soon to be followed by the imprisoned prefect of Pando – after receiving less than a 50 per cent share of the vote in these regions.

This political victory was followed by a victory of a different nature. As the results of the recall referendum were being counted, Morales was busy reaching out to the opposition in a victory speech that appealed to their democratic instincts and asked for unity and consensus building in the process of change. What the country received was exactly the opposite, an audacious move orchestrated by the prefects of the dissident regions under the ironically named Consejo Nacional de Defensa de la Democracia (National Council for the Defence of Democracy, CONALDE), which sent out violent and armed groups of thugs on the rampage. The 'civic-prefectural coup', as the government would dub it, began in earnest on August 15, and had a plan to take control of some regional airports and so prevent the president from travelling around the country. In addition, protesters occupied and destroyed the offices of state institutions such as the National Institute of Agrarian Reform (INRA), nationalised companies like the National Communications Company (ENTEL) and buildings belonging to bodies suspected of having sympathies with the government, such as NGOs that have traditionally supported indigenous demands. The unrest included a number of terrorist attacks on the main gas pipe to Brazil, aimed at damaging the country economically while isolating the dissident regions and creating enough mayhem to either force the intervention of the military or worse, provoke a civil war.

The civil unrest that spread around the country in the middle of September was enough for companies like American Airlines to stop flying to Bolivia for a couple of weeks, and for the government of the United States to issue advice to its citizens to leave the country. The high point of this organised violence took place on September 11 in Pando, when an armed group of workers from the prefecture, following orders from their employer, blockaded the road outside the municipality of Porvenir, stopping a number of lorries carrying indigenous men, women and children, and shooting at them indiscriminately, killing at least 18 people and chasing hundreds of others into exile.[46]

Fortunately for Bolivia, the events of 2003 in El Alto were not repeated. Instead, the government acted decisively but peacefully. First, having accused the US ambassador Philip Goldberg of supporting the armed insurrection, the Bolivian government gave him 72 hours to leave the country.[47] The crackdown had left the opposition prefects without a political rudder, and things soon got back to a tense normality. This is the point at which the international community, led by the Unión de Naciones del Sur (UNASUR), called an emergency meeting. It was hosted by former Chilean president Michelle Bachelet, and expressed its full support for the democratic process in Bolivia.

This timely intervention might well have taken some of the oxygen away from the oligarchy-funded and US-supported armed insurrection, or what MAS has referred to as a civic-prefectural attempted coup, as the president claimed on September 23 at the United Nations.[48] However, the UNASUR intervention also led to a move in favour of dialogue between the government and the political leaders of the opposition, a process of dialogue that international observers monitored and mediated. As a result, these prefects saw their violent manipulation recompensed with an opportunity to dialogue with the government and to negotiate those aspects of the draft constitution they objected to the most. These included the level of resources from the export of gas and oil they would receive in future through the Impuesto directo a los Hidrocarburos (IDH) (a direct tax on hydrocarbons) and the scale of powers and competencies they would hold in their new positions as governors of autonomic regions. Added to this, and in spite of the assembly having the sole authority to produce the new constitution that had to be put to the Bolivian population, a process of negotiation was opened in Congress where the constitutional draft was further tampered with through negotiation between the opposition and the government. This changed the document in some rather significant ways, which according to observers guaranteed increased powers to the autonomous regions and established greater levels of guarantee for private property, even in the case of land that had been illegally acquired.[49] This process can only be explained as a last-minute attempt from the government to secure opposition support for a referendum, but it had the effect of significantly undermining both the new constitution and the legitimacy of the process by which it was produced.

In the end, three full drafts were produced in this less-than-perfect process of writing a new constitution for the refounding of Bolivia. The first was proposed by the unity pact, a coalition of civil society organisations whose proposal served as the basis of discussion in Sucre during the Constitutional Assembly. It essentially reflected the demands and desires of the social movements, representing a majority of the Bolivian population, that had delivered such a new political system and given birth to a broad process of political change.[50] The second draft was produced by the Constitutional Assembly in Sucre, and approved in Oruro, in spite of the boycott of opposition parties and the violent threats that closed the deliberating space provided by the assembly.[51] The third was the constitution that was put to the Bolivian people in January 2009, a watered-down version of popular demand.[52]

In spite of all this sorry history, the new constitution was approved by the Bolivian people on January 25, 2009 with 61 per cent of the vote, significantly less than the figure expected, after a campaign in which the same opposition that had won last-minute concessions from the government tried to convert the referendum into a vote on Morales and the process of change. The campaign was dirty in the extreme, with the bulk of special economic and regional interests dominating the airways and television channels, railing against a constitution they claimed had been written by Venezuela's Hugo Chávez and imposed by MAS. The Bolivian Catholic Church led by Cardinal Julio Terrazas denounced the new constitution. In the process it made allegations that many saw as lies, about the risks this document posed for the future legalisation of abortion or the demise of private education (much of which is delivered by the Catholic Church in Bolivia). Even God, the television adverts warned, disliked the new constitution. But approved it was, and with it began a new chapter in the recent history of Bolivia. It is this the rest of the book aims to explore. The question remains, however, whether the new constitutional text goes as far as it needs to in order to sustain a process that needs to be nothing short of revolutionary if it is to make Bolivia a fairer, more just society.

MAIN PILLARS OF THE NEW BOLIVIAN CONSTITUTION

It seems strange, in light of the new constitutional text, that the Morales administration is almost universally derided in much of the mass media as 'revolutionary' and 'socialist'. The constitution certainly does not include the nationalisation of all private property or the authoritarian imposition of single-party rule, as the recalcitrant right and sectors of the Catholic Church would make people believe. In many respects, the new text is rather moderate, nuanced, and respectful of the country's diversity. Above all, it is based on the consensual discussion and deliberation described above, limited as it was, but representing every sector of Bolivian society. Few constitutions around the world can claim to represent their country's population as well, and even fewer have been drafted with the degree of public involvement, discussion and participation that characterised the entire process in Bolivia. At 411 articles, it is also a very long text. However, it can be said that three main features characterise the new Bolivian constitution.

The first stems from the description made of Bolivia. The preamble says that Bolivia abandons colonial, republican and neoliberal understandings of the nation-state to become a single state that is communitarian, plurinational, and based on social rights.[53] The implications of this statement are many, and they run throughout the length of this book. However, let us concentrate on the meaning of this statement for the reorganisation of the state in Bolivia and of its relations with the people. One aspect of the meaning is related to the creation of new institutions, powers and forms of the state. The three main powers that already characterised the state – the executive, legislative and judiciary – remained in place, although the judiciary was expected to undergo serious reform, including the election of high court judges, whose appointment used to be a presidential prerogative.

The new constitution also declares the existence of a fourth power, constituted by 'the people' – who ultimately hold sovereignty – and the creation of institutional mechanisms so that the people can exercise control of the previous three powers.[54] In a country where the emergence of social movements and organised civil society have seen the levers of power turned upside down, this issue necessitates an assessment of the controls currently exercised by civil society and of any new mechanism that is created in the future. It requires also that we explore the relations of power that exist in a continuous process of flux between civil society and the government, an area considered in Chapter 4. Finally, there are some international implications to the relationship between organised civil society – as it operates through international networks – and governments, something that is referred to in Chapter 8.

The second set of implications that stem from the plurinational nature of Bolivia enshrined in the new constitution refers to recognition of the country's 36 indigenous nations under the principle of 'unity in diversity'. Bolivia remains a single, indivisible state with many nations within its borders, shedding the openly racist nature of its foundation in 1825, the closet racism that fed the 1952 revolution, even the neoliberal forms of multiculturalism that emerged as a result of reforms in the 1990s.[55] In addition to this, the traditionally centralised nature of the Bolivian state will no longer be apparent with the implementation of the new constitution. The new constitution provides for a profound decentralisation of the state into autonomous regions and municipalities, in a way that resembles reforms in other parts of the world including European countries like Spain, which was the source of a number of advisers present in Sucre during the Constitutional Assembly.[56]

What is truly unique about this constitution is that it also permits the autonomous government of indigenous nations within Bolivia's borders. So they win control of their territories as they demanded during the 1990 march to La Paz. Articles 30–32 of the new constitution deal with the collective rights (the individual rights of all

Bolivians are defined in previous articles) of indigenous nations.[57] In these are included the right to manage autonomous indigenous communities, practise their customs and laws, to implement their indigenous forms of knowledge, even indigenous forms of justice, and to be consulted on matters that affect them or their territories. The creation of indigenous autonomies reflects this recognition, and is geared towards the creation of possibilities for the cultural repro- duction of those indigenous communities.[58] It also has implications for a redistribution of power in favour of those who will lose most if plans to introduce direct representation of indigenous groups in the new Plurinational Assembly – the new name for the chamber that replaces Bolivia's Congress – become a reality. Finally, the plurinational nature of Bolivia represents, especially in its intercul- tural facet, a new form of national identity that rescues indigenous ethico-moral principles and values such as *suma qamaña*. Chapter 5 explores this concept in relation to the National Development Plan (NDP) and social policy provision.

The third most important guiding element in the new Bolivian constitution is Part IV on the economic structure and organisa- tion of the country. Divided into three sections, it deals with the dominant role the state will play in the Bolivian economy; the importance of natural resources in the economic development of the country in view of the balancing act that has to take place to protect the environment and biodiversity whilst delivering growth; and the role of sustainable, community-based forms of economic develop- ment for rural areas.[59] The new constitution, which was described by vice-president Linera as 'a vaccine against neoliberalism, against privatisation, against the pillage of natural resources',[60] therefore emphasises the primary role of the state in defining the roadmap for economic development, regulating the actions of economic players, including transnational corporations (TNCs), and ensuring that the benefits of economic growth permeate to all levels of society. It also defines the existence of many different forms of property and of economic practices – market, community-based and coop- erative forms of economic activity.[61] This part of the new Bolivian constitution is explored in Chapter 6.

THE CHALLENGES AHEAD

In Bolivia's highland indigenous communities, community members gather regularly to discuss the selection of authorities, the allocation

of land to families, or even the implications of the new constitution. They all speak and make their points in turn, continuing with
the discussion until people feel there is nothing new to be added,
keeping the debate alive for the entire night if necessary, until a
consensus emerges as part of the discussion that is based on the
strength of the best argument. It is not a gladiatorial and adver-
sarial practice destined to bully the opposition into submission, nor
is it arranged in parties with pre-established positions, where any
individual attempt to break the 'party line' is met with pressure
from the whips to fall into line. It is, in short, about the possibilities of deliberation. These possibilities manifest themselves because
of the ruthless equality of condition and power that characterises
these communities. Collective decision making is therefore possible
under common conditions. The lack of glaring power differences
between individuals and families ensures that community leadership
responsibilities are shared to the point that the various positions of
community leadership are seen as a burden that is taken on a rota-
tional basis, not as the source of power and privilege. This is not a
misty-eyed romantic view of indigenous decision-making processes
but a practice that still works in highland communities.

The Constitutional Assembly was meant to restore some of these
practices by bringing together the greatest range of interests, socioeconomic, ethnic and regional, in a debating arena with the task
of establishing the foundational principles of a new country. The
experience brought into relief the deep divisions that exist in Bolivia
under a thin veneer of normality, prompting some to describe the
process of writing the new Bolivian constitution as a very long
pregnancy and painful birth.[62] Some interest groups with socioeconomic and racial privileges to defend were unwilling to enter into
dialogue with groups they did not recognise as equals. The process
was ugly and turned violent at times, but as at many other times
through Bolivian history, just as the country stared into the abyss,
opportunities for conciliation, negotiation and accords were taken
by those directly implicated. The country slowly retreated into
peace and Bolivia approved its new constitution. Behind it were the
two years of work by the 255 Constitutional Assembly members
elected for the purpose, the deliberate attempts to derail the entire
process, the provocations and the violent deaths, the calls for civil
disobedience and the media manipulation attempting to delegitimize
the debates taking place in Sucre. Violent and messy, the process of
producing a new constitution for a new Bolivia had been imperfect
in both its form and its content.[63] However, the text was the closest

thing possible to a vision of Bolivia that had included every sector of society in its drafting.

With the approval through referendum of a tainted constitutional text in January 2009, matters returned to the more familiar everyday political tussle: blocking of legislation, accusation and counter-accusation in Congress and the Senate, that delivered the paralysed legislative machinery Bolivians had grown accustomed to since 2006. The only way to create and enact legislation was to work through presidential decrees for the rest of the year. In the midst of daily political cynicism, everyone's thoughts began to turn towards the elections to be held in December 2009, the result of which would determine whether the painful process of change that had begun in earnest with the arrival to the presidency of an indigenous leader three years earlier had been a flash in the pan of history and another false dawn – like the 1952 revolution – or the beginning of a new era.

In spite of last-minute attempts to delegitimise the electoral register, elections were held without mishap, and delivered an increased victory for the MAS with 64 per cent of the vote. Now was the time to start the process of implementation of the new constitution, supporting the democratic process that has brought the country to this point, a point of no return in the path of further equality and social justice for all Bolivians. The challenges ahead are enormous, but these are lessened by the implosion of an opposition that, highly divided, could only unite at the last minute behind the controversial figures of Manfred Reyes Villa, a former prefect of Cochabamba who had been ousted in the recall elections of August 2008 and was wanted in relation to fraud during his administration, and Leopoldo Fernández, *cacique* turned prefect of Pando, who is awaiting trial on charges relating to his responsibility for the role of the departmental government in the September 2008 massacre in the town of Porvenir. The question this time is whether the next five years will deliver on people's expectations. What is the valuation that can be made of the government's performance so far? The next three chapters consider three broad areas under the headings of 'new politics', 'new citizens' and 'new economic models of development'.

4 NEW POLITICS

In search of a working relationship between the state and civil society

When, as the Introduction described, hundreds of thousands of men, women and children from every corner of the country descended on La Paz on October 20, 2008 to demand from parliament the approval of a call for a referendum on the text of the new constitution that had been written in Sucre over the previous two years, two key features of the march struck me profoundly. The first was the very serious level of organisation of those taking part, but a type of organisation that did not seem to follow the standard pattern of organisation in parties, trade unions or other form of standard political association. There were groups of miners affiliated to the Central Obrera Boliviana (COB) marching that day, as there were representatives of the teachers' union and of the small traders from El Alto. But there were no political parties marching, and apart from work-based forms of association through trade unions, the vast majority of the participants seemed to be common people who had come from the farthest rural corners of the country, entire communities of indigenous peoples who, led by their leaders, had walked for weeks in some cases to make their demands heard. What were these organisations, and how was it possible that civil society had become so politicised in ways that seem impossible elsewhere?

The second element that struck me was the lack of distance between a civil society pitted against their elected representatives in parliament, and some of those representatives. It is not uncommon to see members of civil society making their voice heard in the streets, as is the case as I write in a number of European countries, at a time of unpopular public funding cuts brought about by the financial crisis. What we would never dream of seeing are prime ministers or presidents joining protesters in the streets. That is exactly what struck me in that October 2008 march in La Paz – the sight of a president of the republic who went much further than simply supporting the demonstrators from his palace, but instead joined them, to enter the city at the head of a multitudinous demonstration that surrounded parliament and demanded their right to vote and decide the fate of the new constitutional text. Had the social movements described above managed to enter the palace, or had the reverse taken place? What are the boundaries that normally separate those who govern from those who are governed and have to resort to protesting in order to be heard?

The story of Bolivia is one of political decline and of resurgence of new and radical political change. The vacuum left by failing political institutions that called into question the viability of democracy in the country during the first few years of the new millennium[1] has been filled by the protagonist role played by organised civil society. This chapter is about assessing how that came about and its implications for the future politics of the country, as they stem from the new constitution approved in January 2009. Three key issues are considered in this chapter. The first is the rise of civil society in Bolivian politics, and the extent to which the balance of forces between civil society and the state (and the market) changed in the period leading to the MAS victory of 2005. The second is to consider the statement, often made by President Morales, that MAS is a government of the social movements. This idea begs questions about the boundaries that separate the government and the social movements in this partnership, when the former is forced to contend with the realities of state governance and the latter have the privilege of not having to compromise their ideological principles.

The final issue is the effects of the new constitutional arrangements for the relationship between the government and the social movements. The key in this chapter is to explore the profound transformation that has taken place in Bolivia, from a liberal model of representative democracy that emphasises individual interests and uses voting systems rigged to various degrees in order to impose certain ideas over others, to a participatory model of democracy. The extent to which this transformation has taken place is important because participatory models of democracy are said to be characterised by much deeper levels of participation from citizens, as a result making them more oriented to public needs as opposed to the needs of the market or of small elites connected to power.[2] The argument is that these deep, participatory or deliberative forms of democracy are, simply put, more democratic. The objective of this chapter is to explain this process of transformation, the implications for it contained in the new constitution approved in January 2009, and the new universe of relations between civil society and the state.

THE FAILURE OF OLD POLITICS

By the end of the 1980s, Bolivia was in crisis. First, there was a profound crisis of the neoliberal economic model, which put a stop to the economic hyperinflation of 1984/5 but at too high a human cost, as it was followed by one of the most radical economic experiments conducted in the region. Second, there was a crisis of what commentators referred to as *partidocracia*, a made-up term that mixes the concepts of party and bureaucracy to mean a political system dominated by self-serving institutions mired in corruption and inefficiency. The confluence of these twin crises spurred a range of sectors of the Bolivian population to embark on a quest to wrest away control of their own country and to transform it beyond recognition. Chapters 1 and 2 schematically described these processes, following the creation of MAS, outlining the reaction of the Bolivian population at key moments of crisis in 2000 and in 2003, and attempting to describe the national euphoria that followed the unprecedented electoral victory of MAS in December 2005 with 54 per cent of the vote, a victory that has been consolidated in subsequent national consultations, including the December 2009 elections in which MAS won more than 63 per cent of the vote.[3]

First up in the sights of Bolivians was the need to rewrite the main governing document of the country, a constitutional document that includes the most fundamental philosophical principles on which Bolivia is based, the basic rights and protections that every citizen can expect, even the specifics of the various powers of the state and of the political, social and economic models that will govern the country in the twenty-first century. Chapter 3 explored this process, explaining its beginnings in the form of indigenous protests and marches for 'territory and dignity' in the 1990s. It was explained how this demand that was first made in the 1990s became more coherently articulated in 2000 in Cochabamba during the water wars and particularly in 2003 as part of the October Agenda, an agenda that was appropriated by MAS and implemented from 2006 onwards. Thus it happened that during a moment of national crisis – and Bolivia, like many post-colonial countries, has had more than its fair share of these moments throughout its history[4] – the constitutional assembly came to be seen as the only mechanism that could deliver national redemption through a process of deliberation and consensus building, imperfect as this was, in order to change the political, social and economic structure of the country. The current chapter and the next two broadly cover these three areas, exploring the role of civil society in Bolivia's new politics, the recognition of the country's indigenous majority and of its conceptual understanding of well-being, and examining the claim that the country's economic model of development is moving away from neoliberalism.

The importance of the role of civil society, and of the social movements in particular, in Bolivia's process of change is unquestioned by commentators, and more than a few academics have tried to make sense of them in literature on governance processes.[5] By the new millennium, the failure to reform party structures that had become unable to represent and channel social demands had led the country into a permanent situation of political crisis. The void in the public democratic space was filled by civil society, led by those indigenous social movements that had already begun to position themselves as valid political actors in the 1990s. Civil society activism and protest have a long tradition in Bolivia.[6] However, instead of acting as part of a growing global opposition to the neoliberal order, civil society in Bolivia became the historical agent of social change, with the ability to propose and build alternatives to the hegemonic model of politics (in the form of a representative democracy that did not represent people's interests), society (in the form of a exclusionary society), and economy (understood as the neoliberal order).

In a paper that explores the contours of the existing literature about the nature of deep forms of democracy, John Gaventa suggests that a variety of approaches exist that can 'deepen' the quality of democratic practice, including deliberative processes, building civil society, and participatory governance.[7] Chapter 3 suggested that the constitutional assembly can be considered a test case for the limits of the first of these aspects of democracy, where the search for consensus was boycotted in the context of high levels of unequal distribution of power and a reluctance to pursue the possibilities of deliberation.

Aspects of deliberative democracy are the daily currency of decision making in indigenous communities up and down the Andes. No elections are required in these communities, where the principle of rotation of community leadership duties applies. Indeed, as with traditional decision-making processes that require the participation of every community member, indigenous values and practices in Bolivia have tended to emphasise close-knit associational forms of work based on community solidarity leading to the benefit of the collective. This forms the basis of much of what constitute the social movements that have played such a crucial role in the Bolivian process of change to date.

This chapter considers the other elements discussed by Gaventa in his paper, namely the strength of civil society as a gauge of the quality of democratic practice, and the role that civil society actors might, through participation, have in the process of governance by sharing power with the state. These aspects of deep democracy are particularly relevant to the Bolivian context given the extent to which civil society has strengthened since the return of formal democracy to the country, in spite of every effort from the neoliberal state to atomise civil society into its individual components.[8] But it is only in Bolivia that a national government has been able to claim that theirs is a government of social movements, as Morales has done on numerous occasions. Testing this claim requires that we ask many questions, not least about definitions, composition, types and roles of social movements, especially in relation to the state and the blurring boundaries that now exist between these two forces.

THE EMERGENCE OF ALTERNATIVE POLITICAL ACTORS

For decades, during the dark years of dictatorships between 1964 and 1982, the main scenarios of political decision making in Bolivia were the military garrisons on the one hand, and the organised workers' movement on the other. The return to democracy replaced the military with elected representatives of political parties. What had not been expected was, as we saw in Chapter 1, the cataclysmic effect that the 'silent revolution' brought about by neoliberalism would have on the trade union movement.[9] Fast forward to the 1990s and the first decade of the new millennium, and we see that the most significant element of change in the Bolivian political landscape in the last two decades has been the protagonist role that new political actors have gained from non-traditional platforms. Indeed, civil society constitutes this new platform, an element that is common to politics in a number of Latin American countries.[10]

Even though the particular mix of power relations between state, market and organised collective action from within civil society remains unique to the individual countries, many have experienced a similar process of empowerment of civil society. In Bolivia, vice-president García Linera has referred to this phenomenon as the rise of plebeian politics, a term which, like in ancient Rome, he uses to refer to the common people, poised to take power from a ruling class of patricians. In Bolivia these 'patricians' are likened to the old elites who reproduced their social position through a party machinery and a system of representative democracy that only represented their interests at the expense of the majority.[11]

Exploring the contours of Bolivia's civil society and the relationship that parts of it, especially the social movements, have with a government that has described itself as a government of social movements is a daunting and complex task.[12] Part of the reason is that civil society, both globally and in Bolivia, is often defined from normative standpoints of what 'ought' to be, presenting characterisations of ideal types that are self-exclusive.[13] For example, some authors have argued that civil society is presented in terms of a variety of paradigms that include 'activist, 'tamed' and 'postmodern' forms.[14] Others however, take on much more reductionist understandings of civil society, providing a judgement on the values and ideologies that are meant to predominate in this sphere of action. In other words, they prescribe for actors operating from within civil society, the objective of working towards a broad set of themes that include social justice and the defence of the environment or human rights.[15]

However, if we take as our objective an outline of the empirical reality of civil society as the space in which multiple forms of activities take place which are organised by citizens and groups that go beyond the state or the for-profit organisations that operate in the market, it is relatively easy to outline the types of associational forms that have been of greatest significance in Bolivia's process of change. What follows is such an outline, taking into account the Bolivian-specific political contours of civil society, rather as Marlies Glasius and others have done in other contexts.[16] We commence with a consideration of Bolivia's social movements and their identities, before considering the role played by non-governmental organisations (NGOs) in Bolivia's civil society.

At this point it is necessary to state that, as befits such a broad understanding of civil society, not all associational forms that are part of Bolivia's civil society have participated in the process of change wholeheartedly. In fact, 2008 and 2009 saw an abrupt increase in the opposition to the MAS political project that came from so-called civic committees, especially in the eastern lowlands of the country. It is indeed a sign of the political success of civil society as a platform for new political actors that the opposition to the process of change spearheaded by MAS appears to have adopted very similar strategies and created civil society organisations to counter the process of change, stopping, derailing or slowing it. A number of characteristics conspire against their effectiveness, however. First, in spite of their ability in 2008 to orchestrate and galvanise opposition to the government, the civic committees of Santa Cruz and their allies represented the interest of small political and economic elites in the region. Second, these committees had little organic support among the population, and when they protested publicly in their region, for example, they often had to rely on cash payments for their 'activists'. Third, they were politically defined by what they opposed (everything the MAS government stood for) rather than by what they proposed. As a result, the 'civic committees' of Santa Cruz and their youth wing, notorious for their racist attacks against indigenous groups in the area, lacked any legitimacy for their actions. More recently their power base appears to have collapsed, and these groups are now less powerful and ubiquitous than during the high point of opposition to MAS in 2008 and 2009.

Indigenous people, class, and popular identities of social movements

First in the importance stakes of associational forms in civil society are the social movements, in terms of both the numbers of people they represent and the qualitative role they have played in Bolivian politics in the recent past. As with the concept of civil society, definitions of social movements appear to encompass a variety of views that depend on the adoption of particular theoretical standpoints. Some authors have identified two opposing schools of thought in the understanding of social movements. One has argued that North American debates have traditionally opted for the adoption of rational actor theories, leading to an understanding of social movements as self-interest groups. New social movement theory, favoured in Europe, has tended to emphasise instead an understanding of social movements as precursors of progressive social transformation.[17] As a result, citizen action through social movements is seen as the work either of unrepresentative, self-selecting and self-interest groups, or the new saviours of democracy who keep in check the undemocratic and unrepresentative practices of governments and corporations that either act with the consent of national governments or are able to subjugate them to their interests.

Others appear to have much simpler working definitions of social movements.[18] If we consider a basic definition of social movements as groups of people coming together for action due to shared political concerns and/or a shared identity,[19] we can see how and why these have proliferated in a country like Bolivia. A similar definition is offered in Bolivia itself, where it is commonly argued that the failure of representative, liberal democracy and the social suffering caused by neoliberal economic policies explains the need for organised civil society in the form of social movements to fill the void, and also to take control of a country on a downward political and economic spiral.[20] If in addition we consider the question of identity as the cement that brings people together into a collective diagnosis and understanding of reality as the basis for social and political action, then we can see how the indigenous social movements in Bolivia are stronger, more numerous and better organised than their urban counterparts.

The political relevance of Bolivia's social movements emerged in the 1980s, as the neoliberal attack on trade union-based forms of collective association opened the doors to neoliberal economic reform. This relevance increased in the 1990s as political parties implemented a decapitation of the state, but social movements came into their own with the new millennium and the systematic collapse of the political system around them, to defend both basic principles and collective resources such as indigenous recognition, and resources like land, territory, water, gas and public enterprises. Bolivia's social movements incorporate indigenous, popular and working-class forms of identity that developed separately and came together with the new millennium to radically alter the political map of the country.

Identity politics and the consequent rise of indigenous social movements have had a strong influence in Latin America over the last two decades.[21] The transnational indigenous movement was aided in its creation by the work of NGOs and the 1989 International Labour Organisation (ILO) Convention 169 on the Rights of Indigenous People,[22] but came to prominence during the protest at the official celebrations in 1992 of five centuries from the 'discovery' of the new world.[23] In Bolivia indigenous social movements take on a new significance, and as we saw in Chapter 3, were instrumental in proposing, and then driving, the process of writing a new constitution. This is in spite of the centuries-long attempts to first enslave, then ignore, and finally assimilate indigenous peoples. The last of those processes took place during the second half of the twentieth century, particularly since the 1952 revolution which, led by an enlightened urban elite, effectively reclassified indigenous peoples as peasants.[24]

The purpose of doing this was twofold. First, it denied an indigenous identity that social constructions of the time considered backward and pre-modern and that had no place in the future of a country that was tied to the global economy through its mineral resources, later joined as a major export by food crops such as soya. Second, it subsumed identity to an economic practice, confirming Marxist-inspired readings at the time that wanted to see in the peasantry a social and economic class, revolutionary or not.[25] As a result, indigenous traditional forms of community organisations were damaged, and much of the wealth distribution inspired by the 1952 revolution took place in ways that reinforced this social construction of the indigenous as a peasant class. For example, land reform did not, on the whole, respect traditional forms of collective land tenure which were common in the highlands, forcing indigenous communities to reclassify their communities as *sindicatos* (trade unions) and receive individual land titles.[26]

Nowadays the term *movimiento campesino-indígena-originario* (peasant-indigenous movement) is commonly used in Bolivia – including by indigenous peoples – to refer to their social movements, and is part of daily political discourse. However, today's peasant-indigenous movement means something very different from a form of political association that is class-based and that works solely within the paradigm of redistributive politics. Today's indigenous movements in Bolivia own their existence partly to the Katarista movement, a political and cultural movement that drew its links from the legacy of Túpac Katari and his wife Bartolina Sisa, symbols of indigenous resistance during the colonial period.[27] Indeed, one of the main indigenous social movements in Bolivia today incorporates women's identity as well as the question of indigeneity, and is commonly referred to as the Bartolinas. Nor are today's most influential social movements in Bolivia entirely driven by identity politics, by a struggle for recognition that is devoid of the politics of redistribution, as a simplistic classification of the literature in this regard would make us believe. In fact, as has been argued before in this book, the Bolivian political map of civil society represents the coming together of the two paradigms of redistribution and recognition, as part of a broader process of change that exemplifies Nancy Fraser's call for a theory of justice that breaks the dichotomy and brings these two elements together.[28]

All of this does not mean that trade union politics, or trade union forms of identity, are dead in Bolivia. On the contrary, within civil society, Bolivia's trade unions probably played the biggest opposition role to the military dictatorships between the 1960s and 1980s, and have written many historic pages in defence of democracy. Firmly associated with the country's mining industry and the COB, a rich trade union history defined political activism from civil society. Yet the trade union movement always suffered from an inability to see beyond its own sectoral demands and a corporatist attitude.[29] As the beginning of this section described, neither the nationalised industry nor the trade union movement it generated was able to survive intact the end of a form of state-driven capitalist development that was symbolised in decree 21060 and the ravages that privatisation and economic neoliberalism effected on the industry. But this does not mean that trade unionist practices did not survive in Bolivia and are not part of today's social movement activist practices. Indeed, the COB still brings together trade unions that represent the interests of miners, teachers, health sector workers and others such as the *fabriles* (manufacturing sector workers). In addition, some of these trade unionist practices became pervasive among new groups of people, and forms of association that emerged with the coca growers' association once thousands of ex-miners moved to the Chapare region looking for new livelihoods. President Morales himself cut his teeth in this arena, becoming the president of the federation of coca growers associations, which would spearhead opposition to the US-inspired coca eradication plan (*plan dignidad*) of the 1997 government of Hugo Banzer.[30]

Further to powerful indigenous social movements and trade unionism, there are what the Bolivian literature refers to 'popular' movements, the youngest form of political association in Bolivia.[31] These tend to include the urban equivalent of the social movements. A strong element of cohesion brought about by a common indigenous identity may be important in these movements, as is the case in the city of El Alto where a strong Aymara identity is pervasive. However, what tends to bring together the poor who constitute the urban popular movements are demands for responses to immediate social concerns such as street paving, lack of basic sanitation, water or other services. Many of these popular movements, organised as neighbourhood associations, now come together as part of a programme for the development of local power, looking at ways of enhancing their participation in public life by increasing their political voice. So groups such as the Federación de Juntas Vecinales (Federation of Neighbourhood Associations, FEJUVE), especially in El Alto, have played key roles in the recent political history of the country, especially during the months of February and October 2003. So have groups like the Coordinadora del Agua y el Gas (Association for Water and Gas) from Cochabamba, that played such a crucial role in the opposition of the city to water privatisation during 2000.

A number of characteristics of Bolivia's social movements are noticeable. First is the wide range of forms of association, identities and demands. They include indigenous organisations that represent different parts of the country and a range of ethnic and linguistic groups, with their own forms of association and decision making, and their own objectives. These movements also include relatively new trade unions (like the coca growers' association), as well as 'popular' movements like FEJUVE. Second, the variety of movements, associational types and strategies of mobilisation have been able to transcend their individual immediate objectives, coalescing at key moments in the recent political history of the country, particularly in 2000 and 2003. As a result, they have been able to move away from protest and demand to become what have been called structures of political action: that is, political agents in a historic process of social change that includes an ability to coalesce and coordinate with other social movements through action networks, diagnose the broader structural societal deficiencies, and put forward alternative policy proposals for changing the system's 'direction of travel'.[32] Such was the strength of Bolivia's social movements and their ability to rock the foundations of the political system in 2003, when they presented an alternative set of demands articulated in the October Agenda.

Third, there are clear relative power differences between the various types of actors outlined. Indigenous social movements that stem from the rural population are the most powerful, and constitute the five main organisations: the Consejo Nacional de Ayllus y Markas del Qullasuyu (CONAMAQ), Confederación Indígena del Oriente Boliviano (CIDOB), Confederación Sindical Única de Trabajadores Campesinos de Bolivia (CSUTCB), Confederación Nacional de Mujeres Campesinas Indígenas Originarias de Bolivia 'Bartolina Sisa' (CNMCIOB 'BS') and Confederación Sindical de Comunidades Interculturales de Bolivia (CSCIB).[33] They have emerged as the strongest mass-based social support for MAS, are the best organised and the ones that give the MAS government the name of 'government of the social movements'. The strong support that the current government received from these social movements is also the reason why some commentators have tried to see contradictions or potential conflict at the heart of government between indigenous and socialist ideologies. The Bolivian opposition made these critiques openly in 2008/9, but serious commentators have also pointed at contradictions between two separate ideologies at the heart of MAS, arguing that Bolivia has seen the emergence of indigenous nationalism as the main ideological characteristic of a number of new forms of power and contestation 'from below' that are taking place in many parts of the world.[34]

Some would even argue that Morales and Linera represent these two sides, one indigenous, the other a white intellectual with a strong Marxist theoretical background. But if we scratch the surface of this view we find that Morales grew politically in the trade union movement – indeed, he is still president of the coca growers' association as well as Bolivia's first indigenous president – whereas Linera was imprisoned for his involvement with EGTK, an *indigenista* guerrilla group operating in the 1990s. Thus the argument could be made that Bolivia's process of change is based on ideological principles that incorporate both the indigenous and left traditions that have in the past followed different paths, as when for example the 1952 MNR-led revolution excluded the indigenous in its midst, or when Aymara-led CONDEPA joined the Banzer government of 1997 at the height of the neoliberal reforms that indigenous social movements now decry.[35]

Other examples exist of leaders who have followed a strong and exclusive *indigenista* ideology, like Felipe Quispe, leader of the Movimiento Indigena Pachakuti (MIP), whose party disappeared after a very poor electoral result in 2005. Instead, what is critical about Bolivia is the mix of these two ideological traditions inside MAS as the determining feature of the current politico-ideological process, as well as the making in civil society – mainly through its social movements but also through NGOs – of the key arena from which a challenge to a delegitimised parliamentary democracy emerged and actors who lead the current, reformed, version of Bolivian democracy were formed.

Fourth, what is of key importance about the social movements in Bolivia is the links they display with other political actors. As befits social movements, they have strong relations with regional and global networks of other social movements that link them and help them operate beyond the limitations of national boundaries, becoming part of new forms of governance in which non-state actors play a crucial role. This is a growing area of interest to academics, who have referred to this style of governance as 'complex multilateralism'.[36] For example, representatives of these movements were among the global civil society organisations that gathered in Copenhagen and Cancún to press for a global agreement on climate change in parallel to the official summits. In Chapter 8, we explore some of the ways in which Bolivian civil society operates across the world, making links with representatives of civil society in the south and in the global north. In addition however, representatives of these movements were also part of the official Bolivian climate change negotiating teams at these climate change and other international summits, begging a question about the blurred boundaries between them and the Bolivian government. What does it mean to be part of a social movement when social movements are supposed to be in power? We examine this question later on in the chapter as part of the relationship between the state and civil society, a civil society that must also include NGOs.

Non-governmental organisations: partners or foes in the process of change?

Taking account of the role of NGOs, and of their international counterparts (INGOs), has to be of crucial importance in the context of Bolivia, where, as is the case with poor, dependent countries, the rise in the number of NGOs has been exponential in the last three decades, with some sources citing more than 500 NGOs operating in the late 1990s, when the number was marginal only a decade previously.[37] NGOs globally have diverse origins, and Bolivia is no exception. In this country, NGOs first emerged to give a voice and provide support to groups of citizens and some of the social movements described above that responded to the illegitimacy of the dictatorships with grassroots social organisation. A second period of increasing influence and growth in the Bolivian NGO sector came at the time of state retrenchment during the neoliberal period discussed in Chapter 1, where NGOs took over the functions of basic service delivery that had until then been the realm of the state, and increasingly started to venture to rural areas further afield in an effort to ameliorate extreme levels of poverty. Further, many NGOs grew to help communities manage the process of local administration of resources that resulted from the application of the 1994 Law of Popular Participation, increasing existing levels of community organisation and democratic decision-making processes.[38]

Neither the place nor the roles that NGOs occupy and play in the universe of policy actors is without controversy. Standard accounts of civil society have referred to them as part of a 'tamed' form of civil society that now operates as a partner of the state, certainly in the global north, having undergone a process of institutionalisation and professionalisation that has increased their respectability.[39] This image fits in with the role currently played by the third sector – and increasingly the Big Society – in the global north, for instance in the United Kingdom where a renewed process of state retrenchment is under way, echoing the actions of the Conservative administrations of Margaret Thatcher and John Major between 1979 and 1997.

In an alternative description of NGOs in Bolivian society, which carries a normative value judgement, some commentators see them as 'a Trojan horse for global neoliberalism, as an agency for helping the guardians of the New World Order secure the political conditions needed to pursue their neoliberal agenda'.[40] Yet others, commentating from within Bolivia, have argued that NGOs are in fact not formally part of civil society. Instead, they argue, NGOs operate in the interstices between the 'legitimate' representatives of civil society – social movements – and the state, delivering goods and services, generating new capabilities, improving the quality of life for particular sectors of society, and promoting political action that follows new readings of reality.[41]

As ever, the reality is hardly ever so uncomplicated as to warrant generalisations of any of these types. An empirical examination of NGOs in Bolivia would show that the NGO world includes as much variety as the concept of civil society explored earlier. It is clear that there are many types of NGO and many ideologies driving their work. Nobody doubts that NGOs implement responses to particular communities on the basis of some definition of need that might or might not be made explicit. It is also obvious that sometimes NGOs take the role of speaking for and representing some of those communities that lack a voice because of poverty or social exclusion, situations that can become entrenched as long as NGOs continue to have a vested interest in maintaining a social purpose.[42] It is indeed obvious that great differences exist between INGOs and Bolivian NGOs. INGOs have an enormous power in the country in so far as they are able to control the budgets over which local partners depend and can therefore define agendas and points of action. This is a point that does not escape the government of Bolivia, judging by the tempestuous relations it has had with USAID. This organisation is regularly accused by President Morales of political meddling and of funding opposition parties, even masterminding the political violence of September 2008.[43]

However, it is also the case that the NGO contribution to the process of democratic and participative practice, better and more transparent governance, and general strengthening of civil society lies effectively at the base of social changes that allowed the current process of change in Bolivia to take place, as the role of NGOs in the provision of technical support for the application of the LPP in the 1990s shows. So NGOs can be a force for good where they contribute to greater levels of democracy, as was the case with the constitutional assembly, where NGOs provided information, technical expertise, advice and resources to assembly members who were part of Bolivia's civil society and in many cases were part of social movements. Similarly, NGOs and their international counterparts are developing a positive working relationship as part of the country's civil society platform on climate change. In addition, the Bolivian state relies on the resources that international governments and INGOs can bring to deliver many aspects of their public policy responsibilities. At the same time, a new, strengthened Bolivian state has every right to ask from the NGO world that they adhere and contribute to the current National Development Plan, so operational coherence can be provided on the delivery of a broad process of change partly by harnessing resources from multiple sources within the INGO world while preventing the common problems of overlap and patchy delivery of interventions.[44]

COMPLEXITY AND CONTRADICTIONS IN THE RELATIONSHIP BETWEEN THE STATE AND CIVIL SOCIETY

Traditional readings of the role of civil society, and in particular of social movements, tend to emphasise the opposition they play to states and markets. This is a view that is expressed in relation to civil society and social movements at both the national and international level, especially among authors who would like to see in civil society the repository of deeper forms of democratic practice and progressive social change driven by values of social justice, peace and environmental protection.

Bolivia's civil society certainly seems to fit the bill. Spearheaded by indigenous/rural social movements, the country's civil society united a broad range of social actors that questioned the dominant political and economic model, confronting the state and demanding a new, re-founded Bolivia that was socially just, ethnically diverse, and politically participative and democratic. The result at the end of the period of mobilisation between 2000 and 2005 was an indigenous president at the head of a broad coalition of social movements under the banner of MAS, opening a period of new possibilities in relations between the new government and civil society. The issue now is to deliver a judgement on the reality of those relations, exploring the process of interaction between the government and civil society. How do these two very different spheres of political practice solve differences? If social movements in particular have traditionally drawn their identity from being a part of opposition politics, is there a risk that they might lose their influence (or their identity) and 'dilute' their message and modes of action in relation to a government they supported?

Given the very heterogeneous composition of Bolivia's civil society, a response to these questions needs to be based on an empirical exploration of a number of cases. Although a political judgement of the current legislative session is premature until it ends in 2014, Bolivian social scientists have attempted interim responses.[45] Taking a broadly Bourdieusian approach that sees social movements as relational categories that draw their identities through processes of struggle for position in what the authors describe as 'fields of conflict' in which the state is a major player, these authors have produced a number of categories for understanding relations between the current government and a series of political actors that emerge from civil society. For them, the last few years of MAS government have shown that some sectors of civil society have effectively become part of the political instrument of MAS, co-opted into the party structure and as a result unable to exercise any independence in thought and action. The key question here is whether these actors have the leadership and influence to shape the policy process from within MAS, or whether they are being used by the government to simply feed back into the population decisions that are made without their contribution. Zegada, Torrez and Cámara argue that other sectors of civil society broadly support the process of change but have no direct links to the government. Finally, others question the MAS government but do not confront it openly.[46]

The corollary of all this must be that in order to be able to maintain an independence of identity and action, civil society must stay outside of government and be able to respond to the changing political conditions. On this, it is clear that there have been developments in the relationship between the government and civil society since 2005 in response to the broader political process. The arrival of Morales as president and his MAS government was clearly not welcomed by the political parties of the past. In a move that demonstrates their adaptation to the new political climate of mobilisation and protest, much of the opposition to the government's agenda was driven by a coalition between these parties in parliament, and a number of 'civic committees' based in the eastern lowlands of the country that the represented the special interests of the landowning and entrepreneurial class. These received increasing support from the Catholic Church on issues of land redistribution and the formal separation between the state and the church, which were evident in the new constitution approved in 2009. As was discussed earlier, 2008–09 marked the high point of violent opposition to the government and societal polarisation brought about by these regional interests, which were bent on derailing the process of change and turning the clock back. In this political climate, all the social movements that originally supported the rise of the MAS government became vehement defenders of the government's record and brought their grassroots to vote en masse in favour of the government at a number of referenda. In sum, their common enemy brought them together.

This opposition was thoroughly defeated in the elections of December 2009, and as a result, has hardly featured as a political threat since. Interestingly, it appears that the government's perception of potential political threats has now turned towards former supporting actors and members of the broad coalition for the process of change, that have come to occupy the vacuum left by the violent opposition from the right. The example of the protest in the city of Potosí in July and August 2010 is a case in point. The city is overwhelmingly in favour of the process of change that the MAS government represents, but the city's civic committee, COMCIPO, which represents small shopkeepers, miners, students and the general population, laid siege to its own city, keeping it closed to the outside world and imposing economic and material hardship on its own population. At issue was a series of broken economic and development promises for the area, and accusations of government foul play in the removal of a popular city mayor who had been critical of the government.[47]

Similar arguments appear to be possible in relation to a CIDOB march in June 2010, which was organised to put pressure on the government to negotiate on the autonomous status of indigenous communities and to demand their right to have prior informed consent before mining and hydrocarbon concessions that affect their territories are signed by the government with multinational corporations. The government reacted with a media campaign against CIDOB, attempts to pit other indigenous social movement organisations against them, and accusations that they were funded by USAID and were 'agents of imperialism'.[48] At the time of writing (September 2011) similar issues were arising in relation to the government's plan for the construction of a road through the Isiboro-Sécure National Park and Indigenous Territory (TIPNIS). The road has economic implications, which are considered in Chapter 6.

It is important to consider here the way in which the government is very much going against the wishes of the indigenous communities and the social movements that represent them, violating the principle of informed consent following consultation that is one of the fundamental rights of indigenous nations inserted into the constitution.[49] Not only that, but it appears that the quintessentially indigenous form of protest, the march, which has always been permitted since 1990 even by governments unsympathetic to indigenous demands, might be blocked on its way to La Paz. In addition, the government seems to be pitting some groups of supporters – such as the coca growers who stand to benefit from easier road access to new lands – against indigenous groups. As a result, the highland indigenous social movement CONAMAQ has openly declared that it supports the TIPNIS indigenous groups.[50]

Many of the complexities and contradictions of relations between civil society and the state are exemplified by a cursory exploration of one particular instance of organised civil society and its relations to the government: the Bolivian climate change platform.[51] This platform brings together representatives of Bolivia's main social movements, NGOs and their international counterparts, including Oxfam, Christian Aid, Trocaire and CAFOD, working together to give expression to the views of the Bolivian population on climate change, something that a government closely linked to organised civil society would be likely to value and accept. Indeed, my own fieldwork at the time would suggest that the Bolivian government relied on the climate change platform in the run-up to the Copenhagen climate change summit in December 2009, as well as the subsequent 'people's conference' that took place in Cochabamba in April 2010. And yet a number of issues emerge immediately from this arrangement that illustrate some of the complexities in the relationship between civil society and a government that is supposedly drawn from the social movements.

The first is the question of legitimacy, especially when INGOs are part of this platform and are in a position (in principle) to exercise influence on a foreign government.[52] The second is a question of the real influence that civil society actually has on government policy. In the case of the climate change platform, its political relevance was demonstrated by the speed with which the government invited its 'political engine', the representatives of the social movements, to join the national negotiating team at international events. There is little evidence however that the presence of indigenous representatives influenced the official Bolivian position, or that the Bolivian government takes a position on climate change at home that is consequent with 'big statements' in international fora.[53]

In short, contemporary Bolivia shows a complex blurring of the boundaries between government and civil society, affecting both social movements and NGOs. In the case of the former, the claim that the MAS is a government of the social movements has seen the entry of many indigenous and peasant social movement leaders into the bureaucratic machinery of the state, while they maintain their positions in the social movements. This is true of the president himself, who retains his role in the coca growers' trade union. The trend could be seen as a 'professionalization' of social movement leaders as part of an effective political leadership in government, but as Hervé do Alto observes:

> This process of maturation of social movement leaders in government also leads to a process of bureaucratisation by which they become disconnected from any form of productive activity and as a result, from their own grassroots members. In sum: if social movements have 'perforated' the state, the latter has also penetrated the leadership strata of the social movements, keeping one foot inside the social movements and another inside the institutions of the state.[54]

A similar conclusion has also been reached by Regalsky, who analyses the cooptation processes that bring social movement leaders into government, effectively decapitating those organisations and their ability to fulfil the roles that led to the creation of MAS in the first place.[55] The irony of a state that co-opts the leadership of the social movements is that these emerged as political actors in order to demand a new type of state that delivered recognition for indigenous peoples and recreated new forms of democratic practice. The new constitution officially converts social movements into overseers of the activities of the state. Indeed, the argument has been made that they represent a 'fourth' power in addition to the executive, legislative and judiciary. In a situation in which the link between the political leadership of MAS in government and the grassroots becomes undemocratic, the danger is that civil society will stop exercising the degree of social control that the new constitution bestows on this fourth power.

Article number 241 of the new constitution explicitly states that 'organised civil society will exercise the social control of public administration at all levels of the state and of all companies and institutions that administer public resources'. In addition, it states that 'the state will help generate the appropriate spaces for civil society participation and effective social control'.[56]

This institutionalisation of the role of civil society, through its social movements, in the running of Bolivian society, would appear to be the zenith of recognition and power bestowed on associational forms that include the common man and woman. And yet a large deal of criticism appears to be levelled from civil society against the specific arrangements for participation envisaged in the constitution. Criticism appears to concentrate on the mechanism created for setting the appropriate spaces for participation. This took the form of an institution dependent on the Ministry of Transparency and Anticorruption. In this way, the state effectively calls on those social movements and associations it deems pertinent to discuss agendas that have been set in advance, capturing and managing their potential for acting as critical voices. The result, according to the critics, is a very poor substitute for the Law of Popular Participation in the mid-1990s. As we have seen, perhaps against the odds, this generated opportunities for the emergence of indigenous concerns in Bolivian politics, first at the local level, and then nationally through the creation of MAS.

At this point, what can be said about the question 'is this a government of social movements'? It could be argued that, regardless of the links, personal and ideological, between members of civil society (both social movements and the NGOs where many of the current government ministers developed their political careers) and the government, the government's current public policies and management do not allow us to see a coherent political project that is led by civil society. To what extent civil society will be able to provide an effective control of the government's activities and policies in the way the new constitution specifies is also an unanswered question, but one that gives cause for concern in view of the more recent squabbles between the government and some of these social movements like CIDOB. And yet it is critical to be able to answer the question in the affirmative, for if Bolivia is to lead the way in the creation of a post-neoliberal alternative that is more deeply democratic, socially just and in tune with nature, it will require a positive contribution from these movements. This can only be made possible by a culture of trust and the availability of spaces to develop these encounters without attempts by either side to dominate the agenda. Neither of these preconditions seems to be in place at the moment.

TOWARDS A NEW POLITY

It had all looked so straightforward as an explanation. The political paradigm of a neoliberal past had been discredited, its policies thoroughly rejected by an enraged civil society because of the human suffering and disenfranchisement they created. And organically, through a myriad of grassroots-level organisations, a new political leadership emerged for a country of increasingly politically aware and participative citizens, be it the Aymara-speaking community leader who attends an *ampliado* (meeting) of CONAMAQ, the university student who is now part of the local civic committee, or the cooperative miner who, with thousands of others, marched for days to La Paz in October 2008 to demand in front of Congress the right to give through his vote his opinion on the draft of the new constitution. In the process, a backward-looking political right of those leaders from the past who had never been able to reconcile their understanding of Bolivian society with the seismic changes taking place in front of their eyes, had been truly defeated in successive elections, which delivered increasing majorities for the MAS movement.

It could therefore be argued that organised civil society – and social movements in particular – play a key role in Bolivian politics in a way that it is difficult to compare with any other part of the world, so crucial has their role been in changing the country's political landscape and so fluid their evolving relations with the state. There are lessons here for other countries, especially those liberal democracies like the United Kingdom, where current political debates on the merits of 'big society' appear to place an inordinate amount of emphasis on the contribution that ordinary people might be able to make to the running of services for their communities. Here all similarities end, however. For, if the Bolivian example shows us anything, it is the depth of transformation achieved by social movements and the challenge they represent not only to the fundamental power relations between civil society and the state, but as Chapter 6 explores, also to the market. None of this is a scenario contemplated in the United Kingdom, where the minister for civil society can only envisage a top-down, carefully managed and uncritical 'doing' (and not thinking) role for individuals, that delivers in areas of state retrenchment but does nothing to challenge the power relations status quo. In spite of the rhetoric of devolving power, the government's policy does not envisage any real empowerment, and many would argue that it has become a smokescreen for the state's abdication of its responsibilities. In sum, it represents what some authorities have referred to as a neoliberal version of civil society, in which individuals arguably provide services in a more flexible and efficient way,[57] and not a real process of deepening democracy based on a redistribution of power between the state and civil society. For, as the Bolivian example shows, if civil society is allowed to take power for real, the real balance of power changes in ways that might not be easily reversible.

This does not mean that, in Bolivia, the role of civil society is anything but complex, and its relations to the state are fraught with difficulties. As this chapter shows, Bolivian civil society gives an enormous role to social movements, which have become heirs to the radical legacy of Bolivia's trade unionist politics, and have added to the trade union organisations an organisationally strong set of indigenous-peasant, and more recently urban, social movements. In the context of a highly heterogeneous civil society, clear differences of status and power exist among a membership that includes indigenous social movements as well as those emerging in urban settings. Relations between the state and the various components of civil society reflect those power differences.

In addition, NGOs are of crucial importance in Bolivia and play a wide range of roles, some of which might support the view that they are an extension of western imperialism. This view is repeatedly pronounced by the government and political commentators in relation to USAID[58] – but as a cursory glance at Bolivia's broad range of organisations, demands and forms of activism shows, the issue is far from clear-cut. For example, a recent open letter criticising the government and demanding a return to the process of change was signed by eminent individuals such as former constitutional assembly member Raúl Prada, land minister Alejandro Almaraz, and former Bolivian ambassador to the United States Gustavo Guzmán. Vice-president Linera accused the signatories of being on the side of NGOs and representing 'the operative arm of transnational interests' that 'reproduce the logic of colonial relations'.[59] This chapter has illustrated the broad range of organisations that belong to the sphere of civil society, and outlined also the range of types of relationships that they have developed with the MAS government since 2005.

That it was the principal role played by the whole of civil society that eventually led to a radical political transformation of the country and the constitutional assembly was established in Chapter 3. What this chapter explores in addition is the result of the assembly and the new constitution, in relation to the roles assigned to parts of this civil society in the form of those social movements that gave birth to MAS. The role, one of 'social control', that the constitution elevates to the category of 'fourth power', has been accused of being much more limited than the name suggests, and subordinated to a definition of themes, agendas and institutional processes that seek to undermine the independence of action of social movements.

Tied to this, there have been criticisms and no little local evidence to suggest that the MAS government is keen to direct agendas and their relationship with social movements by co-opting leaders into key government positions. This threatens to break the organic nature of the links that are meant to characterise leaders and the communities they represent, and it suggests that what was once a disparate collection of social movements has become a traditional party, with all the consequences this entails in terms of ideological orientation and democratic participation.[60] Whether these are just the normal teething problems of a new, more participative form of deep democracy or warning signs of a lack of democratic accountability, only time will tell. The long-term success of Bolivia's profound process of change depends in no small measure on the government's ability to reflect and implement those policies that respond to the deepest desires of the Bolivian population, including both redistribution and recognition.

5 NEW CITIZENS, WELFARE AND WELL-BEING

Living in the metropolitan area of La Paz, a modern city with the economic development and the cultural offer to rival any major conurbation, one could be forgiven for assuming a lifestyle for *paceños* that fits in with expectations that would not be out of place in the Global North, given the wide avenues, oversized cars and homes, and chic boutiques of the neighbourhood of San Miguel. Except for two things, that is. The first is that the south part of La Paz, also the lowest in altitude, does not represent the common Bolivian living standard. Indeed, as one travels up, always up from San Miguel, it becomes clear that as the temperature drops, so does wealth, reflecting the national extremes in inequality. This means that, whereas some Bolivians look to Miami as the model of their material aspirations, most make do with annual incomes below US$2,000. The second thing one notices in this most economically segregated city, where the rich live in gated communities with their own private security and the mass of the poor from El Alto in self-built homes with corrugated iron roofs and no basic services, is that poverty and indigenous people go hand in hand. In a country where two-thirds of the population are poor and two-thirds – 62 per cent, to be exact – indigenous, these two groups largely overlap. Not surprisingly, every year in the month of August, as winter stops agriculture and the land is allowed to lay fallow before the next planting season, one sees in La Paz elderly women with small children who come to beg from Norte Potosí, the poorest of all poor Bolivian regions, to add to their families' meagre annual incomes. That this annual migration should only have been known to urban Bolivians since the mid-1980s is a sign of the social damage perpetrated by the same economic policies heralded around the world as the mechanism for economic growth and the solution to poverty.

This chapter considers a number of key elements that, brought together, explore the way in which the Bolivian government is attempting to make social justice a reality in a context of extreme inequalities built on the back of profound divisions between ethnic groups. First, given the intrinsic link between indigeneity and poverty in Bolivia, we explore the great qualitative transition that has taken place in the country in recent years in the inclusion of the indigenous majority.[1] Previous chapters have outlined the political role played by indigenous organisations that have been instrumental in the rejection of neoliberal models of politics and in the proposal of a new model, through MAS. Previous chapters also explored the transition that the new constitution represents in principle: that is, a transition that leaves behind the republican notion of the nation-state in favour of a plurinational state, with what this means in terms of political representation, voice, participation and respect for the rights, knowledge and customs of indigenous groups. This chapter advances this story by considering the qualitative transition in definitions of citizenship that this political revolution entails, moving as it has from definitions that excluded a majority of the population and denied their social rights in everyday practice, to definitions that, as part of a plurinational Bolivia, recognise equality in the context of difference. The new constitution provides a good starting point for considering the way in which these definitions play out, as they were expressed in the writing process as much as in the final text.

The second point considered in this chapter stems from the above, as it explores one of the fundamental implications of the greater levels of power, representation and voice that have been achieved by previously excluded indigenous majorities. This is the way in which indigenous forms of knowledge inform the current administration's public policies. Among them is the concept of *suma qamaña* or 'living well'. Bolivia's indigenous peoples have a range of these concepts in a number of languages, as do those in Ecuador, but only these two governments (Bolivia and Ecuador) have openly embraced this key concept and attempted to integrate it into policies designed to improve their citizens' lives in a way that is qualitatively distinct from the hegemonic paradigm of traditional economics, which equates well-being with economic growth and sees this at the base of every attempt to improve the material, social, even the spiritual basis of life. The term 'living well' is certainly different from the western concept of well-being, but Bolivians tend to oppose it to 'living better', a concept they claim underlies imported models and practices to achieve well-being that focus on the individual and the material at the expense of the collective, the spiritual, and of nature. The chapter outlines the various dimensions of *suma qamaña*, but concentrates on the way in which the concept informs a number of social policies in the form of cash transfers introduced by the current government to tackle the many aspects of poverty through redistribution programmes.

The third part of this chapter presents the government's strategy for tackling many of the country's ills as they are presented in the National Development Plan (NDP). This section outlines some of the challenges facing the government in 2005, and the various areas of provision that have been prioritised in a concerted effort to meet the Millennium Development Goals (MDGs) and rid Bolivia of the pejorative condition of being the poorest and most unequal country in South America. The final section explores some of the specific policies destined to make a reality these lofty aims, concentrating on redistributive policies in the form of the cash transfers Bolivians call *bonos* for a range of social groups such as mothers and babies, school-age children, and old people. This section pays particular attention to the new universal pension, *renta dignidad*, as it has received a great deal of attention abroad as part of a renewed interest in the virtues of social pensions. The section also explores what difference these policies have made and the extent to which they are sustainable in the long term.

UNITED IN DIVERSITY

Article 1 of the new constitutional text declares Bolivia to be a single state with a plurality of nations in its midst that can exercise their social rights.[2] The plurinational nature of Bolivia might appear self-evident to many, but during the writing of the constitution, this question caused one of the earliest and most intractable clashes between opposing points of view. The social movements and the *indigenista* section of the constitutional assembly wanted Bolivia to be described in terms of the 36 indigenous nations and languages that are part of the country, something criticised by opposition parties generally.

For the former, the old Bolivia they wanted to erase represented a centralising nation-state that denied their identity and had imposed imported linguistic, cultural, religious and social norms during its colonial, republican and neoliberal phases. The argument defended by social movements, MAS and the forces of change was that the colonial and later republican nation-state they decried had abjectly failed to incorporate indigenous communities into the state of

Bolivia, creating instead second-class citizens who, throughout the country's history, had suffered from poverty, abandonment, and most importantly, lack of recognition.[3] Their demand was that the new constitution acknowledge Bolivia's ethnic, cultural and linguistic richness as a precondition to equality, a demand that they saw as intrinsically linked to the political struggle for recognition that they originally began with the march to La Paz in 1990 under the banner of land, territory and dignity.[4] For the latter group of opposition parties, the claim of plurinationality was denied by what they argued was the reality of a *mestizo* country that resulted from five centuries of mixing of Spanish and native populations, who now share a common language, religion and identity. Their argument followed the mantra of the 1952 revolution and the vision of a homogenising nation-state generated as a result, which was used to justify an appeal to equality of citizenship condition, including rights and responsibilities, for all Bolivians. In sum, in their view there were not many Bolivias but one Bolivia, and not many categories of Bolivian citizen but one single category.

It did not take long for indigenous *constituyentes* to find out the truth about the newly declared sense of brotherhood from their counterparts. For when opposition to the work the assembly was conducting became most radicalised, leaders from the same opposition parties who had claimed brotherhood with their indigenous counterparts, along with thousands of citizens from the city of Sucre and, most shamefully, not a small number of university students, resorted to the all too familiar racist abuse and violence that characterised the country during 2007–08, looking for ways in which to, as the saying went, teach a lesson to *indios* – a term often used pejoratively by whites and *mestizos* – who 'didn't know their place'. Some of these acts of violence, including the events that led to the production of the documentary entitled *Ofendidos y humillados*, were explored in Chapter 3 and will not be repeated here. Suffice to say that two significant elements characterised the racist violence from this recent period of Bolivia's history. The first is that the violence was directed and often perpetrated by 'respectable' members of the social, economic and political elites in the city, with positions in national and local government or leading the local university in Sucre. The second element is that the violence was fed by a deep-seated belief in a fundamental inequality of condition between themselves and those against whom the violence was directed.[5]

As an outside observer of these events, it seemed to me that these acts were enough to invalidate any claims to 'sameness' between all Bolivians when this was patently not believed by those who made the claim themselves. The thesis of the *indio permitido* (the permitted Indian) can help explain how early national legislation was used to adopt and recognise indigenous cultural rights – as was the case in Bolivia in 1991 with the adoption of ILO Convention 169 on Indigenous Rights – as a way of limiting the aspirations for real transformation in their lives.[6] Both the content of the new constitution and the process by which it was written represented a threat to these limits, and could only ultimately be resisted through violent means.

The qualitative transition in definitions of national identity and citizenship that the current process of change entails has been best explained by Xavier Albó.[7] For him, the 'indigenous question' is an unresolved one in Bolivia, in part because the country was born with what he regards as the racist 'original sin'. The colonial period disregarded the indigenous majority and excluded it not only from the corridors of power and the economic life of the country, but even from urban spaces, exclusion that continued during the republican period.[8] Only in the 1952 revolution, the argument goes, was there acknowledgement of the unresolved nature of this question, a question that was brought into relief by the experience of the Chaco War in the 1930s when many indigenous men were conscripted, and indigenous peoples were finally given the vote. This is, however, at the cost of ignoring the country's ethnic and cultural diversity to create an imagined national *mestizo* identity that converted all indigenous peoples into a new peasant class.

Albó's argument fits well with the empirical evidence and current interest in the growing political struggle of indigenous groups for recognition and their right to exercise their citizenship. Critics might argue that the 1990s represented a step forward in terms of the recognition of multiculturalism in Bolivia and beyond. However, as with the thesis of the permitted Indian, commentators have argued that neoliberal forms of multiculturalism have in fact reinforced the power of traditional and new actors at the expense of indigenous peoples.[9] Only the current process of change has delivered what Nancy Postero has termed 'postmulticultural citizenship' and others 'postneoliberal plurinationalism', a citizenship regime that holds the promise of a new beginning that no doubt observers will evaluate in due course.[10] However, the premise of indigenous identities necessary to maintain this argument is denied by Bolivian authors such as Carlos Toranzo, who refute the reality described by the 2001 census and denounce what they see as the dangers inherent in an extremist version of indigenist ideology.[11] The question is further complicated by those from Bolivia who have advocated the relevance of theories of complex identity,[12] stipulating the need to understand the multiple facets of identity in Bolivia with reference to not only their ethnic-cultural forms but also their class, region and ideological counterparts.[13]

In the end, imperfect as it is, the new Bolivian constitution represents a great leap forward in this regard. The text takes the country away from a definition of what constitutes a Bolivian that was ethnically blind but systematically excluded a majority of the population, to one that accepts difference as part of a plurinational Bolivia and recognises equality of condition in the context of difference.[14] This acceptance of what the literature has referred to as complex equality as the basis for constructing a new form of social justice is something Bolivians have described in terms of 'unity in diversity' to explain the meaning of a refounded Bolivia that the new constitution declares to be plurinational. Seemingly a contradiction, it constitutes the best hope for a philosophical foundation to progressive social change that reduces poverty and increases life chances for the most excluded in society. There are many implications of this for Bolivia.

The first set of implications that stem from the plurinational nature of Bolivia enshrined in the constitution refer to a new understanding of the structure of the state. Bolivia remains a single, indivisible state. However, it now acknowledges the existence of many nations within its borders. What this means is that this constitution recognises the country's indigenous majority in its entire diversity. With this, the country sheds both the openly racist nature of its foundation in 1825, which ignored the existence of indigenous citizens, and the closet racism that fed the 1952 revolution. The principle of equality in diversity that informs the new constitution means equality of rights and duties of every citizen. The principle also includes an acknowledgement and acceptance that within Bolivia, a diversity of languages, cultures, beliefs and knowledge systems coexist. The creation of indigenous autonomic territories reflects this recognition, and is geared towards the creation of possibilities for the cultural reproduction of those indigenous communities. It also has implications for a redistribution of power in favour of those most discriminated against, as it introduces direct representation of indigenous groups in the new Plurinational Assembly – the new name for the chamber that replaces Bolivia's Congress – and accepts different forms of knowledge, including indigenous forms of knowledge, to inform the education and health systems, even the administration of justice in those territories that can now follow traditional indigenous practices.[15] Finally the constitution recognises the right of indigenous groups to hold territories collectively and to be consulted on issues that might affect them.

The second set of implications is that, with the implementation of the new constitution, the government of Bolivia expects nothing less than a redefinition of the social contract, of the relationship between the citizen and the state. This redefinition of relations itself includes two aspects. First, emerging from the previous chapter that explored the new-found power relations between citizens and the state (through the social movements and the increased levels of citizens' political participation), the corollary is the inclusion of a large majority of the country in the social rights of citizenship. Bolivia is now the country of all Bolivians, not of a minority. So this is an aspect of inclusion to all and the extension of social rights to all, something that had clearly been denied to many until now, either formally or in everyday practice. Second, the redefinition of relations between the state and the citizen is taking place in the context of a wider redefinition of the size, responsibility and place of the state in the state–market–community triangle.[16] The meaning of this, at least in theory, is that individuals are no longer abandoned to the vagaries of the market, as happened during the neoliberal period. The aim then was to create a type of 'active, empowered and entrepreneurial citizens who will take responsibility for their own and their families' welfare, and who are prepared for the market rather than the state to provide for their social rights', often through the work of international non-governmental organisations (INGOs) and their emphasis on microcredit as a tool for developing entrepreneurial activity.[17] Instead, according to the new constitution, the state will now take on responsibility for its citizens. It promises a new era of well-being and social cohesion based on a concerted effort to minimise poverty and reduce inequality, while organised civil society has a legitimate role to play in delivering social control of the state's activities.

Third, the plurinational Bolivia that has been enshrined in the new constitution brings together both indigenous politics and citizenship. It is the development of a strong indigenous movement in the last two decades that has partly delivered the process of change that this book explores. One of the consequences of the formation of this new political actor has been the incorporation into Bolivian society of a previously excluded majority. What follows the inclusion within Bolivia of a number of indigenous nations is that this inclusion incorporates new social rights for citizens, and crucially, these rights operate at both the individual and collective levels.[18] It is this link between the debate on democracy and citizenship that is interesting in Bolivia. We can argue that citizenship is the expression of the quality of democracy, because people who can exercise their political, social and civil rights are more able to construct a better quality of democracy. In this sense, Bolivia has made enormous progress in the last few years by incorporating the collective demands of indigenous nations in its (new) constitution. And yet, as any Bolivian could explain, applying for and receiving an identity card as a precondition to being able to exercise citizenship rights such as voting, receiving benefits such as the *renta dignidad* and finding employment, is still an extremely complex process. It proves impossible for some, illustrating the strange distinction between the advanced possibilities for exercising collective citizenship rights and the difficulties that follow sometimes in exercising individual ones.[19]

What the plurinational nature of Bolivia represents, especially in its intercultural facet, is the acceptance of new forms of identity based on common principles and values. Values hitherto submerged and sidelined to the margins of society are now rescued and given new meaning by a government led by an indigenous president. Andean values of equality, reciprocity and *complementariedad* (roughly meaning the principle of building relationships that bring holistic units together) are seen as the building blocks of *suma qamaña* or *vivir bien*, a concept that translates as living well together. Living well, an idea that has also been adopted recently in Ecuador's constitution, could well be compared to the contested notion of well-being. The next section endeavours to make sense of this concept, especially in terms of what it means for the provision of universal basic services. For the first time in the history of a country infamous for the brutality of economic reforms in the 1980s and the degree of social suffering they provoked, the state undertakes a responsibility to provide basic health care and education for all, a dignified retirement through the implementation of a universal pension, and the access of all Bolivians to safe water, described for the first time as a basic human right.[20] The provision of basic protections, it has to be remembered, is the basis on which European countries were rebuilt after the Second World War. These are fundamental to their welfare states. How are these new social rights rationalised in the context of Bolivia?

SUMA QAMAÑA, OR AN INDIGENOUS UNDERSTANDING OF 'LIVING WELL'

When I was listening to Bolivian foreign secretary David Choquehuanca, giving a speech in La Paz, discuss *suma qamaña–vivir bien* (living well) with a group of Europeans, a number of things became clear to me about a concept that can be difficult to grasp.[21] On that occasion, he chose to compare *vivir bien* (living well) to *vivir mejor* (living better than). The former represents an Andean model of human development based on a sustainable relationship to natural resources in a framework of values of solidarity, mutuality and reciprocity, whereas the latter refers to increasing living standards based on unsustainable levels of consumption in market conditions that lead to high levels of inequality. As the argument goes, in an interrelated world, pretending to be in a race against others and outpacing their economic performance can only deliver success as the direct result of the failure and misery of others, and this cannot ultimately be the answer to happiness, satisfaction or self-fulfilment. The idea includes lessons for governments as much as for individuals. For the former, it criticises mainstream economic ideas of ever-increasing growth based on the unsustainable exploitation of natural resources, the domination of nature and the deployment of the capitalist system. For the latter, it proposes collaboration over competition, sharing over accumulation, solidarity over disagreement, cohesion over discord.

The fact of the matter is that *suma qamaña* is about relations and living in harmony. The first aspect of this is about social relations, about living well with others. In this, the term should be distinguished from well-being. People continue to struggle to make sense of what well-being means for groups of people rather than for individuals. The western conception of well-being is highly contested, but has often been dominated by economic measurements – as when policy makers equate it to the absence of poverty as measured in per capita income – and utilitarian views that reduce multiple aspects of life to the maximisation of pleasure.[22] Only an Aristotelian tradition of philosophy has explored well-being as well-living, moving beyond the concept of well-being as a state of being to one that takes account of the multifaceted nature of our humanity as is expressed in our daily lives, in relation to others. Thus, having, doing and interacting are seen in this tradition as key elements in the pursuit of a good life.[23] Only in the last few decades have the principles of an ethic of care appeared to have made headway in the academic literature. Originally proposed from a feminist perspective, they argue against dominant philosophical foundations that see us as autonomic individuals compelled by universal standards of moral behaviour, and present instead a view of humans as highly interdependent, where our behaviour takes place in response to the interconnected networks of needs, care and avoiding harm.[24] In sum, headway is being made in our understanding of what constitutes well-being in ways that reflect the indigenous principle of *suma qamaña* that includes forms of conviviality based on reciprocity.[25]

Western conceptions of well-being do not yet seem to take account of the fact that a harmonious life has to go beyond the purely social. In addition to the social, a multitude of indigenous understandings of *suma qamaña* in other regions appear to put emphasis on the importance of the natural world, including complementary understandings of *suma qamaña* from the Mapuche, Maya and indigenous groups in Colombia.[26] That is, living in harmony and sustainably with and within nature is as important as the principles of solidarity, cohesion and care that rule human relations. So *suma qamaña* is also about living well with and within nature. The importance of this aspect of *suma qamaña* has been underlined by the very vociferous and active international role played by the Morales government on climate change. This role is supported by legislation on the Rights of Mother Earth, which was introduced just in time to be announced to the world during the international conference on climate change held in Cancún in December 2010. This conference also supported the Bolivian campaign to create an international environmental tribunal to protect the rights of Mother Earth.

It would be easy to dismiss these policy positions for being idealistic in the extreme and difficult to implement in the real world, especially when the MAS government is being increasingly accused of a double discourse that promotes Mother Earth abroad but encourages an unsustainable development model at home.[27] However, we would be mistaken if we dismissed *suma qamaña* entirely. One of the most exciting things about this concept is the extent to which it lives on among indigenous communities in Bolivia and has a very practical place in everyday life. So, for example, some Andean communities have opted for collective land titles (as opposed to individual ones. which was the preferred option of the post-1952 revolutionary government) in the spirit of traditional ways of life that embody the principles of *suma qamaña*.[28] The reason is that their holding comprises several different types of terrain at different altitudes, and a community pooling land resources in this way is able to minimise the risks associated with poor weather and crop pests, maximising food production and the continued survival of the community. In addition to this, traditional decision-making practices that aim for consensus building rather than majority impositions are able to allocate plots to families according to changing circumstances and needs, such as the number of children. Thus, *suma qamaña* comprises respect for the environment and an attempt to maintain a sustainable relationship to it, as well as harmonious social relations, resulting in collective natural resource management and food security.[29] Instead of a quaint set of traditional practices, *suma qamaña* shows us perhaps a different future, one that marries human needs with those of the earth.[30]

Discursively at least, the new era inaugurated by the election of the MAS government in 2005 has ushered in a new focus on redressing the excesses of human suffering created by the neoliberal period. For that, Bolivia is taking a look at itself, reverting back to Andean ethical principles and values that express the ideal of the good life. The result discussed here includes a revitalisation of indigenous value systems – including *suma qamaña* – that put an emphasis on harmonious social and environmental relations. This principle is arguably being adopted by the state in its new capacity as promoter of the population's well-being, and is proving decisive at a discursive level in providing a coherent programme for state intervention in areas as wide apart as land redistribution, economics, international relations and social policy. The next section focuses on the social policy implications of living well.

WELFARE, WELL-BEING AND THE ROLE OF THE STATE

Critical for a government that celebrates the presence of indigenous communities at the heart of Bolivia has been the insertion of the principle of *suma qamaña* at the core of the country's master plan for leaving behind the neoliberal state and for delivering a new model of development for the country, which includes dealing with its considerable social policy challenges. The NDP carries in the subtitle its objectives, including the creation of a dignified, sovereign, productive and democratic Bolivia that delivers 'living well'.

The NDP argues in its introduction that discrimination, poverty and inequality in Bolivia have deep historic and structural causes

that have been built on the back of development models that have
been imposed on the country, first in the colonial and republican
periods, and then by the more recent neoliberal phase in the 1980s
and 1990s. The former created a model of export of primary
products that did not deliver wealth accumulation at home whereas
the latter weakened the state and subordinated national priorities
to those of transnational corporations (TNCs) and international
financial institutions (IFIs). All imposed political and social structures that denigrated local forms of knowledge and practices. The
result of these models has been the predatory exploitation of natural
resources, the accumulation of wealth in the hands of a small
minority, and the subsequent social exclusion and marginalisation
of the majority of the population. The NDP is the current government's strategic blueprint for reversing this situation, and provides
a roadmap for Bolivian development that is holistic and includes
economic, political, social and cultural components.

According to the introduction to the document, the NDP
emerged from Bolivia's multicultural capacities and from the daily
practices of community-level organisations and resources. These
practices have led to the creation of a new set of institutions in a
new plurinational country that is decolonised, socially focused, and
works as an expression of Bolivia's communities' determination to
make the concept of living well a reality.[31] The new plurinational
and decolonised state is meant to play a particularly important role
in the construction of this new society and development model.
The state is viewed as the main political actor, able to establish the
guiding principles of the process of change and police their implementation. This is, however, a new type of state, one that emerges
from social movements and local forms of community organisation,
an autochthonous state with new, decolonised institutions, and the
NDP is a new paradigm built on the bottom-up reassessment of the
role of the state in promoting and contributing to the well-being of
society.[32]

In addition to the state, the NDP carries the implicit acknowledgement that actors at many levels carry responsibilities for the delivery
of the plan. The state's role in providing a unifying framework for
the implementation of a single, universal system of provision goes
hand in hand with an NDP based on the objective of regaining
national sovereignty. However, the state is relatively weak in Bolivia,
making the extent to which it can achieve this objective difficult to
forecast.[33] Besides the state, other key actors in the delivery of the
NDP are the communities. Bolivia is a fairly decentralised country

in which the various levels of government have responsibilities for the delivery of services. In addition, the 1994 Law of Participation and the nature of the current political paradigm make civil society – in the form of social movements, community organisations and interest groups – a powerful actor in Bolivia.[34] This said, the evidence on the extent to which popular participation at the municipal level has improved democratic practice is mixed.[35] The same can be said for the extent to which indigenous-specific health views are expressed and reflected in the provision of services, an area that, with few exceptions, remains under-researched.[36] Finally, international solidarity networks and global civil society constitute another key actor in the mix of influences on local implementation of the NDP. This point is acknowledged in the document itself, which stipulates that all external sources of help, including international NGOs and foreign aid, will have to conform and contribute to the national framework itself.

The NDP itself outlines the main characteristics of the strategic plan. Under the heading 'democratic Bolivia', the document explores the value of community organisation and the levels of decentralisation required. Under 'productive Bolivia', the document outlines the main guidelines for the implementation of the new economic plan. Under 'sovereign Bolivia', the document explores some of the main principles of the country's foreign policy. In the case of social policy, the plan outlines, among others, proposals for tackling poverty, poor health, education, and access to basic services like water and sanitation, by delivering a significant increase in expenditure in social policy for programmes that aim to provide universal and free access. All of these principles and the strategies that accompany them become the state's responsibilities, and are part of a dominant ideological principle enshrined in the idea of living well. The guiding principle in the implementation of these policies is the idea that social policies will no longer be seen as derived from economic policy (in other words, as a burden) but an intrinsic part of the state's responsibilities and an investment in human capital.

For example, Bolivia's new NDP contains details of the educational and health challenges present in the country as well as the plans to tackle those needs. The section on Bolivia *saludable y formada* (a healthy and well-educated Bolivia) seeks to create a new educational system that is decolonising, intercultural, community based, and that regains the knowledge and technologies of indigenous communities. For its part, the health plan is built on the principles of universality of provision that is free at the point of delivery, regaining the state's responsibilities in the management of the health system, social participation in the management of the health system, heath promotion, and the creation of a national alliance to combat malnutrition and the exclusion of groups living in extreme poverty. These are particularly important interventions given that Bolivia in 2005 continued to be a country where two-thirds of the population did not have access to free health care, especially in the rural areas, infant mortality rates hovered around 60 per 1,000 live births, chronic malnutrition affected a quarter of all children, and many children were forced to abandon school in order to contribute to the household's income.[37] Following internationally agreed MDGs, the Bolivian state puts a big emphasis on plans to eradicate extreme poverty by 2015 under the 'living well' banner. Although it is acknowledged that poverty is a multidimensional social problem, and that many of the policies in health, education, food sovereignty and access to basic services go some way into tackling aspects of poverty, the Bolivian government has received international attention for a number of specific cash-transfer policies implemented since 2006, directed at schoolchildren, mothers and infants, and older citizens.

LIVING WELL AND ANTI-POVERTY CASH TRANSFERS

Social cash transfer programmes are increasingly becoming the policy instrument of choice in many less developed countries (LDCs) in the Global South. They constitute permanent programmes that regularly provide cash to households that meet the relevant eligibility criteria, provide basic social protection to large numbers of people, and help make rapid progress towards meeting the MDGs. Social cash transfer programmes are currently being praised for their effectiveness, and are encouraged by many international development institutions such as the World Bank and the UK Department for International Development (DfID).[38] Where the 1980s were dominated by targeted assistance and social forms of insurance, more recently social cash transfers have been used in countries as far apart as Brazil and South Africa.[39]

Bolivia is not the first Latin American country to introduce social cash transfers: Mexico, Nicaragua and Brazil were the trailblazers in the region. However, the Morales government has gained much political capital at home and abroad through the introduction of three types of social cash transfers, or *bonos*, as they are usually referred to in the country. The first is the Bono Juancito Pinto, a conditional cash transfer that takes its name from a twelve-year-old drummer who died in 1880 during the Pacific War. The sum of Bvs200 (around US$30, to be increased to US$45 in 2011) is given to primary school children up to eighth grade at the end of each year provided they meet a minimum attendance requirement. It constitutes a key form of economic support that diminishes the need for children to work, and covers the costs of school materials, transport and other expenses. According to the Bolivian Education Ministry, the Bono Juancito Pinto is responsible for halving disengagement from primary school between 2005 and 2009 to a figure of 2.5 per cent of all enrolled children.[40]

The second is the Bono Juana Azurduy, also known as the *bono madre–niño* (mother–child). This cash transfer was introduced in May 2009 and delivers cash to mothers – up to US$260 if they attend every appointment – on condition that they attend check-ups and have a hospital birth.[41] The idea behind this cash transfer is to incentivise access to a holistic health service provision for both mother and child, increasing the family's economic resources during the first two years of life and reducing chronic malnutrition (which still affects 25 per cent of children) and Latin America's second-highest maternal and infant mortality rates. The programme has encountered problems in its introduction, not least the lack of health provision in many rural areas, and has spurred the Ministry of Health to recruit up to 800 new doctors to provide the required attention. The second problem encountered is the lack of identity cards and the difficulties of obtaining birth certificates, issues that the current government is working towards resolving by sending outreach teams that can provide these services in the furthest reaches of the country. Delivering cash directly to mothers and providing health attention sensitive to multicultural needs, the Bono Juana Azurduy is expected to contribute significantly to a number of the MDGs, including the eradication of extreme poverty and hunger, reduction of child mortality, improving maternal health, and promoting gender equality and the empowerment of women.[42] In 2011 the programme received international attention and recognition from the United Nations Institute for Training and Research (UNITAR).[43]

The example for which Bolivia has received most international attention is the social pension, or *renta dignidad*. This is in line with the interest created by social pensions elsewhere.[44] The Bolivian version is a payment of Bvs2,400 p.a. for those who receive no other (contributory) pension, and Bvs1,800 for those who do (around US$340 and US$257 respectively) to citizens over 60, who constitute almost 7 per cent of the population. This universal pension was decreed on November 28, 2007 through law 3791, and began to be paid out in February 2008.[45] The *renta dignidad* constitutes a commitment by the government to pay out around $190 million per year, a not insignificant amount of money for a country like Bolivia, and is paid for through new taxes levied on gas and oil companies.[46] Again, the single biggest obstacle for elderly citizens in obtaining their *renta dignidad* lies in obtaining an identity card. The difficulties of achieving this have been reduced considerably since the introduction of biometric identification to compile the electoral lists for the 2009 presidential election.[47] As a result the *bono* reaches around 700,000 people, 60 per cent of whom are said to live on less than US$1 per day. This particular cash transfer to elderly people who make up a large percentage of the poorest sections of society has been the biggest and most warmly received by a country where, given the high levels of informality in the labour market, only about 15 per cent of the economically active population have access to a contributory pension.[48] Thus *renta dignidad*, small as it is, constitutes an enormous help to elderly people, with its benefits extolled by a jubilant population and its merits celebrated by international organisations and NGOs alike.[49]

Critics point out that the principle of *renta dignidad* is not new in Bolivia because this cash transfer effectively replaced another state pension, Bonosol, which had been introduced by Sánchez de Lozada in 1996.[50] However, besides offering a smaller cash transfer and suffering from multiple administrative problems and interruptions, the funding of Bonosol was limited because it relied on the income generated by the privatisation of utilities in the 1990s. These generated less income than expected, so there was a shortfall early on.[51] For a left-leaning government like MAS that was aiming to 'recover' previously privatised companies and not to make further privatisations, this form of funding was neither desirable nor workable. In terminology, the *renta dignidad* is much more in tune with current government rhetoric and ideology.

The idea of recovering the people's assets, their natural resources, in order to use them for the benefit of all is key to the ideological repertoire of the MAS.[52] The ultimate aim of 'living well', which does not imply high levels of consumption so much as dignity, is common in Morales' speeches, and the 2009 constitution includes a guarantee of a universal pension for the Bolivian elderly.[53]

There is some evidence that the combined effect of these redistribution programmes is delivering positive social and economic
results. The three forms of cash transfer discussed reach 29.8 per
cent of the entire Bolivian population, and three out of four families
receive at least one form of cash transfer.[54] Although it is too early
to be conclusive, non-contributory universal pension systems have
been argued to be both affordable and politically beneficial for
those governments that introduce them.[55] The limited evidence
available from Bolivia suggests that the social pension contributes
to the generation of economic activity among the poorest, helping
family incomes even though by itself it is not sufficient to lift individuals out of poverty altogether. A study conducted on the effects
of *renta dignidad*'s predecessor Bonosol suggested that the elderly
in receipt of this social transfer tended to share it with the wider
household, and were able to convert financial capital into social
capital, strengthening their condition as citizens, increasing their
autonomy and reinforcing the intergenerational contract.[56]

Back in 2006 the NDP spelled out an aim to reduce extreme
poverty to 22.2 per cent by 2015 as part of Bolivia's commitments
to the MDGs. The *renta dignidad,* along with the Bono Juancito
Pinto and the Bono Juana Azurduy, was seen as the core of the
government's anti-poverty programme, which aimed to reduce
socioeconomic inequality through progressive redistribution. Recent
statistics suggest that moderate progress has taken place in the last
few years. Almost 64 per cent of the Bolivian population living
in rural areas in 2007 lived in extreme poverty, with per capita
incomes of less than US$1 per day.[57] However, according to the
Unidad de Análisis de Políticas Económicas y Sociales (UDAPE)
(a unit for the analysis of social and economic policies), there was
a notable reduction in poverty between 2000 (66.4 per cent) and
2010 (49.6 per cent). The reduction in extreme poverty was from
45.2 to 25.4 per cent in the same period.[58] These are national
figures, and although poverty levels continue to be much higher in
the rural areas than in cities, the downward trend is apparent there
too. The Gini coefficient, the standard international measure of
inequality, also decreased greatly in the same period.

Along with the introduction of social cash transfers, social
expenditure increased enormously in that period, with expenditure on health and education doubling between 2000 and 2008.
However, given the economic growth experienced by the country,
specially since 2005, these figures represent a barely perceptible
increase in percentage of GDP expended. In health, the figure only

moved from 3 per cent in 2000 to 3.2 per cent in 2008, whereas in education the increase was better but still modest, from 5.8 per cent to 7 per cent.[59] Just as the Gini coefficient continues to be double the average European figure, Bolivian social expenditure can still only be described as moderate compared with richer countries.

TOWARDS A NEW DEFINITION OF THE GOOD SOCIETY

Five years after the arrival in power of MAS and the announcement that the new government aimed to carry out nothing less than a refoundation of Bolivia, the signs are that some progress is taking place. The refoundation was meant to take place to redress the histories of injustice that have seen the majority of the Bolivian population socially, economically and politically excluded. This chapter has explored the meaning and the difficulties of new understandings of the multicultural nature of the country, and the novel ways in which, in spite of recurrent difficulties, Bolivia has embraced unity in diversity.

One of the ways in which the indigenous core of the Bolivian identity is expressed in the new constitution lies in the adoption and reinterpretation of indigenous understandings of living well. These understandings informed the 2006 NDP, including its social policy chapter. Under the heading 'a dignified Bolivia', they lay the foundations for policies that include the universal provision of health, education, basic services such as water, sanitation and electricity, and the creation of social cash transfers in order to deal with the country's extreme levels of poverty.

The resulting policies have received international attention and much congratulatory commentary, as there is some evidence that human development indicators (poverty, literacy levels, maternal and infant mortality rates, vaccination levels, levels of chronic malnutrition and so on) are all improving. However, with poverty figures that put the country only ahead of Haiti in Latin America and the Caribbean, the overwhelming evidence is that Bolivia has a very long way to go before living well is realised. There is, then, a mismatch between the rhetoric of *suma qamaña* and the daily experience of the average Bolivian. In terms of the difficulties being faced by the country to create a welfare system of sorts, one important element is that, as an underdeveloped economy with a large informal labour market, it is very difficult to tackle large inequalities and structural poverty because the state has few tax revenues to sustain an increasing welfare budget. This has created a system of social protection that is highly vulnerable to the international economic climate.[60] The next chapter explores the Bolivian government's response to the transformation of the economy in the national quest for achieving 'living well'. Even if the Bolivian government accepts the indigenous principles of living well with others, can it realise this vision in the context of what some authors have referred to as 'the new ecological paradigm'?[61]

6 NEW ECONOMICS

The promise and the limits of post-neoliberal development

It is said that the famous Cuban intellectual and hero of independence José Martí (1853–1895) once declared that 'the nation that buys commands, the nation that sells serves'.[1] He was referring to Cuba and to a colonial economic experience that had made the Caribbean island dependent on the export of a main product: sugar. He wrote this line in 1891 as he participated as a delegate at the International Monetary Commission in Washington DC representing Uruguay. He could have been referring to Bolivia of course, and to the rest of the Latin American countries that refused to be drawn economically closer to the United States at that event, for their economic histories were similar then and would continue to be so in the twentieth century.

In the case of Bolivia, in the colonial period of dependence on Spain, an enclave economy built on the extraction of mineral resources was paralleled by a mass of rural and indigenous people practising subsistence and small-scale agricultural production. This economic period was extended and entrenched during the republic. It was still the dominant dual economic model well into the middle of the twentieth century. Later, with the triumph of the 1952 revolution, there was a concerted effort to modernise the country, establishing a nation state and superseding these premodern and precapitalist forms of production. The economic period dominated the three decades following the 1952 revolution was characterised by the ascendance of the state as the driver, financier and executor of the main economic forms of production: that is, a form of state capitalism.[2] The state therefore sought to nationalise the production and transport of the main source of wealth in the country: the mines and the railroads. In addition, state-driven

capitalism brought about land reform in order to liberate indigenous labour power that was still tied to the land as bonded labour
in a remnant of the colonial forms of production. And as the great
haciendas disappeared, their labour was freed and their land distributed for the purpose of creating a small, rural-based economy that
could sell its surplus.

This was the period of dominance of the left, who sought to
unionise the entire population, whether in the mines or in the rural
areas, where some of today's indigenous social movements started
off their political life as trade unions. In short, the dream of the
urban-based intellectual elite of the 1952 revolution was to create
a mass working class. The result of these economic policies was
successful in some ways but limited in others. This was a period of
state-capitalist production and investment in the mining industry,
with a leap forward in production and especially in security at
work. Workers' rights were recognised and Bolivia achieved social
rights that put the country on a par with others in the region,
with reasonable levels of educational achievement for example and
pensions for workers. These rights did not however extend to the
entire population, as the economy continued to be divided between
an extractivist, export-driven sector and a mass of poor rural
workers dependent on agricultural production mostly for national
consumption.

The neoliberal period began with the return to democracy in the
1980s and ended, the current government argues, in 2005. Chapter
1 explored this economic era which, it has been argued, acted to
deliver high levels of human suffering. Coupled with this, a growing
ideological reading of the neoliberal economic era has explained it
in Bolivia and increasingly in left circles as the deliberate result of
a concerted effort by an elite home-grown capitalist class linked to
international economic interests and financial institutions intent on
'freeing' Bolivia's natural resources for the benefit of international
capital, an agenda ruthlessly supported by northern countries, especially the United States. The result of this reading is that increasing
popular uprisings throughout the 1990s rejected both the economic
model and the political system to which it was tied, producing as a
result the MAS era for which we are now trying to evaluate various
areas of performance. It is worth reminding ourselves of the main
characteristics of the neoliberal model that the government of MAS
claims to have left behind.

Neoliberalism between 1980 and 2005 essentially privatised the
state monopolies, starting with the mines in 1985 and continuing

with the gas and oil industries, the main state electricity company, the state airline and telecommunications. These privatisations were imposed on the country as part of the conditions for receiving external aid. In many cases, as with the mines, privatisation essentially meant that state assets were sold at heavily discounted prices to private investors that either creamed off the rich pickings – leaving behind everything that required investment – or asset-stripped these cheaply bought companies and left the carcasses to rot, as in the case of the national airline. Second, the neoliberal era in Bolivia meant market liberalisation and the introduction of a flat tariff regime that freed imports and tried to encourage the export of natural resources and agricultural produce. Third, the system demanded a great level of deregulation to create one of the most flexible labour markets in Latin America. Labour flexibility reduced costs but also made work highly precarious without necessarily increasing the levels of formal employment. Finally, the system imposed an individualisation of risk and the introduction of market-based forms of self-help. In the case of the pension system, developed during the period of state capitalist domination and based on a model of intergenerational solidarity, the individualisation of risk essentially meant that the pay-as-you-go system introduced in 1996 forced workers to save for their retirement in individual savings accounts, and severely reduced the contribution to their pensions from employers.

The results from this system, introduced apparently to rescue Bolivia from economic meltdown in the 1980s, were not all what the international community was made to believe. Perhaps the most positive element to it was the increase of foreign investment in the country. However this increase was concentrated mostly in the hydrocarbons industry, and in any case, as we saw in Chapter 1, the period will be forever associated with a serious externalisation of profit which, as a result of privatisation contracts that were highly advantageous to transnational corporations (TNCs), left Bolivia without natural resources and also without royalties or taxes to compensate for the exploitation of its resources. The country's railways were closed as a result of privatisation and the national airline lasted no more than ten years as a private company before going bankrupt. The only positive note of the period was the growth of the agricultural export industry, particularly soya. However its production delivered other problems in environmental and social terms. For example, agricultural production for national consumption decreased during the period and worsened the country's food self-sufficiency. The economy did grow after the dramatic period of 1984/5, but not by more than 3 per cent on average, and this period included the recession of 1999. What grew beyond control, in spite of the praise that Bolivia was receiving from the International Monetary Fund (IMF), the World Bank and the International Development Bank (IDB) was the size of the national debt. By 2005 it was at least US$7.5 billion.[3] Beyond that and the extractive industries, the Bolivian economy continued to be divided into a peasant and community-based rural economy and a highly insecure informal economy based in the cities.

The human suffering caused in this period constitutes a salutary tale. Although Bolivia has joined the group of medium human development as defined by the United Nations Development Programme, the country is still ranked 97 out of 165 countries and is below the median level of human development in Latin America.[4] In 2005, when the MAS came to power, 60 per cent of the Bolivian population had been plunged into poverty, while 38 per cent of the population lived on less than US$1 per day and were classed as living in extreme poverty.[5] The levels of inequality in the country were also extreme even by the standards of Latin America, the most unequal of continents, reaching a Gini coefficient of 0.60.[6] Education and health figures were also severely depressed, with an average of only four out every five children completing primary education, and only a third of adults having completed secondary education.[7] Health figures suggested one of the lowest life expectancies in Latin America and highest indices of infant and maternal mortality.[8] The challenge was therefore a big one for the new regime in 2005. How could the MAS create a better economic system that delivered growth together with higher levels of human well-being?

TOWARDS A NEW NATIONAL PRODUCTIVE ECONOMIC MODEL

The economy is a fundamental element of the new Bolivian society, not because the material base is fundamental to determining social relations in Marxist terms but because the penury that the neoliberal economic model caused for the Bolivian population (with both more poverty and more insecurity), and its consequences for the Bolivian economy (poor performance, asset privatisation and flight of profits) were crucial to the discursive strategies employed by the popular uprising to justify the transition to a new era. This was the paradigmatic shift that delivered the government in the December elections of 2005 to a coalition of civil society organisations. The result in discursive terms is that Bolivia is the only country where the adjective 'neoliberal' is used as a term of abuse by the MAS against anyone who dares to question the government's economic programme.

Given that the recent political history of MAS and of Bolivia is the history of the popular struggle against the widespread privatisation of public services – like the water services in Cochabamba – and of natural resources that sparked the Gas War of 2003, it is easy to understand the message of opposition to neoliberalism that characterised the arrival of MAS to power. In effect, the message from MAS and from the president at the beginning of 2006 was that the MAS government would invest its efforts in a repeal of article 55 of decree 21060 and the desire to proceed without delay towards establishing what MAS refers to as 'national sovereignty' over natural resources, especially in the oil and gas sectors. Not surprisingly the MAS reacted quickly and began to put into practice these ideas, some of which have been claimed to have symbolic rather than real importance. So, on May 1, 2006, armed forces 'took over' oil installations around the country in a highly reported and symbolic move that might have shouted 'nationalisation', but fell short of this in reality.

Some of the ideas of the new economic framework are central to the National Development Plan (NDP) 2006–10 in so far as the plan takes a strategic overview of the role of the economy as generator of employment and wealth with which to achieve greater levels of social well-being.[9] But the finalisation of the theoretical framework for the new economic model which the government refers to as the new national productive economic model would have to wait until the writing of the new constitution, which incorporates a number of key strategic points. So what does the new constitution establish for a change of economic path for Bolivia?

In a document that describes the key elements of the constitution discussed in Chapter 3, vice president García Linera argued that the new economic model is built on five interconnected main guiding principles.[10] The first is the preponderant role of the state in the new economy, described as a new plural economy at the head of which the state will take the leading role in investment, job creation and strategic development. The emphasis is on the adjective 'productive' to characterise the new role for the state, something that symbolises the transition from a neoliberal phase in which the state was seen as an obstacle to economic growth and the private sector the only saviour of Bolivia's economy, to a post-neoliberal paradigm that emphasises the positive contribution the state has to make in creating a nurturing environment for delivering a productive economy. The key here is to move the state away from a purely rentier role, based on taxing natural resource exploitation, which had been the pattern in Bolivia throughout much of its history.[11] The neoliberal revolution substantially decreased the participation of the state in the economy, to the point where by 2005, only 11 per cent of the economy could be attributed to the public sector. By 2008 this had gone up to 22 per cent, and the objective is that by 2012 it will be as much as 35 per cent. Thus the state regains an important role in the economy but will not be the only player.

One area in which the state has taken a leading role has been in regaining overall control of natural resources. Under the new national productive economic model, key natural resources are defined as of national strategic importance. Thus the new economic model includes the nationalisation of natural resources as demanded by the Bolivian people in such a way that this cannot be reversed unless the constitution is changed. In this case, natural resources and land are described as of national strategic importance and the preserve of the state. So, for example, article 359 of the new constitution establishes that hydrocarbons are the property of the Bolivian people regardless of the state in which they are to be found. It also establishes that the Bolivian state, as the representative of the Bolivian people, exercises the right to exploit hydrocarbons in the Bolivian territory. This is reinforced in article 124, which establishes that it will be regarded as betrayal of the motherland to, among other things, contribute to the expropriation of natural resources in favour of TNCs, foreign states or people.[12] Only the Bolivian state, in as far as it is the representative of the Bolivian people, has the authority to commercialise these resources.

One of the areas in which the state is expected to play a key role is in the so-called industrialisation of natural resources. This constitutes the second principle of the new national productive economic model.[13] One of the main critiques of the anti-neoliberal resistance developing in Bolivia since the 1990s was that the neoliberal economic model was based on the export of raw natural resources in a way that was highly detrimental to the interests of the Bolivian population. Effectively, the argument goes, during the neoliberal period natural resources were being 'given away' to TNCs, which benefited mostly from their sale and commercialisation. The new national productive economic model establishes that the way to maximise the earning potential of these natural resources is to 'industrialise' them: that is, produce derivatives with added value. This might mean, for example, not just exporting natural gas in its 'raw' form, but processing it to produce liquid fuel and fertilisers. Plans for this type of development were announced by the Bolivian government in 2011.[14] It could equally mean refining oil to produce diesel, something Bolivia currently has to import, or instead of exporting wood, manufacturing and selling wood products like furniture. The idea behind this drive is that the country can derive a twofold benefit from this process: one, creating thousands of new jobs, and two, producing goods with added value. Similarly, this plan means that instead of repeating the historic pattern of exporting natural resources, the country might one day make use of its vast lithium deposits to produce the electric car batteries that the international market requires to make the transition to a post-oil economy.[15]

The third principle of the new national productive economic model is based on the modernisation of small and medium-sized enterprises (SME) in both rural and urban locations. In addition to this, the challenge is to infuse a sector that is crucial to the Bolivian economy because it accounts for the vast majority of jobs in the country, with the credit, business support and technology to become more efficient and increase its overall size in the economy. Thus this principle is based on the acknowledgement that, in addition to a strong state-led economy that delivers direct jobs through its control of natural resources and links with international markets, the Bolivian economy includes a small-scale entrepreneurial sector which consists of artisans and small-scale producers concentrated in the cities, and also an important community-based rural economy. The argument is that the various areas of the economy contain a variety of forms of economic organisation such as statist, private, community based and cooperative. Bolivia's economic system is in other words plural in nature, and articles 311 and 312 of the new constitution guarantee the equality of rights that the various forms of economic organisation now have under the law.[16] This, it is argued, will lead to a very different pattern of state support from the neoliberal period, when big export-led sectors like agro-industry were seen as of prime importance, and almost all state support was focused on them. From now on, the new constitution acknowledges the importance of other sectors and ensures that all will receive support from the state for their development.

The fourth and fifth principles of the new national productive economic model are related to each other because they express a fundamental value of the current government's approach to economic organisation. This is that the main purpose of the economy is to deliver and sustain growing levels of economic well-being and what Bolivians refer to as 'living well'. This is again a principle that Bolivians consider to be paramount, and one that was 'forgotten' during a neoliberal era that delivered enormous economic wealth for a small minority but large levels of social injustice, inequality and poverty for the vast majority. In relation to this fundamental value, the fourth principle of the new national productive economic model is the principle of satisfaction of national needs in the first instance, before exports to international markets can be considered. This principle has strong implications for the production and sale of food and basic necessities, and is linked directly with some of the experiences of the Bolivian population during the neoliberal era and beyond. For example, because of the emphasis put on the production and export of cash crops during the neoliberal era, Bolivia became dependent on the import of some basic foodstuffs such as fresh fruit. Equally important is the experience – which still continues – of shortages of gas for domestic consumption when Bolivia is a country that produces and exports gas in vast quantities. The new economic model is supposed to end this and ensure, following the precepts of economic nationalism, that Bolivia's natural resources and production benefit Bolivians in the first instance.

The final principle of the new national productive economic model is the principle of redistribution. As was explored in Chapter 5, the new government led by MAS has put a strong emphasis on the redistribution of the wealth generated by the exploitation and commercialisation of natural resources. This includes the provision of conditional cash transfers that was outlined earlier, but it is important to appreciate that behind these lies a major change in perception. The MAS belief is that social policies, and by implication the taxation to pay for them, can no longer be conceptualised as a 'burden' on the productive sector, something that can only be afforded in times of surplus. Instead it sees their provision as an intrinsic part of the state's responsibilities towards its citizens and an investment in human capital.[17] Again, in making this emphasis, the new government aims to show a clear break with the neoliberal past, when the government appeared fixated on ensuring macroeconomic growth regardless of the social cost, which included increasing levels of poverty, inequality and a growing urban/rural gap.[18]

In sum, the new national productive economic model aims to expand the role of the state in the economy and its broader social role as well. The state will function as an employer, as the provider of a framework for investment, and by giving strategic leadership. In addition, it gives the state overall control of the country's natural resources and their commercialisation, a principle that is integrated into the new constitutional text. At the same time, the new economic model supports other forms of economic organisation which are dominant in urban and rural areas (such as community and cooperative models as well as SMEs), and is designed with the objective of delivering economic growth but not at the expense of social well-being. It includes a strong emphasis on the satisfaction of basic human needs and the redistribution of wealth, eroding the country's high levels of informality in the labour market, inequality and poverty, which were the social consequences of the recent neoliberal past. What is the assessment that can be made of Bolivia's economy halfway through the second term of MAS government?

A STORY OF SUCCESS?

Let us now examine some of the major decisions (and their results) in Bolivia's economic policy since early 2006. Without doubt, they seem to point towards an unremitting story of success that has gained regional and international praise, even from the country's former critics in the IMF.[19] Results so far are good in many areas, including a healthy economic growth and budget surplus that reflect a series of policies pursued by the Morales government since 2006 in order to redress the enormous influence of the market on Bolivia's economy.

In the case of gas and oil companies, things did not start well when plans for nationalisation were announced in early 2006. At the time, companies like Repsol, Petrobras, British Gas and the French Total announced freezes in their investment programmes in Bolivia until clarity about the meaning of 'nationalisation' had been achieved. Others threatened to leave the country altogether or to take the country to international arbitration in an effort to resist having their exploitation contracts renegotiated.[20] The Bolivian government needed to strike a careful balance, fulfilling the promise of regaining control of natural resources that had been made to the electorate, but setting against this the need to keep both the investment and the technology that comes with TNCs operating in Bolivia. As a result, a 'selective nationalisation' of the hydrocarbons sector has been pursued since 2006. What 'selective nationalisation' means in practice is that, since May 2006, different levels of state involvement have been applied to these industries. So, for example, whereas the transport and production of derivatives from gas and oil (such as the separation of gases and the production of diesel) are concentrated in state hands, the exploration and exploitation of gas and oil fields is conducted in a number of partnerships between the Bolivian state and private companies. This includes associative forms of working, where the Bolivian state keeps a majority stake in a company created for the purpose, or gives a contract to a private sector company to work a gas field.

The underlying idea of all these initiatives is to move from a situation where TNCs effectively own the raw materials below the Bolivian subsoil and have the power to commercialise them, to one where the state sets the rules in such a way that it can maximise and keep the profits generated in the exploitation of Bolivian gas and oil. The arrangement during the neoliberal period effectively meant that oil multinationals operating in Bolivia were able to set extraction quotas, prices, and significantly, the commercialisation policy. Indeed, TNCs effectively had the power to decide how little to pay the exchequer in royalties and taxes, since all they had to do was submit a sworn annual statement of production. No wonder these companies had the lowest costs for production, exploration and taxes in the whole of Latin America.

The policy changes since 2006 have brought the commercialisation of gas under state control. As a result, new, much more favourable prices have been set for the existing export contracts for natural gas that Bolivia has with Argentina, and more importantly Brazil. Second, the Bolivian state declared unconstitutional the 1990s legislation that had allowed the reduction of the state's stake in YPFB, and forced a market buyout of the various companies that were 'capitalised' in the 1990s. In this way it regained control of YPFB and of its transport and storage infrastructure.[21] As a result, YPFB has now extended its gas pipeline to Argentina in an export deal that lasts until 2029. Third, the Bolivian state has imposed a much heavier levy on gas and oil production, with a royalty of 18 per cent on the value of production, in addition to a new 32 per cent direct tax on hydrocarbons (IDH). Taxation has therefore gone from 18 to 50 per cent overall, resulting in a fivefold increase in state income from this source, from Bvs2.2 billion in 2004 to Bvs11 billion (US$1.6 billion) in 2011.[22]

In addition to this much increased stake in the gas and oil sectors, the Bolivian government has pursued a policy of heightened involvement in other strategic areas of the economy. This includes the provision of essential services like water, electricity and telecommunications. Access to these is seen by MAS as a human right which must not be limited by the ability to pay. The state telecommunications company ENTEL, founded in the 1960s, had undergone the same process of capitalisation as other state monopolies, with 50 per cent of its shares being sold off to Telecom Italia in 1995. The new government of Bolivia regained up to 97 per cent of shares in the company in 2008, and is now working to ensure that mobile coverage is available throughout the entire country.[23] The move was not without cost to the Bolivian state, as it had to pay over US$100 million for the buyout in order to avoid the Italian owners of the expropriated company taking a complaint to the international courts.[24]

The Bolivian state has pursued similar policies in the case of electricity companies and the mineral extraction and smelting sector. Following what has now become an annual tradition, May 1, 2010 signalled the takeover of four electricity companies, some of which were subsidiaries of TNCs such as the French GDF-Suez. This regained state control of about 80 per cent of the country's electricity generation and distribution capacity.[25] Mining and smelting was under the control of the formerly state-owned mining company COMIBOL, which had been sold to foreign investors including Glencore International and Pan American Silver Corp. The Morales government managed to recover the Vinto tin smelter from Glencore International in 2007, but has come up against a number of difficulties more recently in trying to extend the renationalisation process. This includes the opposition of workers at the affected mines.[26]

The second area of state-dominated intervention in the Bolivian economy includes the industrialisation of raw materials. The state now mostly has control over the manufacture of gas and oil byproducts. It is committed to the creation of a basic petrochemical industry, based on Bolivian investment, which can produce diesel, jet fuel and key raw materials for the production of plastics and fertilisers.[27] It lacks both the resources and the technology to be able to commercially exploit the lithium reserves in the Uyuni salt flats, and is still looking for 'equal partners' with whom to pursue this. This is a major opportunity for the country, and there is a determination in the government to not repeat the mistakes of the past and fail to realise the potential profits.[28] The major international companies with whom discussions have been held (they include French, Japanese and South Korean companies) now appreciate that the government is looking for a proper return on the exploitation. At the time of writing, no agreement had been reached. Meanwhile, the government has funded a pilot plant to develop knowhow and assess the viability of industrial-scale exploitation of this resource in the future.[29] Similarly, the Bolivian state aims to rebuild the national energy industry – through a programme of investment in new hydroelectric energy capabilities – and has established policies to encourage investment in small-scale food production. A state company, EMAPA, has been set up to provide soft loans to small producers and rural communities that are willing to invest in food production and processing, but are not attractive customers for private banks or investors.

There are a number of reasons for this policy, beyond the obvious economic benefits to be obtained through control of natural resources and the development of the country's industrial base. The new national productive economic model also aims to control the process by which basic services are made universally available, following the chapter on basic rights in the new constitution. This drive stands to benefit at least 100,000 households, especially in rural areas. Food sovereignty is also cited by the national development plan as of key strategic significance. The significant economic resources devoted to food production aim to ensure universal and subsidised access to basic foodstuffs, while aiding the economic development of rural communities. All of these policies, from the nationalisation of natural resources to the increasing levels of state intervention in the economy, are based on the recognition that Bolivia has a plurality of economic systems – small artisan producers, community-based rural producers, and export-led industrial sectors – and that they should all receive the same degree of support.

The macroeconomic results of this strategic economic direction since 2006 have been nothing short of extraordinary for a country that had become used to a perennial fiscal deficit, weak growth, high levels of debt and runaway inflation. In that time, Bolivia's economy has grown on average by 4.8 per cent per year, including a peak performance of over 6 per cent in 2008, and there is a projected growth level of 4.5 per cent for 2011.[30] It is important to note that the country has been able to maintain these high levels of growth in spite of the global financial crisis, which has affected Bolivia severely in two respects. The first is a decrease in demand for some of the country's export commodities, but more important is the effect that growing unemployment in the traditional destinations for Bolivian migrants – the United States, Argentina and Spain – had on their ability to continue to send remittances. In 2006 foreign remittances made up to 10 per cent of Bolivia's GDP, so their falling-off seriously affected internal purchasing power.[31]

Another negative effect was created by the US cancellation in 2008 of preferential trade status under the Andean Trade Promotion and Drug Eradication Act (ATPDEA) arrangements. The new regime also led to a major fall in foreign investment in Bolivia. International assessments of Bolivia's economic performance during this period highlighted this: the IMF considered it might be related to uncertainty over the country's regulatory framework.[32] Even so, GDP doubled between 2006 and 2011 to over US$9 billion, making Bolivia officially no longer a poor but a middle-income country. It is recognised that the strong economic growth experienced by the country would not have been possible without high prices for hydro-carbons, high levels of production, and the leadership role taken by the state in investing in capital and infrastructure projects.[33] As a result of the strong lead by the state in the economy, exports tripled over the period under consideration, to almost US$7 billion by the end of 2010.[34]

Inflation figures have been generally lower than during the neoliberal period, even after the stabilisation in 1986, and fell to 4 per cent in 2009. However, inflation increased to as much as 11 per cent in the spring of 2011 following the so-called *gasolinazo* of December 2010. This was a planned reduction of subsidies to fuel, which could have increased prices by as much as 80 per cent. It was reversed at the last minute, but might have had a residual effect on food prices.[35]

Bolivia has also only recently (in 2011) achieved a fiscal surplus, estimated at 4 per cent of GDP.[36] As a result public expenditure, including the kind of social policy provision discussed in Chapter 5, has increased significantly in the last six years. This, however, continues to be inadequate. Figures for 2009 suggest that social spending represented no more than 2.7 per cent of GDP, a woefully small amount given the structural challenges of extreme inequality and poverty that plague Bolivia.[37] In spite of this, according to the Bolivian Central Bank, international reserves in June 2011 were the highest ever in the history of the country, and stood at US$10.7 billion, an increase from US$1.7 billion in 2005.[38] Finally, the health of the Bolivian economy is reflected in the sharp reduction in international debt experienced by the country in recent years as a result of the heavily indebted poor country (HIPC) and multilateral debt relief (MDRI) initiatives.[39] Estimates vary, but it is argued that Bolivia's debt went from representing 64 per cent of GDP in 2003 to 15 per cent in 2010, leaving a much larger share of the budget for investment in economic growth and human development. However, although the combined IMF/World Bank debt relief might reach US$1.7 billion, Bolivia is still highly indebted. Much of its debt with the IDB has not been reduced, and the country is also increasing its multilateral debt with countries like Venezuela. As a result, servicing this debt puts limits to what the country can invest in essential areas of development of the economy and of human well-being. For example, interest payments on the national debt cost more than the country is able to devote to its education budget.[40]

In sum, the Bolivian official discourse about the rapid economic progress made by the country would emphasise that a new national productive economic model based on the nationalisation of natural resources, coupled with a state-led process of investment in strategic sectors of the economy using the increased resources generated by the process of nationalisation, has delivered economic growth and stability as well as serious advances in public spending and human development. This represents a reversal of a historic economic experience of debt, economic contraction or poor growth, and increasing levels of social suffering.[41] And yet increasingly loud voices in Bolivia and beyond appear to be pointing to the limitations of this picture of economic renaissance.

THE LIMITS OF POST-NEOLIBERAL DEVELOPMENT

There is little point in accusing Bolivia of having implemented an economic policy that is not socialist enough, or that has failed to follow patterns or ideas that are not practical or implementable in the real world. However, increasingly critics have been pointing to limitations in the economic model presented by the Bolivian government. These criticisms can be classified in terms of the extent to which they are made about the government's own claims for the new economy, or more broadly, about the internal contradictions it creates between fundamental guiding principles of the process of change that is to deliver a refounded Bolivia.

It is the government's claim to have nationalised the country's natural resources. This is clearly not the case. Bolivia has not nationalised foreign-owned companies in the same way that Cuba did in the early 1960s, taking over their capital and assets, and creating ripple effects in market and political circles. In fact, as many commentators have pointed out, the so-called nationalisation is in effect a market buyout that has been achieved by paying compensation at market rates and through negotiation with the affected companies. In some cases state companies have been created, but in many other cases, the process of 'nationalisation' has meant that the Bolivian state has reached majority shareholder status in companies that were part of, for example, YPFB and had been privatised in the 1990s. Nor does this process of nationalisation reflect a radically new or revolutionary legislative framework stemming from the new constitution. In fact, many of the buyouts in the gas and oil sectors were conducted with the legislation in existence before the new constitution was approved in January 2009.[42] It is important that, in spite of a number of cases going to international arbitration, virtually no foreign companies have left Bolivia as a result of the government's intervention. So the Bolivian government has increased its share of the profits in the exploitation of gas and oil, but TNCs still have every chance to make profits in Bolivia, and continue to do so, at the government behest.

In fact, the Bolivian government is acutely aware of its dependence on foreign investment and technology to continue to develop the exploitation of natural resources, and must walk the tightrope between a presentation to the electorate that emphasises the use of natural resources for the benefit of the Bolivian population – rather like the 2003 October Agenda demanded – and a series of soothing messages to foreign capital that encourage investment. Sometimes the rhetoric is accompanied by theatrics, as when President Morales sent the military to 'take over' gas installations on May 1, 2006. But the fact of the matter is that this does not add up to renationalisation.

Take for example mining, the industry on which Bolivia's modern economy was founded. Foreign companies such as Sumitomo, Glencore, Coeur D'arlene Mines Corporation, Pan American Silver Corporation and Republic Gold still dominate economic activity and receive most of the profits. The state's involvement in the sector through COMIBOL is still far from what it was between 1952 and 1984.[43] In addition, it appears that the contribution made by these mines to the treasury through taxes and royalties is still low, particularly for a country in which the government claims to be spearheading a socialist transformation of society. It should be taken into account that in 'neoliberal' Chile, transnational mining companies contribute on average 51 per cent of their gross profits in tax.[44]

Nor is the contradiction between what the government says and what it does limited to the place that TNCs currently occupy in the economy. Bolivian official discourse about the need to emphasise the industrialisation of natural resources is based on two convictions. The first is this will permit the export of added-value products that can increase earnings, and the second is that the process of industrialisation can deliver the dream of creating an economy that goes beyond a narrow-based economy of single-product exports. The dream is to encourage instead a broad-based economy that is diversified, includes a manufacturing base, creates the tens of thousands of jobs Bolivia needs, and helps to move the country away from the dangers intrinsic to path-dependent forms of development.[45] However, as Bolivian economist Fernanda Wanderley has argued, the state has continued to show:

> preference for growth based on exploitation of natural resources ... aimed supposedly at strategic sectors, such as hydrocarbons, mining, and electricity. At the same time, a broad swathe of the Bolivian economy has lacked the sort of incentives and conditions that would help it become part of a sustained export-diversification strategy.[46]

So much then for the plural economy emphasised by vice-president Linera, which includes a small-scale artisan productive class and a rural economy. In fairness, the Bolivian government is acutely aware of the dangers and limitations posed by path-dependent development trajectories, but it cannot always change direction quickly. The country's reliance on gas exports is determined not only by the readily available gas deposits, but also by the long-term effects of the economic policy developed during the neoliberal era, which was driven by the dominance of this particular resource.[47] Long-term contracts for the sale of gas to neighbours Brazil and Argentina make it difficult for Bolivia to route the gas to support the country's 'industrialisation' process. In addition, the dominant distribution pattern of income from the IDH to the regions and the municipal level mean that most of the national budget is spent on roads and infrastructure, rather than on human development or the development of other areas of the economy. Furthermore, there is a lack of capacity in YPFB to invest in further exploration and development, a problem that developed during the neoliberal era because of the short-term approach implemented by TNCs to gas extraction.[48]

However, the real problem that an economy dominated by a

single form of natural resource exploitation creates is the rent-seeking approach that develops at all levels of the economy and society, including the regions dependent on their share of IDH, which in turn limits the ongoing development of this sector of industry. Add corruption to the mix, as the Santos Ramirez scandal that shook YPFB in 2009 shows, and Bolivia's economic dependence on gas exports no longer looks so attractive.[49] Furthermore, the curse of natural resources has long been understood to lead to 'Dutch disease' in the form of currency appreciation and damage to a country's chances of developing a manufacturing base, further locking economies into a vicious circle of increasing reliance on natural resource exploitation. Bolivia's economy is no stranger to this problem.[50]

Perhaps the most fundamental contradiction between the new Bolivia's guiding principles and the direction of the economy lies in the country's commitment to the principles of *vivir bien*, and especially respect for *Pachamama*, or Mother Earth. Bolivia is playing an important international role in support of a robust global agreement on climate change. It claims that indigenous knowledge and experience can contribute to a better understanding of nature and the part that humans play in it, and supports an endogenous and indigenous model of community-led development built on food sovereignty and sustainability. This challenges the basic economic precepts of capitalism, a system Morales has continuously critiqued at international fora.[51] Yet the country's main economic model of development is based on the extraction and export of natural resources.

The contradictions between these two models operate at many levels. Not only is the extractivist industry unsustainable in the sense that all economic models based on the extraction of finite resources are unsustainable in the long term by definition, it is unsustainable in ecological terms, contributing to the global rise in carbon emissions and the industries the Bolivian government claims to fight against. The contradiction goes beyond the merely symbolic level. Where the two have come into conflict in Bolivia in recent times, the TNCs and global capital have appeared to be winning, often with the support of the government. This has led to accusations from CONAMAQ that Morales employs an empty rhetoric in respect of the environment.[52] Examples abound, for example, of communities whose access to clean water is compromised by the excessive water usage of mining concessions and by the pollution they generate.[53] The issue is particularly ironic because the United

Nations recently declared water and sanitation to be a basic human right, a resolution spearheaded by Bolivia.[54] Bolivia is proud of the new-found voice and power of indigenous peoples, something that is clear for all to see in the content of the new constitution. Indigenous peoples are also seen as guardians of knowledge and traditions that can protect nature. In 2009, Morales himself handed over the collective land titles for an area of over 1 million hectares of the Isiboro-Sécure National Park and Indigenous Territory (TIPNIS) which is home to over 1,500 families from the indigenous Yuracaré, Chiman and Mojeño nations. Yet the state appears to favour steamrollering through its plans for 'development' against the wishes and traditions of indigenous communities by building a road through the middle of primary rainforest, something that environmentalists claim could facilitate rapid deforestation.[55]

All of this suggests that there is a clear difference between what the Bolivian government claims in terms of the creation of a post-neoliberal economy and the reality. Certainly economic growth in the last six years has been spectacular by all measures, even if Bolivia is here following in the footsteps of more powerful regional economies which are living through a golden age, at the same time as the Eurozone and the United States cannot seem to shake off the global financial crisis. Yet, as a number of commentators have argued, although Bolivia has achieved these levels of economic growth by means of a higher involvement of the state, it has on the whole been following rather mainstream economic tools and thinking. In the case of the limited nationalisation of the hydrocarbons sector, commentators have referred to it with the seemingly contradictory term 'neoliberal nationalisation'.[56] Others have referred to the entire MAS economic programme as a form of reconstituted neoliberalism because of the party's reformist approach and commitment to fiscal austerity and close partnership with TNCs for the development of natural resource exploitation, demonstrating a failure to take the revolutionary steps demanded by the grassroots.[57]

This chapter began asking how the MAS could create a new economic system that delivered growth with higher levels of human well-being. The country has managed to deliver growth but often by compromising many of its own principles in the process, including its commitments to sustainability as part of *vivir bien*. As Chapter 5 argued, another aspect of *vivir bien* is related to the way in which the new Bolivia confronts its deep injustices and social problems. Bolivia has made some strides into this territory but poverty, lack of formal employment and deep socioeconomic inequalities remain the Achilles' heel of the economic policy because of the slow pace of change and, some say, the Bolivian government's commitment to low-cost and 'flexible' labour. It is this part of economic policy that is increasing the sense of frustration in a population that was prepared to unite against the political assault of the right during 2008 and 2009.

Since the electoral victory of December 2009 which delivered MAS its biggest majority yet, the population have been growing restless. From the conflict in Caranavi to the siege of Potosí, to the *gasolinazo* events of December 2010 and indigenous protests in July to October 2011 against a road through TIPNIS, it is clear that social unrest since 2010 has taken place in MAS heartlands, and that it had at its root economic demands. It could be argued that the government must meet these demands during the current legislative session if it does not want to find itself on the wrong side of history.

7 BOLIVIAN–US RELATIONS

Breaking the stranglehold

It was September 11, 2008 and my wife and I were due to travel from the United Kingdom to Bolivia with American Airlines (AA). Except that we couldn't, because, according to the airline there was a civil war in that country and all flights had been suspended. However the reality on the ground was very different from what the airline was claiming. What the airline had reacted to was a spate of organised violence towards the end of August that culminated in the massacre of indigenous people in the town of Porvenir, in the northern region of Pando, by armed officials working for the local prefect. It now seems clear that all these actions were systematically organised as part of a wider strategy to derail the process of political change. The strategy included exaggerating the 'spontaneous' nature of the social unrest – echoed only by the US State Department and AA – which fizzled out almost as soon as the US ambassador in Bolivia, Phillip Goldberg, was expelled from the country, accused by President Morales of conspiring with the opposition to bring about a civil coup against the elected government.[1]

This episode in recent Bolivia–US relations is symptomatic of the way in which very different readings are made of the 'other' by these two countries. For Americans, September 11, 2001 carries a deep meaning as the day when the world changed and a global 'war on terror' began. The war on terror since 2001 has been played out mainly in Iraq and Afghanistan, but it was used by President Bush to tarnish Latin American countries – as when Cuba was included in the axis of evil – and Morales was painted by the Bush administration as an extension of the axis of evil alongside President Chávez of Venezuela.[2] This might explain why, when my wife asked an AA member of staff at Miami airport how long it would be before the airline resumed flights to La Paz, she received the following response: 'As long as that Evo guy is alive, I don't think American Airlines will be flying to Bolivia.'

Readers will be able to draw their own conclusions on that response. What is significant is that an image that portrays certain Latin American leaders as troublemakers or simple obstacles to US interests in the region – as Castro, Chavez and Morales are – gives justification to their removal by foul means if necessary. This justification then becomes part of a widely shared belief system that has no room for dialogue or compromise. As Bush declared after the attack on New York's Twin Towers, in this war 'either you stand with us – or against us'.

For many Latin Americans, September 11, 2008 marked a very different significant event, as it was the 35th anniversary of the US-sponsored coup that overthrew the democratically elected government of Salvador Allende in Chile.[3] Unfortunately for Latin America, that is far from the only episode of US intervention south of its borders. US policy has shown a certain degree of continuity since the end of the cold war, as we explore in this chapter. Latin Americans, and Bolivians in particular, are much more likely to interpret US policy towards their region through the prism of imperialism. Given the widely shared belief that US interests are at odds with Bolivia's best interests, the thrust of the country's policy towards its northern neighbour during Morales' first term has been one of critical engagement, seeking to maximise benefits wherever possible – such as maintaining privileged access to US markets or continuing hitherto unsuccessful efforts to have Sánchez de Lozada extradited for trial – while increasing the volume of anti-US rhetoric in international forums. Here Bolivians blame the United States for what it represents in terms of capitalist development and imperialist domination.

This chapter builds on the context of historical relations of domination that have characterised the role of the United States in Latin America, including political, economic and military aspects. The chapter then explores relations between Bolivia and the United States during the Bush administration, putting an emphasis on the background of the war on drugs that characterised and continues to play an important role in this relationship. Third, the chapter explores the breaks and continuities that can be noticed in the relationship that has developed between these two countries since the election of Barack Obama to the presidency of the United States, an arrival that was heralded as a new beginning in Bolivia but has delivered precious little in terms of tangible changes in relations between the two countries. The final section of this chapter turns to the Bolivian reaction to the United States at the regional level. Here it has joined forces with the rest of Latin America in what is a much more assertive regional policy towards the United States through organisations like the Unión de Naciones del Sur (UNASUR), and the creation of new institutional mechanisms such as the Alternativa Bolivariana para las Américas (ALBA) with key allies like Venezuela and Cuba. These are redefining regional politics and the relationship between Bolivia and the United States. This section sets the scene for the next chapter.

A HISTORY OF IMPERIALIST RELATIONS

When US secretary of state John Quincy Adams penned the Monroe Doctrine in 1823 he would have been unable to foresee the extent to which his work would become central to defining US foreign policy towards Latin America for almost two centuries.[4] The document stated a claim on the part of the United States to defend the independence of states in the Americas from European interference, but in essence it was part of a global carve-up of territories and areas of influence that separated European powers like Spain and the Holy Alliance of Russia and Austria from the Americas. The declaration was supported in practice by a British crown keen to develop privileged economic relations with the Southern Cone at the expense of Spain, and enforced by the British navy at a time when the United States had no means to do so. This military support was in effect crucial for the independence of Latin American countries in the first quarter of the nineteenth century.

The doctrine, written in language that declared brotherhood between the people of the Americas who shared in the freedom from monarchic and colonial rule, was in fact invoked early on to feed the expansionist ambitions of the United States, demonstrating its belief in the competing ideologies of anti-colonialism and imperialism.[5] It is often associated with a belief in manifest destiny: that is, that there is a self-evident and inexorable process of expansion towards the west. It was in this spirit that the United States annexed Hawaii in the 1840s and even tried to bring Cuba into the fold a decade later.

The United States intervened militarily against Spain to 'preserve the freedom' of its Cuban 'brothers' during the 1898 Cuban war of independence. Upon victory however, the United States promptly invaded the island and claimed Puerto Rico, while wresting control of the Philippines from Spain. US forces stayed in Cuba until 1902.

In the meantime, the United States secured Guantanamo Bay and set the legal framework for the unrestrained domination of US capital in Cuba's economy, something that would stay in place until the revolution of 1959.

The limited independence associated with the birth of the Cuban state and the North American annexationist tendencies had been accurately predicted by José Martí before his death in 1895.[6] These tendencies were also discussed by Lenin, who observed in the role of the United States in Cuba the birth of a new imperial power.[7] His theory of imperialism essentially posited it as necessary for the very survival of capitalism, and as forming a special stage in its development. No longer was imperial power necessarily brought about by means of direct political control over colonial lands. Instead, economic relations of domination between more developed and less developed countries created a new phase of global capitalist exploitation.

The Leninist theory of imperialism became very influential in Latin American academic circles and in Marxist reinterpretations of imperialism, which in the 1960s took the form of dependency theory and world systems theory. These schools of thought shared a vision of the world capitalist system as biased in favour of the core capitalist countries, so that it created a one-way flow of capital from the periphery to the developed countries.[8] These theories went beyond the purely economic argument discussed in Chapter 1, as they included an understanding that the exploitation of poor, dependent countries was backed by a strong military power. This in turn justified its existence by the need to police the world and bring into line any attempt by dependent countries to opt out of this hegemonic system. The Latin American left has explained US–Latin American relations in these terms, and continues to do so when it refers to US imperialism, presenting the major source of conflict in society not in traditional Marxist terms but as one between an imperialist Global North represented by the United States and an exploited Global South represented by Latin America. This basic contention continues to be explored, currently in the guise of critical globalisation theory.[9]

The Monroe Doctrine and the logic of the cold war came together for a large part of the twentieth century. Both were invoked by successive presidents to justify US intervention, covertly or not, and to maintain US interests – that is, the interests of US capital in the region – often at the expense of democracy and human rights.[10] The list of US-inspired interventions is extensive. It includes secretary of state John Foster Dulles invoking Monroe to justify the 1954 overthrow of President Arbenz in Guatemala, and Kennedy's interventions in 1960s Cuba. Henry Kissinger, secretary of state in the Nixon administration, demonstrated the measure of his administration's disregard for democracy when, referring to Chile's soon to be democratically elected president Salvador Allende, he was quoted in the *New York Times* as saying 'I don't see why we need to stand by and watch a country go communist due to the irresponsibility of its own people.'[11] US meddling in Latin America continued during the Reagan presidency, which intervened in Central America's 1980s conflicts. The involvement also included invasions of the Caribbean island of Grenada in 1983 and of Panama in 1989. Not surprisingly, critics of US foreign policy such as Noam Chomsky have argued that in practice, the Monroe Doctrine has been invoked to justify unilateral intervention in countries unwilling to subject themselves to the hegemonic control of the United States.[12]

The context of US–Latin American relations that frames this argument is one in which, from the early part of the nineteenth century, the United States developed the policy and ideological instruments to exercise hegemonic control over the region.[13] The dominance of these relations has been exercised militarily on multiple occasions, either by invoking the Monroe Doctrine, or during the cold war, by claiming to prevent the growth and influence of communism in the region.[14] The main purpose of these interventions, however, went beyond the mere demonstration of power, as they served to make the region safe for US capital and to enmesh exploitative relations of production which were beneficial to the United States, something that has been denounced by critical Latin American voices recently in relation to recently failed US–sponsored neoliberal integration agendas. US imperialist domination in Latin America during much of the twentieth century also developed at the cultural level, becoming unconscious and permeating everyday language and creating taken-for-granted values in societies and governments alike.[15]

Bolivian–US relations during the second half of the twentieth century fit into this global and regional context. Indeed, Chapter 1 outlined Bolivia's economic development in the context of dependency and insertion into the global economy, including the role played by international financial institutions (IFIs) such as the International Monetary Fund (IMF) in the prescription of economic policies[16] that have ultimately failed to deliver social well-being.[17] Chapter 2 explored some of the political consequences of this dependency in terms of the poor quality of the democracies achieved in the region following a successful transition from military rule.[18] These were the consequences of US–Bolivian relations during this period as they were mediated by a strong US policy objective of preventing the spread of communism throughout the region. In order to achieve this policy objective following the 1952 revolution in Bolivia, the United States selectively used direct diplomacy, as well as financial and military aid, with successive Bolivian governments.

Through its embassy in La Paz, the State Department initially backed the Movimiento Nacional Revolucionario (MNR) as the most effective brake on the potential spread of communism in Bolivia. It made particular efforts to support the centrist tendency in the party, ensuring that the country remained open to foreign investment and its mineral wealth accessible to the United States, while preventing the deepening of revolutionary change. This essentially constituted a continuation of long-standing policies that had ensured the steady supply of Bolivian tin to the United States during the (Second World) war effort, and set the basis for a dependent economic relationship that failed to diversify the economy. This happened in spite of the fact that Bolivia was one of the countries that fell within Kennedy's 1961 Alliance for Progress, a ten-year policy of US economic aid designed to foster economic development in Latin America.[19] The Alliance for Progress was in effect the policy instrument that was supposed to make a reality of the 1960 modernisation theory of Walt Rostow, academic and advisor on national security to Presidents Kennedy and Johnson.[20] During this time relations were close between these two countries, and Bolivia was publicly heralded as the good US pupil in Latin America for overtly supporting this policy, as would be the case in the 1980s with structural adjustment. The good relationship was extended to the personal level, with President Paz Estenssoro visiting Kennedy in 1963.

The United States changed tack soon after the death of Kennedy that same year. Officially the Alliance for Progress continued until it was seen to have failed in the early 1970s.[21] The reality however is that the United States began to take a more active interest in the Latin American military as the better safeguard against communism, and actively supported the Brazilian coup of 1964. In the case of Bolivia, some authors have viewed the coup led by General Barrientos that same year as an accident that took place as a result of a split in the MNR.[22] Others however have argued that the United States actively supported this takeover through the CIA.[23] It was the beginning of a long period of US support for Latin American juntas throughout the continent, support that was facilitated by increased levels of military aid and the wide availability of military training for officers in the United States.

The School of the Americas (SOA) is a US military training facility in Fort Benning created in 1946. Over the decades, it played a key role in training military officers from most Latin American countries, including a large number of would-be dictators and torturers. Documents released by the Pentagon in the 1990s appear to confirm that training in counterinsurgency included the use of torture and executions. The list of Bolivian officers trained at the SOA and accused over the years of drug trafficking, armed insurrection and torture is long. It includes Hugo Banzer and two generals accused of responsibility for the deaths of protesters in El Alto in 2003.[24] During 2008, Morales announced that Bolivia would not be sending any more officers to the SOA.

US support for military rule in the region was motivated by a 'revolutionary offensive' launched from Cuba in the second half of the 1960s. Following the foco theory proposed by French intellectual Régis Debray, Cubans basically aimed to reproduce their own revolutionary transition to socialism in other Latin American countries such as Bolivia, and in 1967 they began a guerrilla campaign led by Ernesto 'Che' Guevara that included Bolivian and Cuban fighters.[25] As in other countries where the Cuban example had inspired guerrilla tactics, the United States quickly stepped into action. In addition to putting Bolivian interior minister Antonio Arguedas on the CIA payroll, the United States sent a group of Green Berets to train a special counterinsurgency battalion, and had a number of CIA agents operating in the hunt for Guevara.[26] However, not all the military governments that ruled Bolivia between 1964 and 1982 were docile to US demands. Following a nationalist current in Peru's military leadership, Bolivian General Ovando and his successor General Torres nationalised Gulf Oil in 1969, expelled the Peace Corps in 1971, and allowed the Central Obrera Boliviana (COB) and the miners' trade union (FSTMB) to take virtual control of Congress. These actions displeased the United States, and led to their support for other military leaders more pliable to their interests, such as Hugo Banzer.[27] At this time, a new policy priority was added to the war against communism, which would come to redefine US relations with Bolivia.

THE TRANSITION TO DEMOCRACY AND THE WAR ON DRUGS

Since he had been trained in the SOA, Banzer's ideological allegiances and anti-communism were not in question. They were instrumental in maintaining a US foreign policy driven by cold war and anti-communist concerns. Globally, the 1970s was defined by the cold war, the Vietnam conflict and détente with the Soviet Union and with China. In the Latin American region, cold war policy making translated into interventions in Chile and, during the Reagan administration, in Central America. This however did not detract from a new policy line driven by an anti-drugs agenda, which the United States has expanded mainly in the Andean region.[28] It was during Banzer's leadership that the United States initiated its anti-narcotics and coca eradication policy in Bolivia, which Banzer was instrumental in supporting. However, open conflict between support for anti-communist military rule (however violent and illegitimate) and the need for allies in the war on drugs did not emerge until the leadership of García Meza (1980–81). His was the most brutal and violent of Bolivian dictatorships. What finally convinced the United States of the need to rescind its support for Meza's regime was not the illegitimacy or brutality of his rule, though, but overwhelming evidence of his direct involvement in the drugs trade.[29]

In fact, Meza's regime epitomised the ideological link that has existed historically in Bolivia between the narcotics mafia and the military. This was evidenced by the misuse of state loans by military governments during the 1970s, intended to develop the cotton industry in Santa Cruz, but which ended up financing cocaine production. In return, the cocaine mafia supported financially the coup led by Meza in 1980. According to some authors, 'there was a virtual symbiosis between drug trafficking and the state under Garcia Meza's regime ... an ideological affinity between the mafia and the military ... and a common fear that democracy would undermine these values'.[30] These were the days of cocaine producers like Roberto Suárez, who became a folk hero in Bolivia's popular imagination because, unlike most political villains who used their power to make fortunes from the state's resources, his wealth came from taking advantage of what Bolivians consider is the depravity of cocaine consumption in the United States.[31]

No one was in doubt of the pernicious effect drug trafficking had on Bolivian politics. Governments from 1982 onwards felt threatened by the combined power of the military and the drug-trafficking fraternity, and turned to supporting the expansion of US anti-drugs efforts in the country. Through successive US presidents, coca eradication policies provided continuity and defined relations between these two countries during the 1980s and 1990s, with US aid increasingly tied to milestones in the war against drugs. Thus from 1986 onwards, the US Congress gave itself the right to 'certify' the degree of cooperation that Andean countries were providing in the war against drugs, with aid and the support of the United States for multilateral loans from organisations like the IMF being dependent on the perceived progress being made.[32] The biggest and most sustained policy in the war against drugs was the coca leaf eradication programme called *plan dignidad* (dignity plan). Unfortunately for the United States, it would also sow the seeds of the rebellion against US hegemonic domination in the region.

The coca leaf has been grown in the Andes for millennia, and plays a very important practical and symbolic role, as it is consumed directly (chewed), in tea, and used in all manner of ceremonies and social rituals. Thus, miners for example will chew the leaf to combat exhaustion and hunger, and use the leaf to make offerings to *el tio*. During meetings, a bag of coca leaves will be passed around the table for all to consume.[33]

The *plan dignidad* policy was introduced in 1997 by Banzer, the military dictator (1971–78) who became elected president of Bolivia for Acción Democrática Nacionalista (ADN) in 1997. In effect, the policy constituted a continuation of coca eradication programmes created and imposed by the United States and implemented for decades in Latin America, notably in the Andean region. In Bolivia, the criminalisation of coca production took place at the height of the neoliberal economic revolution in the late 1980s, and became official government policy, although with limited results, during the Paz Zamora (1989–93) and Sánchez de Lozada (1993–97) administrations.[34] The timing of this criminalisation is interesting because, as we saw in Chapter 1, it took place just as tens of thousands of Bolivians were losing their jobs as a result of the economic policies dictated by the IMF. When the Chapare region started to increase the production of coca, many relocated ex-miners were in effect entering the only form of economic activity that could help them survive. In fact, it is estimated that in the 1980s the value of illegal exports of cocaine paste was close to that of all Bolivian legal exports.[35]

Of course all attempts to eradicate coca production were met by increasing resistance from the strengthening coca growers' movement, where one Evo Morales rose through the trade union ranks to become the leader of all six federations of coca growers.

However, in 1997 Banzer's *plan dignidad*, directed by the US Drug Enforcement Administration (DEA), intensified the militarisation of this area of Bolivia, persecuting poor coca farmers – as opposed to targeting the large narco-trafficking rings – and sowing the seeds of the national rebellion that would take the country into uncharted territory of social and political change.

It is noteworthy that the indictment from some academics, but also from the social movements that rose against the *plan dignidad*, was that, along with similar US-sponsored coca eradication plans elsewhere in Latin America, such as plan Colombia and plan Puebla Panamá, *plan dignidad* was part of a neoimperial strategy that had little to do with the eradication of coca production and everything to do with making Latin American natural resources 'safe' for US business and markets as part of the wider strategy of imposing a neoliberal framework in Latin America through the Free Trade Area for the Americas (FTAA, or ALCA in the Spanish acronym).[36] According to this view, *plan dignidad* ensured the smooth export of Bolivian gas through the Chilean ports of Arica and Iquique.[37] It is also noteworthy that a US State Department press release from 2000 in support of *plan dignidad* makes the connection between the implementation of the plan and the economic benefits that were likely to follow for the country as a result, in the form of direct foreign investment and debt cancellation from the United States.[38]

Chapter 2 discussed how the rebellion against US hegemonic domination in Bolivia was led by the coca growers through their trade unions. Given that US and the coca growers' interests were diametrically opposed, the US response to this affront to its chief policy in the region was not surprisingly to intervene actively in the internal political processes of Bolivia, giving support to every effort to act against Evo Morales. Enter a period of US intervention against the process of change.

FIGHTING THE PROCESS OF CHANGE

Officially, the war on drugs never changed as a driver of US foreign policy in Bolivia. However, from the moment the Movimiento al Socialismo (MAS) began to play a formal political role and to challenge the status quo, US policy in the country switched to preventing its rise by means of active support for alternative candidates and deliberate attempts to discredit the MAS leader. This level of intervention in Bolivia's politics coincided with the presidency of

George W. Bush. For example, actively promoting a portrayal of Evo Morales as a drug baron, US ambassador Manuel Rocha publicly warned the Bolivian population during the 2002 election that their support for Morales would damage relations with the United States. This threat had the opposite effect in a Bolivian population that was growing increasingly anti-imperialist in its reading of the political reality of the country, and in that presidential election Morales came second, less than two percentage points behind the US favourite candidate, Sánchez de Lozada. After the election, Morales publicly thanked the US president for his ferocious attacks on him and his character because of the way in which they translated into renewed support from the electorate. The direct intervention in the internal politics of Bolivia to prevent the rise of Morales during the Bush presidency shows that the United States has not understood the strength of anti-imperialist feeling in Bolivia that feeds the process of change.[39] The more they tried to get rid of Morales, the greater his appeal for the wider Bolivian population. As a result Morales has made anti-imperialism the discursive trademark of his leadership challenge and rise to the top of Bolivian politics.

Relations between these two countries have changed significantly since 2006. Morales' ascendance to the presidency of Bolivia did much to confound the United States. In spite of, or perhaps because of, the best efforts of the United States and its interference in the presidential campaign in 2002, the Bolivian population turned out en masse to support MAS in the 2005 election, delivering a clear vote for a president in the first round for the first time since Bolivia's return to democracy in 1982. In spite of previous US attempts to characterise Morales as a dangerous individual, both presidents initiated their relations amicably enough. Indeed, the United States took a view of 'wait and see' that included a congratulatory personal phone call by Bush to his Bolivian counterpart. And in spite of MAS claiming to represent a revolutionary process of change – the first since MNR in 1952 – US policy towards Bolivia represented an attempt to move away from the failed cold war framework of meddling in the internal affairs of other countries. A study by the US Council for Foreign Relations supported the development of working relations with both the government and the opposition in Bolivia, arguing that closing down trade, military and diplomatic relations would only bring the country close to Cuba and Venezuela, feeding the anti-US sentiment in the region.[40]

Unfortunately the recent history of US–Bolivian relations has failed to live up to expectations in the early days of the current process of change. The United States has become increasingly restless at the Bolivian unwillingness to show pliancy in Morales' use of anti-imperialist rhetoric, Bolivia's refusal to support US plans for Latin American economic integration, and its independence of thought regarding the coca eradication policy. Thus the United States increasingly used its leverage in the country – that is, military and development 'aid' as well as trade policy – to intervene in support of the Bolivian opposition and try to bring about political change.

The critical period in the collapse of relations between both countries came in the autumn of 2008. This showed that, with Bush at the helm, little had changed in the US attitude to critical Latin American voices. The *golpe cívico prefectural* is the term used by MAS to describe an attempted coup in which the main leaders were the prefects of the 'half moon' opposition. Following the historic victory of the president in a recall referendum in August with more than 67 per cent of the vote, coordinated riots expressing opposition to his regime took place in the dissident regions, and state institutions were sacked. The civil unrest peaked on September 11, in Pando, when a paramilitary group of officials from the prefecture massacred a number of indigenous people.[41]

Because of the suspected involvement of US ambassador Goldberg in fomenting this unrest, he was expelled from the country. Relations between Bolivia and the United States deteriorated from that moment onwards. Later that month at the United Nations, President Morales publicly accused Goldberg of being a co-conspirator in the attempted coup, claiming he had supported the opposition leaders and had tried to use Peace Corps volunteers and a Fulbright scholar as spies in Bolivia.[42]

Relations between both countries deteriorated further when the United States reciprocated the expulsion of Goldberg with the expulsion of Gustavo Guzmán, the Bolivian ambassador to the United States. In addition, the State Department 'decertified' Bolivia's anti-narcotics policy, branding the country 'uncooperative' in the war against drugs, a judgement that carried serious penalties like the withdrawal of aid and lack of US support when applying for loans from international lending institutions. Further, decertification effectively led to an automatic suspension of Bolivia from the Andean Trade Promotion and Drug Eradication Act (ATPDEA), a favourable trade agreement with the United States that supported thousands of jobs in Bolivia. The decision hurt Bolivia economically, and there were attempts for a while to negotiate with the United States in an effort to reinstate the trade arrangements. However, a year later the Bolivian government announced that it would no longer be seeking to reverse the situation with the United States, as it had found alternative markets for the country's textile products in Venezuela.

The suspension of Bolivia from ATPDEA only reinforced critics' accusations that the US war against drugs in Latin America is in effect part of a broader policy to control the region's markets and natural resources through a process of militarisation. Given that Colombia, the largest exporter of cocaine in the world, maintains its preferential trade status with the United States, the argument can be made that decertification was in effect a political decision taken in Washington to punish Bolivia for the audacity of expelling its ambassador. Unfortunately, the sorry saga of retaliation continued with the expulsion from Bolivia of the Drug Enforcement Agency (DEA) in November 2008 after the agency was accused of supporting the near-coup that took place two months previously. Thus a policy that started with a 'wait and see' approach from the United States deteriorated further than at any time in the history of relations between both countries. There was a new low in US–Bolivian relations. Towards the end of 2008, in the *palacio quemado* there was a feeling that no progress could be made in trying to repair relations with a US president who was on his way out. With US presidential elections barely weeks away, Bolivia would have to wait for the results before resuming a concerted strategy of trying to develop a collaboration with the United States that was in both national interests.

UNCHANGING RELATIONS AND FRUSTRATED EXPECTATIONS

Obama's victory was generally received with enthusiasm in Latin America. It could not be otherwise, for in his two terms at the helm Bush Jr. had managed to acquire a reputation as the worst president in the history of the United States. He left the White House with the lowest approval ratings recorded for any US president, after eight years that would be remembered for a policy on terror that delivered two wars in distant places, the application of illegal inter-rogation techniques in illegal detention camps like Guantanamo, and the biggest economic crisis in 70 years. Even in Bolivia, Morales spoke about changing times when a black president could be elected in the United States, and renewed his commitment to improving relations between the two countries.[43]

Almost inevitably in situations when high hopes dominate, the reality ends up disappointing. So far, Obama's administration has failed to improve relations with Bolivia, and risks marginalising its position with much of a Latin American continent that is moving on, confident in the future and with a number of shared values that make the US positions on drugs, coca leaf, democracy and trade seem out of touch. Part of the problem might be the unwarranted desire for presidents and analysts alike to believe that a single individual can stamp his authority and bring about a dramatic change in the hegemonic power structures that drive US foreign policy. No matter how capable, willing or ideologically predisposed they are to do so, it is perhaps impossible.

During the first chance that Latin American presidents, including Morales, had to meet Obama, at the fifth Summit of the Americas in April 2009, the US president delivered a convincing performance, distancing himself from the policies of the previous administration and stating his desire for good relations with the region.[44] However, a number of incidents since 2009 have ensured that US–Bolivia relations remain firmly chilled. Obama was sworn in barely a week before Bolivia confirmed by referendum a new constitution which crystallised the enormous ideological gap between the two countries. So, for example, instead of extolling the virtues of individual freedom, the Bolivian constitution refers to the state's responsibilities towards the well-being of its population; instead of private property and capitalist development, the new constitution echoes a national desire to regain sovereignty in the management of the country's natural resources. In addition, the new Bolivian constitution refers to principles of solidarity in its relations with other countries and to the pacifist aims of its military, ruling out any foreign intervention and, in article 10.3 forbidding foreign military (read US) bases on its soil.[45] Most importantly, article 384 of the constitution refers to the coca leaf as part of the cultural heritage of the Bolivian people and not a narcotic in its natural state.[46] These are fundamentally different positions that could not but spell trouble for the future of US–Bolivian relations.

In February 2009, barely three weeks after Obama took office, his secretary of state Hillary Clinton unveiled a policy of 'direct diplomacy' to the Senate Committee on Foreign Relations. The driving principles behind the new US foreign policy in Latin America included the use of language such as 'Venezuela and Bolivia pursue policies which do not serve the interests of their people or the region'.[47] This tone was confirmed by a later report to Congress on Latin American human rights, which singled out Venezuela and Bolivia and reprimanded them for human rights abuses, whereas countries such as Colombia and Peru received a 'pass' grade in these areas in the eyes of the United States.[48] Further, the statement seemed to be unaware of the depth of legitimacy enjoyed by the Bolivian and Venezuelan governments in the region. It served to create a cleavage between Latin American countries and the Obama administration very early on. Ignoring the democratic mandate of the governments in question and lecturing them on human rights while Guantanamo is still open was rightly seen as an insult, reminding them of the ever-dominant 'carrot and stick' approach used by the United States to further its interests in the region. This view was reinforced June 2009 when there was a coup in Honduras which ousted President Zelaya. Bolivia accused the US government of supporting or at least tolerating it.

The interventionist nature of Obama's presidency was further demonstrated when the administration maintained Bolivia's decertification in September 2009, 12 months after Bush had imposed it as retribution for expelling Goldberg. The move prompted the Washington Office on Latin America (WOLA) to view this decision as a continuation of the political use of the decertification process, and to point out that this had important foreign relations implications. It argued that 'Bolivia's decertification indicates that the Obama administration is out of step with developments in the region, and missing opportunities for more constructive relations.'[49] This is not the only recent accusation of interventionist foreign policy. In the case of USAID, commentators decry its lack of transparency and argue that the United States has spent millions of dollars in Bolivia on 'democracy promotion', which is a codeword for supporting US interests in the country by bolstering opposition parties. In addition, the 2010 appointment of Mark Feierstein as the USAID administrator for Latin America was controversial in Bolivia because of his links to former Bolivian President Lozada, whom the US government refuses to extradite to Bolivia to face charges for his role in the Gas War massacre of 2003. Both issues have put further obstacles in the path of re-establishing cordial relations between both countries.[50]

Another issue that has soured relations between Bolivia and the Obama administration is the ideological battle surrounding the war on drugs, and more specifically the role played by the coca leaf. The 1961 Single Convention on Narcotic Drugs mistakenly classifies the coca leaf as a narcotic. Bolivia has done much to challenge this, citing the scientific evidence that shows the coca leaf poses no danger to health, as well the various UN conventions that protect the right of indigenous peoples to express their cultural heritage and traditions. Ironically, the United States is a recent signatory of the UN Declaration on the Rights of Indigenous Peoples, but it led a minority objection to Bolivian attempts to correct the 1961 Single Convention and reclassify the coca leaf in January 2011.[51] As a result, Bolivia proceeded to withdraw from the convention. This is problematic for relations between Bolivia and the United States and will also damage US relations with the rest of Latin America, given that UNASUR supported Bolivia's amendment.[52]

In sum, Obama's administration has so far proved incapable of repairing the damage caused by Bush. This does not mean that the United States and Bolivia are not interested in resuming diplomatic relations. Bolivian foreign minister David Choquehuanca has been working to restore them as part of a broad frame of understanding and respect between these two countries that is expected to be signed in the near future.[53] And yet it seems that during the period since the collapse of relations between the two countries, an accelerated process of decline has taken place that challenges the undisputed leadership position the United States has enjoyed in the region since 1898. The twenty-first century clearly signals the decline of US might and a shift in the global axis of power towards the east.

The period of US economic crisis since 2008 has been characterised by the opposite situation in the Latin American region, where developments speak of growth, confidence and a new-found voice in the international arena. Not surprisingly, some have spoken about a 'Bolivianisation' of relations between the two countries, whereby US foreign policy towards Bolivia is defined as an extension of Bolivia's regional politics.[54] Bolivia's foreign policy priorities are now driven by a new-found confidence in the world and a closer alliance with like-minded nations in South America. So whereas Obama seems to be finding it difficult to steer the United States away from a classic imperialist foreign policy, Latin American countries, including Bolivia, are starting to see increasing relevance in developing new relations with emergent powerful global players, and are no longer afraid of the United States.

THE END OF THE MONROE DOCTRINE?

The backdrop to the new low in US–Bolivian relations that developed in the autumn of 2008 was provided by a global crisis that affected the United States in a number of ways. First, as Bush's term in office came to an end, there was the inescapable realisation that his presidency would be forever associated with the war on terror initiated after the September 11, 2001 attacks on New York. This is highly ironic given that during the 2000 presidential campaign Bush was seen to represent an inward-looking candidate, uncomfortable with foreign policy and lacking in experience. When he gained the disputed nomination, it seemed that his presidency would be focused almost entirely on domestic policy. Yet the legacy of his eight years in power would be two long and expensive wars, fought thousands of miles away from US shores, and defining not only the Bush presidency but US foreign policy in the early part of the twenty-first century.

Attempts have been made to link the so-called 'war on terror' to Bolivia and other Latin American countries, apparently with the aim of providing a coherent narrative of the role of the United States in the world. But the inescapable conclusion from Bush's time in office is that the United States took its eye off the ball in its Latin American backyard. It failed to engage with the region in new and meaningful ways beyond the war on drugs and attempts at further economic integration.

True to a reputation for pragmatism, Obama soon announced a reduction of troops in Iraq accompanied by a temporary surge of troops in Afghanistan, aimed at a producing a withdrawal timetable that would put to an end the military quagmire in which the United States found itself. Part of the reason for aiming to end US involvement in these long wars was their political and economic cost. The political cost of the war in Iraq – which many people worldwide saw as illegal – has waned since 2003. The economic cost of these wars continues to grow, however, at a time when the United States has narrowly escaped defaulting on its sovereign debt. This provides a link to the second element of the backdrop to Obama's presidency. Obama arrived at the White House as the initial stages in the biggest global financial crisis since the 1929 Wall Street crash were being played out. If the war on terror was Bush's legacy, the global financial crisis will define Obama's first term.

The financial crisis that began with the banking sector extended into the wider economy, taking the country into recession and eventual (weak) recovery, increasing unemployment, and most significantly, resulting in record levels of public debt. The resulting national economic problem is the most serious the United States has had to face since the 1930s, and has forced the Obama administration to concentrate on national policy. An agreement was reached with Congress on August 2, 2011 which was based almost entirely on cutting expenditure on health services to the poorest sectors of society, while taxes continue to be at their lowest for 35 years and military spending remains untouched. Many feel that this offers an inadequate solution to the country's debt crisis. It is a bad remedy not only for the majority of the US population, but for Obama's chances of re-election – his popularity at home is waning as a result of the continuing economic problems – and for the standing of the United States in the world. When the country's economic viability is called into question it cannot unquestioningly dominate the international stage.

The global financial crisis provides a critically important context to the international role of the United States and to its foreign policy in Latin America. Just as North Americans have been getting used to lowered expectations in their living standards, the White House is having to come to terms with an economic vulnerability that translates into a real loss of influence at the international level. This loss of influence is magnified by the rapid economic progress in much of the Latin American region in parallel with the recession the Global North. While the Eurozone and the United States struggle, countries like Bolivia, Argentina and crucially Brazil have been able to weather the storm and grow strongly. The startling contrast in experiences serves to further vindicate the critical stance that much of Latin America has taken towards the US-inspired economic integration agenda and the 'Washington Consensus'. Instead, the region has seen a broad political turn to the left, which has been accompanied by nationalist and anti-imperialist discourses, together with attempts to create its own forms and institutions of integration that exclude the United States. At the same time, Latin America has seen one of its own, Brazil, join the elite club of key global economic powers, along with Russia, India, China and recently South Africa (collectively the BRICS). This group of countries is now playing an increasingly important political role at the global level. Bolivia is riding partly on the back of the new global leadership position achieved by Brazil during Lula's presidency, which looks likely to continue under Dilma Rousseff, and its new alliances with countries like Venezuela, Ecuador and Cuba.

The summit of Latin American presidents in the Brazilian city of Bahia in December 2008 was symptomatic of the new-found confidence of Latin American countries. As President Correa from Ecuador argued, the gathering was symbolically important as it was the first time in history that leaders of all Latin American countries had met without the United States. Key resolutions at this gathering challenged US power in the region. The first was the decision to accept Cuba as member of the Rio Group. This came on the eve of the fiftieth anniversary of the Cuban revolution, and after Cuba had spent 46 years as a political pariah in the continent from when following US demands, it was expelled from the OAS in 1962. Now the tide is finally turning, beginning the political rehabilitation of the country at the Latin-American level.

Second, the meeting in Bahia created a Latin American Security Council (LASC) and common defence programme. This marked the last rites for the US Monroe Doctrine. Since 1823, the United States had claimed the right to intervene in Latin America both directly and indirectly, supporting those administrations and factions (including dictatorships) that it felt best served US interests.[55] The move could be explained as a Latin American riposte to the re-establishment in 2008 of the US Fourth Fleet, with a brief to patrol Caribbean and Latin American waters, as well as to the militarisation that has followed the war on drugs policy. Latin American countries are starting to question every bastion of US power, including its self-appointed role as the world's policeman, challenging the hegemonic power it has exercised since the end of the nineteenth century.[56] The next chapter turns to Bolivia's place in this changing Latin America.

8 BOLIVIA'S PLACE IN LATIN AMERICA

This chapter explores Bolivia's place in the world and the inter-national dimensions of the country's process of change, in a way that aims to make the most of the key elements that explain the loss of influence the United States has suffered in Bolivia since the ascendance of Evo Morales to the presidency. It does this by adding the regional political context to the new set of international power relations operating in Latin America, and by looking beyond the traditional mechanisms and logics of power in operation between states at the international level, putting emphasis on Bolivia's new-found interconnection and exchanges with like-minded governments in the region and with global civil society networks.

The first part of this analysis includes an exploration of present and past attempts to bring about a degree of integration, economic or otherwise, in Latin America. The chapter examines the two most recent significant regional integration attempts that concern Bolivia, in the form of the Comunidad Andina de Naciones (CAN) and the Mercado del Sur (Mercosur). The chapter presents them as inte-gration attempts that have seen their potential largely unfulfilled, and asks to what extent they are related to North-American-driven exercises in neoliberal forms of economic expansion that can be observed in initiatives such as the North American Free Trade Agreement (NAFTA).

A second element to this analysis concerns the extent to which the ideological principles that steer the process of change in Bolivia are in tune with the Unión de Naciones del Sur (UNASUR) and the Alternativa Bolivariana para las Américas (ALBA). Bolivia's participation in UNASUR is explored in terms of the direct benefits it brings to the poorest country in South America in the context of a new-found Latin American confidence on the international stage that reinforces the geopolitical aspirations of the region and challenges international interference in countries hitherto too small to counteract economic, political and military meddling from the Global North.

Bolivia's place in the world is also explored in terms of the political, ideological and social benefits its participation in ALBA brings to the country. This includes the international political support Bolivia receives, the symbolic possibilities of self-presentation as a leading progressive anti-capitalist state, and the very real support Bolivia has received from ALBA in terms of funding and expertise to carry out a universally celebrated literacy campaign and bring Cuban-sponsored health care provision to the poorest and most isolated areas of the country. ALBA is thus presented as a hybrid type of associational arrangement that brings together like-minded governments, but has also been able to develop intricate links with civil society both at home and abroad.

The third strand in this chapter consists of an exploration of Bolivia's links with global civil society networks, presenting a case study that examines both achievements and limitations.

A LATIN AMERICAN BLOC?

Mercosur and CAN have for a long time been the dominant institutional instruments for Latin American integration (or at least, represent the processes of South American integration). However, both are failing and have stalled for a while, representing an image of the past, not the future of Latin America's geopolitical birth into the world.

CAN is problematic because it brings together countries with polarised ideological positions. Bolivia and Ecuador stand at one extreme of the ideological spectrum whereas Colombia stands at the other. For example, Colombia was the only Latin American country that expressed formal support for the coup that ousted president-elect Manuel Zelaya of Honduras in June 2009, while Uribe's right-wing presidency was mired in civil and human rights violations at the side of paramilitaries. Peru stood in a similar position, as former president Alan García ditched the left-wing populism that had characterised his leadership first time round between 1985 and 1990, to have serious and recurrent disagreements with Morales between 2006 and 2011. These divisions were based on ideological differences, and became most salient from 2008 onwards, with Garcia accusing his Andean neighbour of trying to support an indigenous uprising in Peru, after serious clashes between indigenous groups and the police took place in the jungles of northern Peru as the people tried to defend their lands from oil and mining exploitation.[1] Peru is rapidly privatising assets, opening the country to foreign investment, and opening its jungles to mineral and oil prospectors. Whereas it is not entirely clear what direction successor Ollanta Humala's economic policy might take, it might still differ greatly from Bolivia's state-controlled (if not nationalised) and managed process of exploitation of natural resources. In addition to this, two of the original members of CAN are no longer part of the group. Chile left during the Pinochet years, but Venezuela's departure in 2006 (it joined Mercosur shortly afterwards) delivered a much greater blow to the long-term aspirations of this regional integration initiative.

CAN suffered its worst period in 2009 because of internal disagreements about the process and nature of its relations with the European Union. Although comprehensive bloc negotiations that include political and economic aspects are meant to be the *raison d'être* of both CAN and the European Union, the process of association between these two blocs which began in 2007 broke down two years later because of internal divisions – exacerbated by EU meddling – that resulted in Colombia and Peru going solo and looking for bilateral free trade accords with Europe, something entirely rejected by Bolivia. (Peru and Colombia had also sought bilateral free trade agreements with the United States a few years earlier.[2]) Bolivia rejects free trade agreements generally and the prospect of a free trade agreement with the European Union in particular because, the argument goes, the European Union demands the inclusion of patent rights and the deregulation – meaning privatisation – of utilities as part of the deal. For Bolivia, a country in which the privatisation of water in Cochabamba led to a popular uprising in 2000 and where the new constitution explicitly forbids the privatisation of basic services such as water and electricity, these demands are unacceptable. In addition, Bolivia's new constitution explicitly states that the country's natural resources are for the benefit of the people, not multinational corporations.[3] At the height of this crisis, Bolivia directly accused the European Union of trying to undermine the integrity of CAN by opening bilateral trade negotiations with Colombia and Peru at the end of 2008. Although renewed attempts to quick-start bloc negotiations took place in 2010, little progress has been made, and in the last few years the relevance of CAN has been called into question.

Mercosur, including Brazil, Argentina, Uruguay, Paraguay and more recently Venezuela, is the best known of the Latin American integration attempts. Mercosur follows in the steps of a long and unsuccessful history of Latin American economic integration initiatives that began as early as 1960 with the Latin American Free Trade Association. However, the project of integration that Mercosur represents has also recently run into the sand to some extent, because of an endless set of political disputes between Argentina and Uruguay over the pollution effects of a paper factory on their common border river, disputes between Brazil and Paraguay over their shared hydroelectric dam, and the collapse of the Argentine economy back in 2001. Some of these disputes are having to be resolved by means of international mediation, a sign of weakness for any process of integration. Other difficulties are that the potential global role of a regional trade and economic institution is limited as long as the World Trade Organization (WTO) trade talks which began in Doha in 2001 continue to be paralysed,[4] and that, as some studies have pointed out, Mercosur member states have always prioritised domestic policy considerations – retaining a large degree of national sovereignty – over those of regional integration.[5] Thus, as a number of commentators argue, it is unlikely that Mercosur will deliver on its initial promise.

Amid these slow attempts at what constitutes a mainly economic form of integration – but with political aspirations, as was demonstrated by CAN's declared intention to create an Andean parliament – UNASUR has become the latest institutional mechanism to bring about the reality of integration for the countries of South America.

THE EMERGENCE OF UNASUR

Whereas previous integration attempts have floundered, arguably at core because of their distinct lack of founding principles and a sense of direction, UNASUR has both these assets. It represents Latin America's coming of age, gives the strongest hint yet of its desire to play a strong geopolitical role. Led by Brazil, a country that under Lula's presidency has claimed centre-stage in the international arena through its leading role in the G20 and the Brazil, Russia, India, China and South Africa (BRICS) group, UNASUR represents Latin America's desire to play a role in the new multipolar politics and diplomacy of the twenty-first century. UNASUR's founding principles and sense of direction are clearly delineated by the presidential summits and declarations in 2004, 2005 and 2006 in Cuzco, Brasilia and Cochabamba respectively. They state the desire to move further than the purely economic dimension – which limited NAFTA and the previous Latin American processes of integration – in order to create an integrated regional space that converges at the political, social, economic, cultural and environmental levels, emphasising the existence of a shared collective identity and citizenship.[6]

UNASUR brings together the existing regional subgroups that have limited chances of succeeding individually in their projects of integration. With around 400 million inhabitants, this project has taken the lead from the European Union, and is exploring methods of deepening the democratic accountability of the integration process by creating a new UNASUR parliament in Cochabamba, Bolivia. This was announced at the same time as the resolution that officially created UNASUR itself in 2008 in Brasilia.[7] However, as the difficulties to achieve the ratification of the European constitution by its citizens show, it is hard to make people fall in love with the idea of political integration. In Europe, the financial rescue packages for Greece and for the euro that were agreed in the spring of 2010 demonstrated the emergence of a two-speed bloc, with northern countries led by France and Germany speeding towards economic recovery and a southern Mediterranean fringe, the PIIGS (Portugal, Ireland, Italy, Greece and Spain) holding the eurozone back. The result is increasing division and resentment from Europe's affluent northern citizens towards their poorer counterparts, as they feel forced to shore up other people's economic mismanagement and corruption. This has led to division and a loss of legitimacy at the heart of the European project.

In a radical departure from the EU model of integration, UNASUR is trying to increase the legitimacy of its integration proposals. Thus a key aspect of the new South American parliament is, in principle, the full participation of civil society in the process of integration, an element emphasised by left-leaning governments of the region like those of Ecuador and Bolivia. One aspect of this is the acceptance of a vision for UNASUR inspired by the coming together of social and indigenous movements around the continent, a vision that demands social justice in the form of the recognition and implementation of indigenous rights. The proposed vision is free from neoliberalism, is deeply participatory, and is sustainable in the spirit of *suma qamaña* introduced in Chapter 5.[8] Whether it succeeds in these aspirations to deepen the quality of democratic practice in the process of Latin American integration is something that only time will tell. Meanwhile, UNASUR had more than its fair share of crises early on in its life, and these have tested the institution's strength and sense of purpose.

UNASUR's first serious political tests took place in 2008, its first year of existence. The first and most serious test involved Bolivia, when the country's political turbulent atmosphere degenerated into all-out violence in the lowlands (see page 71).[9] At that point UNASUR called an emergency meeting, which was hosted by then Chilean president Michelle Bachelet, to express its full support for the democratic process of change in Bolivia. In addition, a UNASUR-led high-level human rights commission was sent to the country to investigate the massacre in Porvenir. This timely intervention and the leadership shown by UNASUR might well have taken some of the oxygen from the oligarchy-funded and US-supported armed insurrection, what MAS has referred to as a coup attempt that stemmed from the opposition prefects. The move allowed the police to arrest the chief suspect in the masterminding of the massacre – former prefect of Pando Leopoldo Fernández – who at the time of writing was in prison awaiting trial.

That UNASUR was able to come together with a single voice over the Pando massacre – and so help to prevent a worsening internal political situation in Bolivia – speaks volumes for this institution's ability to steer a way out of crises, further increasing the region's desire to construct and uphold a democratic future. Unfortunately, this positive early record was besmirched when, in spite of every effort to speak with one voice in support of Zelaya at the time of the June 2009 coup, UNASUR was unable to force a reinstatement or to prevent a presidential election later that year in Honduras that did not meet minimum democratic standards.[10]

In spite of this mixed record, UNASUR represents a real leap forward in the process of Latin American integration, and a major advance on the previous attempts. This is because, during 2009, UNASUR leaders managed to bring Latin America together and to speak with one voice in a way that has no precedent in the modern history of the region. Some of UNASUR's achievements during 2009 might indeed be seen in the future as Latin America's contribution to a global realignment of power that the United States is unable to stop or control. This global realignment certainly looks very different from the triumphalism that followed the end of the cold war and the vision of a US-led post-communist unipolar world in the 'end of history' thesis popularised by Francis Fukuyama.[11]

The United States is still by far the most powerful military force in the world. However, the geopolitics of capital point in the direction of China, the new creditor of the United States, which currently holds the biggest reserves of US dollars in the world, and to other emerging nations such as Brazil, India and Russia.

In the rapid transfer of power to the east and to the global south, Latin America appears to have found a new assertiveness and unity of voice in a process led by UNASUR. During the spring of 2009 a mega summit brought together the meetings of the two major organisations of Latin American and Caribbean countries, Mercosur and UNASUR, led by President Lula of Brazil, now seen as a world statesman. Its achievements are outlined on pages 156–7. Bolivia suggested that it go even further, and demand that the United States either accepts Cuba back as a member of the Organization of American States (OAS) or leaves the organisation. Lula disassociated himself from that position, arguing that as a new incumbent, Obama should be given time to outline his policies towards Latin America. He did, however, condemn the US embargo on Cuba and joined a chorus of support for the island, voicing the expectation that the new US administration would review the failed policy of isolation.

Second, during the 2009 Bahia summit, UNASUR presidents formally received the report by the investigative commission they had set up in September 2008 to explore the recent events in Pando. They unanimously confirmed that what took place was a massacre and a serious breach of human rights, and were united in supporting the democratic process of change in Bolivia. The declaration was a clear rebuke to extreme right-wing groups in Bolivia and their supporters in the United States. The United States was conspicuously silent about these events.

Third, the meeting in Bahia created a Latin American Security Council and marked the start of a common defence programme. This is of enormous importance for Latin America for the reasons outlined on page 157. These, and Ecuador's refusal to renew the three-decade-old lease to the United States of its military base in the coastal city of Manta, might be the clearest signs yet of the United States' loss of clout the region.[12]

Clearly then, the creation of UNASUR marks a new departure for a region that seems to be finally proceeding towards accelerated political, economic and military integration. In the process, Latin America also aims to be more independent from the United States. Similar trends lie behind the proposals to create a single

Latin American currency, first discussed in the spring of 2009 at the ALBA meeting in Caracas. These were reinforced by the creation of a development bank, the Banco del Sur, that replaces the dependency of countries in the region on Bretton Woods institutions such as the World Bank and the International Monetary Fund (IMF). Since the 1980s debt crises, these institutions had been viewed with suspicion by Latin American governments. They were perceived as the financial arm of an international system of domination that according to Correa had inflicted on Latin America illegitimate, immoral and illegal debts. Their supplanting signals the emergence of a more assertive and self-assured – even openly hostile and rancorous – Latin America, that seems poised to follow her own path.

And yet the process of integration being led by UNASUR might be less radical than it seems at first sight. It is true that it goes further than previous integration attempts. It signals a new Latin American confidence to play a role in global politics that is independent of the US position. And there might indeed be space for new economic exchanges that blunt the worst of the rapacious neoliberal economic relations, based on supposedly free market economics, but which have rarely seemed free to the countries of Latin America. As Fernando Solanas's 2004 documentary film *Memoria del saqueo* (Social genocide) portrayed, this economic model has been responsible for the worst excesses of plunder of Argentina's natural resources and national assets by an unholy alliance between a corrupt local political class – with the help of multinationals – and international financial institutions. Argentina's experience chimes with that of other Latin American countries including Bolivia.[13]

In spite of these positive aspects, some commentators argue that UNASUR does not represent a model of integration that is truly radical or new. This is because, for all its potential as a source of political independence for Latin America, its internal relations are dominated by a traditional model of exchanges between nation states, what has been referred to as the 'club model' of international relations.[14] Another hybrid process of collaboration taking place in Latin America resembles much more the sort of political changes that characterise Bolivia, and represents an expression of those changes at the international level because it brings together a plurality of like-minded actors that include governments but also, crucially, international non-governmental organisations (INGOs) and social movements, in what could be referred as a network of solidarity.[15]

A POST-NEOLIBERAL PARADIGM

If the story of Bolivia, as retold in this book, is one of resistance to the neoliberal order that was imposed on the country in the 1980s, the same pressures can be said to have affected the region in general. It was after all the human consequences of these neoliberal economic policies that led to strong rejection of them by the electorates in a number of countries. The 'pink tide', as it is often called, represents a number of national-popular governments with a message of social protection and job creation based on the nationalisation of their vast natural resources. However, it is now clear that even when anti-neoliberal groups achieve power at the national level, it does not necessarily deter the forces of global neoliberalism.

Since the 1990s the United States and global financial institutions have been supporting proposals for regional integration that are more or less overtly based on neoliberal economic principles. The most significant of these is NAFTA, an agreement between Canada, the United States and Mexico, which the United States has attempted to expand into the Free Trade Area for the Americas (FTAA), encompassing other Latin American countries. The government of Venezuela has been the most vociferous in the region in arguing that NAFTA represents a new market mechanism, the purpose of which is to maintain exploitative North–South relations.[16] As a result, the pink tide and other countries in the region have so far resisted these attempts. Negotiations collapsed at a meeting in Argentina in 2005, and have been stalled ever since. From this perspective, it could be argued that the call made by the Zapatista uprising (which began on January 1, 1994) against Mexico's entry into NAFTA has been heeded by other Latin American countries.[17]

Just as the political turn to the left in Bolivia was inspired by civil society, now the Latin American direction of socioeconomic policy is being articulated through an alliance of actors under the banner of the hemispheric social alliance. This is a transnational coalition of actors such as indigenous social movements and trade unions. Operating from within civil society, this alliance opposes the FTAA and the principles that govern it, and is instead working to develop a democratic and sustainable alternative.[18] At the same time, regional relations are now being redesigned through the example provided by ALBA.[19] Originally proposed by Venezuela and Cuba, ALBA now includes eight member states (Venezuela, Cuba, Bolivia, Nicaragua, Dominica, Ecuador, St Vincent and the Grenadines, and Antigua and Barbuda), with Paraguay as observer. The organisation is working to develop a series of key policy instruments, such as a regional energy infrastructure, a development bank of the south, a digital television news network, TELESUR, and even plans for the creation of a single currency.[20] Bolivia's contribution to ALBA to date has been to propose the creation of a 'trade treaty of the peoples' (TCP in Spanish). Thus these countries have been able to portray ALBA-TCP as the result of a popular rejection of the neoliberal policies of unfettered free-market capitalism and privatisation. Instead, they argue, ALBA-TCP provides an alternative based on a model of development that demonstrates concern for humans and their well-being in the context of participative forms of democracy and environmental sustainability.[21]

There are a number of reasons why ALBA is an important institutional mechanism. First, it represents a form of integration between countries in the Latin American region that is based on different values from the neoliberal, market-driven forms of integration adopted by NAFTA and FTAA. Rather than the market-driven exchanges on the basis of comparative advantage which are dominant in mainstream economics, ALBA represents a 'trade plus solidarity' form of integration that is built on the basis of 'collaborative advantage'.[22] Collaborative advantage is an important principle in this case because it puts the emphasis on values of solidarity and common benefit over and above those of profit maximisation. ALBA appeals to the principles of social justice, well-being and human development, as well as solidarity between the poorest peoples of the Americas. It is this value-driven ideological base and the emphasis on collaboration, solidarity and human development that characterise what have been described as networks of solidarity.[23] It has been argued the distinctive values that dominate ALBA have emerged from the popular revolutionary processes that have recently delivered new paradigms of social development in Venezuela and Bolivia. They are based on a critique of northern-sponsored frameworks for economic integration as new forms of US domination in the hemisphere. Indeed, as the next section shows, solidarity exchanges between the peoples of two or more countries simply take to the state level the principle of reciprocity that is said to characterise community-level exchanges and human relations, in the idealised vision of the *ayllu* that the Bolivian government uses as an example in order to promote decolonisation and a return to supposedly Andean values.

Second, in addition to the characteristic of exchange and collaborative arrangements driven by common values, ALBA represents a new institutional framework because of the important role that, at least nominally, civil society has when operating as part of ALBA. The term 'network of solidarity' has been used to refer to political actors that operate from within civil society, and constitute a counter-hegemonic bloc with a potential for taming neoliberal forms of economic globalisation.[24] ALBA is, in this sense, an attempt to forge links with global civil society as 'a complex social and spatial terrain' in which various types of globalisation projects are being struggled over.[25] New actors are thus the hallmark of an institutional arrangement that allows for bottom-up participation. Formal summits of the umbrella collaborative arrangement that is ALBA operate at state level through their presidents. However, they tend to be accompanied by parallel gatherings of transnational networks of civil society operating at the continental level. For instance, the 2009 ALBA summit in Cochabamba included these parallel gatherings. These were topped by a public ritual at the end of the summit in which representatives of the indigenous social movements handed over to President Morales a document containing the resolutions taken in their summit.

Cynics might see this as a purely representational exercise that masks the lack of real social movement power in ALBA. However, it is a symbolically powerful illustration of the often quoted line that Morales exercises his power by obeying the people. Certainly in Bolivia, and to a lesser extent in Venezuela, there is a close relationship between civil society and the current governments, suggesting that ALBA goes much further than a simple set of state-level relations, and includes instead a network of civil society agents closely linked to the state.[26]

Finally, ALBA constitutes a new institutional framework in that it brings together countries in the global south through exchanges of solidarity. Policy transfer and aid are common features of a globalised world in which policy making and delivery take place. These processes are often explored in relation to transfers of policy ideas and resources between the North and the Global South. ALBA represents an example of South–South policy transfer that illustrates the principle of solidarity and non-market-driven policy delivery.

Besides establishing the economic basis for an alternative to neoliberal forms of economic integration, ALBA's primary areas of social policy activity lie in education and health. An example is the health and education support that, in the context of ALBA, Cuban solidarity-driven aid to Bolivia is contributing to the delivery of the country's National Development Plan.[27] Bolivia has been a net recipient of ALBA's social policy 'aid' since 2006, and it has contributed directly to the MAS government's aspirations of making a reality the principle of living well by eradicating illiteracy and achieving universal and free health care provision.[28]

ALBA AND BOLIVIA'S SOCIAL POLICY[29]

Following the principle of solidarity-based aid, ALBA's contribution to social policy measures in other Latin American countries, particularly in health and in education, is being carried out mostly by Cuba. This follows a fundamental principle of Cuba's revolutionary ideals, establishing contacts with other countries in order to export the ideals of the Cuban revolution. When exporting the method of revolutionary transition to new societies failed after the death of Guevara in the Bolivian jungle in 1967, the establishment of networks of solidarity with the poor peoples of the world took hold. This practice has been dismissed as propaganda.[30] However, Cuba has engaged in solidarity exchanges in the health and medical fields with other countries since the beginning of the revolution, responding to emergencies and natural disasters such as hurricane Mitch in the 1990s in Central America. Cuba has tens of thousands of medical personnel in more than 70 countries around the world, and receives thousands of medical students from many of those same countries to train as doctors.[31] Suggestions about the motivation for these solidarity-driven forms of international aid have therefore ranged from benefits in 'symbolic capital'[32] to the opportunity they afford the island to exercise 'soft power' – that is, to gain influence in countries that receive Cuba's help, even when international aid is delivered without strings attached.[33]

In Bolivia, what could be termed ALBA's post-neoliberal social policy aid has taken place mainly in the fields of health and education. The relationship between these two countries in the public health area began in 1987, and was based on academic exchanges between the Higher Education Institute of Medical Science in Havana and the University of La Paz.[34] This piecemeal arrangement was extended in 2005, and included the Cuban health ministry and the municipal government of La Paz, establishing the first Cuban ophthalmological teams in the country. This project would eventually grow to deliver Operación Milagro, a humanitarian ophthalmological programme delivered by Cuban doctors around the world, which aims to reduce preventable blindness.

In Bolivia, Operación Milagro has conducted more than 200,000 cataract operations, including tens of thousands on people from border areas in neighbouring countries, who have also been able to take advantage of the Cuban health care provision.[35]

The formal Cuban contribution to Bolivia's system of health care provision that emerged as a result of negotiation with ALBA in the context of shared values and ideological principles which began in 2006, at the same time as the first MAS administration. The Cuban contingent of health professionals in Bolivia is currently around 2,000 strong, including 1,300 doctors.[36] In addition, Bolivian students have privileged access to free medical training opportunities in Cuba at the Latin American Medical School (ELAM) that was created in the wake of hurricane Mitch to train Latin American doctors who were prepared to return to their areas of origin to practise.[37] In addition, by June 2009, the ALBA-sponsored Cuban medical presence in Bolivia included equipment for 40 hospitals, 30 of which were established in rural areas on the basis of need. It also included mobile health teams that can reach every corner of the country. As a result of these efforts more than 3 million consultations were provided in the first three years of the programme.

The principle of resource allocation according to need goes against the logic of insurance-based systems that tend to provide health care to those in formal employment. These individuals constitute a minority in a country like Bolivia, and are almost exclusively based in cities.[38] As a result, rural areas have suffered a chronic lack of health care facilities. The patchy health care provision still fails to reach at least 25 per cent of the Bolivian population.[39] Current explanations for this continuing failure include the degree of fidelity with which Bolivia followed World Bank recommendations between 1986 and 2006. These included the restriction of access to anything more than a basic care package for those unable to pay, coupled with high levels of decentralisation in the administration of the health system. It has been argued that as a result of these reforms, segmentation of the health system increased significantly while accessibility to care and its quality decreased in equal measure.[40] This is a factor that the current health system does not seem to have tackled, in spite of the increase in free provision linked to the Cuban presence in the country and of a number of cash benefits such as the Bono Juana Azurduy (discussed in Chapter 5) which is conditional on new mothers and their babies accessing health care.

ALBA's contribution to education policy in Bolivia is almost exclusively linked to the literacy campaign headed by around 200

Cuban and Venezuelan advisors. This began in 2006 and officially ended in December 2008, after UNESCO had declared the country free of illiteracy.[41] Given the way in which the MAS project of national rebirth is constructed as part of a democratic and cultural revolution, it is easy to understand the priority that was assigned to the literacy campaign as early as 2005 during the presidential electoral campaign.[42] The illiteracy rate at the time according to the 2001 census was 13.3 per cent. The state of the Bolivian educational system was such that up to a quarter of children were in effect unable to attend secondary school because of the lack of facilities. Many did not complete primary school because they were forced to work and contribute to the family income from an early age, an issue that remains a problem today. Following his historic victory in December 2005, President Morales signed an agreement with Cuba to implement what would be the biggest literacy campaign in the continent since the Cuban literacy experiment back in the 1960s.

The literacy programme was based on a Cuban teaching method that had been made relevant in content to a Bolivian audience. Named *Yo si puedo* (Yes, I can), this programme was based on 65 hours of face-to-face teaching in small groups. It was designed to be satisfactorily completed by illiterate adults in the space of three months, at a rate of five to six hours of group work per week.[43] The programme incorporated lessons learned during Cuba's celebrated literacy campaign of 1961.[44] However it took advantage of the technological advances since that time, so the Bolivian version was audiovisual, with a set of videotaped lessons accompanied by a reading book for each participant. This made the programme very easy to deliver by Bolivian teachers and trainees. In addition to a small number of advisers, the Cuban contribution to the programme included a large number of television sets, recorded videos, teaching materials (including books and manuals for teaching staff), and solar panels for use in rural areas without electricity. Eyesight tests showed that reading glasses were also needed for over 50,000 adults before they were able to join the course.

The results of the literacy campaign are many and diverse. First, as many as 820,000 Bolivian adults – 70 per cent of them women – achieved the basic objectives of the programme, and learned to read and write. Most opted to learn in Spanish, but 14,000 and 25,000 people respectively chose to study in Quechua or Aymara – the two most widely spoken indigenous languages, in which the literacy programme was made available.[45] It could be argued that there is an inherent contradiction when in a country in the midst of a process of decolonisation, the majority of adult learners chose to learn to read and write in a language other than their mother tongue. Even so, the results constitute an important achievement towards the Millennium Development Goals, and mean that less than 4 per cent of the Bolivian population can now be considered illiterate. However, the biggest gains in this campaign were probably social and political.

The literacy campaign increased national cohesion in a country riddled by divisions. It also served to deliver basic messages of citizenship, spreading some of the fundamental values that are part of Bolivia's national rebirth, with messages such as 'Education is a human right', 'All Bolivian cultures are equal in value' and 'Bolivian women have a right to a life without fear of violence'.[46] These are key values of the process of change, and the Cuban-inspired literacy campaign supported their diffusion among the poor masses of the country. In more narrowly defined political terms, the government gained renewed support from the poor because this popular campaign was squarely identified with the MAS.

Many factors were responsible for the trumpeted success of Bolivia's literacy campaign. It is clear that the political will of MAS was crucial to the success of the campaign, but it would not have been possible without Cuban expertise and Venezuelan financial backing. Ultimately however, the success of the literacy campaign is testament to the degree of grassroots organisation and desire in the population to undertake this personal challenge. In particular, social movements crucial to the Bolivian social and political organisational fabric that took MAS to power, have now become part of local educational authorities (Servicios Departamental de Educación, SEDUCAs) and closely monitored progress in the implementation of the campaign on a monthly basis, providing social control of the campaign and popular ownership. This is in spite of the fact that a number of commentators have taken a critical view of the real possibilities for social control that the social movements are afforded, and view them instead as part of a mechanism in the chain of top-down command.[47]

Indeed, the argument from government sources is that the social movements constitute the inspiration and driving force behind new educational developments that aim to go beyond the original literacy campaign. A post-literacy campaign called *Yo sí puedo seguir* (Yes, I can continue) began in March 2009, aiming to reach much greater numbers than the original campaign (with up to 1 million people taking part), including all adults who had not finished primary school. The plan is to introduce four curriculum subjects – geography, history, maths and natural science – and to develop them until students reach the educational level of a typical eleven-year-old. The post-literacy campaign is being followed by a third educational phase, which includes the introduction of an accelerated secondary education curriculum and system for working adults.[48]

ALBA: THE FUTURE OF SOUTH–SOUTH COLLABORATION?

At a time when neoliberal models of development are criticised for their deleterious human consequences in many parts of the Global South, alternative ideological frameworks and forms of practice are starting to emerge. This tendency appears to be strongest in Latin America, the stage of some of the earliest and most dramatic attempts to export the neoliberal experiment around the world. The significance of the post-neoliberal developmental paradigm and its evolution in Latin America can be explored through the example represented by ALBA as an alternative to the neoliberal attempt of economic integration represented by FTAA. There is an emphasis on ALBA-sponsored key strategies for bringing about human development and provisions such as health care and education.[49] Some authors have argued that ALBA represents a network-type relationship that brings together a mix of third world nationalism and ideological perspectives from global civil society in the aim to develop a post-Washington consensus.[50]

ALBA can be understood as an example of a network of like-minded countries based on common ideological values of solidarity as well as on cooperation and collaboration. As such, it is argued that ALBA represents a practical as well as an ideological alternative to neoliberal models of development. For delivery of health care and education, these have traditionally advocated a retrenchment of the state, resorting to the market principles of privatisation of services and competition between providers.[51] ALBA is different as it proposes the principle of 'collaborative advantage' in its practice instead. This echoes the values of reciprocity and *suma qamaña* that are said to dominate life in an idealised version of the Bolivian *ayllu*. The result is that ALBA can be seen to represent a new paradigm that permits the creation of a counterhegemonic network-like set of relations dominated by values of fairness, social justice and solidarity.[52] Add to this the increasing evidence of the key role played by civil society – particularly in the form of social movements – and ALBA can be seen to represent a solidarity network characterised by South–South cooperation and trust-based forms of development that espouse the values of cooperation and solidarity, mutuality and respect, and an ethic of care and social responsibility.[53]

One of the early key aspects of ALBA's collaboration has been to contribute to making a reality the health and educational objectives in Bolivia's National Development Plan. Bolivia's high-profile literacy campaign and the new health system in the process of construction have depended on Cuban expertise and resources. Cuban professionals have fulfilled very different roles however, limiting themselves to the provision of advice in the case of the literacy campaign, but constituting the main workforce in the delivery of health care, especially in rural areas. In both cases however, ALBA's contribution has exceeded expectations. In the case of health care, limited but freely available care is now a reality in the most isolated rural areas of Bolivia. In addition, the Bolivian Ministry of Health is creating a new medical speciality in family and community intercultural medicine that, following a social model of health, sees the logic of medical intervention in preventive terms and in the well-being of families and communities, instead of in the mere absence of disease at the level of the individual. It is expected that the new Bolivian family doctors will adopt traditional forms of health knowledge in daily practice, and that this new figure will come to replace the Cuban presence in the rural areas of the country, becoming the backbone of a new universal form of health provision.

In the case of the education, whereas the original plan was a one-off campaign to end illiteracy, policy aims are much broader and ambitious now. These include extending the literacy campaign to a new post-literacy phase that links in with a universal secondary education system for adults. This degree of ambition is linked to the political realisation that, in order to deal with illiteracy and prevent its resurgence in the near future (as happened in Nicaragua at the end of the 1980s war), the country's structural conditions of inequality need to be tackled. One element of this challenge includes creating the infrastructure to ensure that secondary educational facilities reach 100 per cent of the population and that entire rural communities are not left behind, as is currently the case. The second, more difficult challenge is to ensure that students do not feel forced to abandon their education in order to find work to survive. Until the challenges posed by the pervasive structural inequalities in

Bolivia are met, functional illiteracy and poor levels of health and well-being will continue to be found in the country.[54]

Can ALBA's contribution to Bolivia's national development plan constitute a successful example of South–South forms of solidarity-based collaboration? Although results for these two programmes appear to have been positive, they point the need to address the serious structural inequalities that characterise Bolivia. This challenge can only be tackled by the country at the national level, and international networks like ALBA are unlikely to be of much help in that endeavour. However, there is a realisation that there is much more at stake than the success of Bolivia's health and education programmes. The point of ALBA's contribution to Bolivia is to show the world a working alternative to social development that succeeds where other models have failed. In this sense, according to the Cuban director of the literacy campaign in Bolivia, the point of ALBA's contribution in the country is to successfully put into action a new set of ideological values that permit the principle of collaboration to snowball throughout the Global South. So if Cubans and Venezuelans have provided advice to the Bolivian literacy campaign, the expectation is that Bolivian advisers will now be able to put into practice some of their learning by providing expertise in the forthcoming literacy campaign in Paraguay, converting South–South collaborative efforts into a self-sustaining reality through networks of solidarity. This is the principle of reciprocity at work in the international arena.

A key characteristic of ALBA's workings is the way in which it appeals to social movements to lead the demands for a new 'people's internationale' that bypasses national boundaries. ALBA works with the emerging global networks of civil society to develop a strong third power that can take on the current dominant forces: markets and capital on the one hand, and states – the dominant political and administrative unit of the current international architecture of power – on the other. Bolivia is a key player in the development of this alternative third force that aims to redraw the balance of power in international governance, because it makes claims to having a government of the social movements.

After the debacle of the Copenhagen Climate Change summit of December 2009, Bolivia made a call to the 'peoples of the world' to gather in Cochabamba in April 2010, before the follow-up international summit took place in Mexico later on that year. Bolivia's call for the celebration of the World People's Conference on Climate Change and the Rights of Mother Earth was a major coup in positioning the country as the defender of the values and aspirations of progressive forces from civil society throughout the world.[55] As with major national and regional political events, the gathering ran parallel timetables that saw governments and social movements work side by side.[56] The meeting also included a public event in which the president accepted the 'policy' drawn up by social movements and gave some credence to the often repeated principle that this is a government that leads the country by obeying its people. However, this celebration was tarnished by government officials' refusal to include a discussion panel on the climate change challenges faced by Bolivia. The unofficial 'panel 18' went ahead on the fringes of the official gathering, putting the spotlight on the government's double discourse on the environment and climate change. In spite of this, commentators have defended the democratic credentials of the World People's Conference on Climate Change and the Rights of Mother Earth.[57]

In spite of this, it has to be accepted that the very audacity intrinsic in the idea of holding a global gathering such as the People's Conference on Climate Change is precisely what international commentators are heralding as the key to saving the international institutional structures for decision making, like the UN Framework Convention on Climate Change (UNFCCC). This is especially true after the US chief climate change envoy, Jonathan Pershing, made comments that seemed to suggest that in future these global negotiations should include only those countries that 'matter'.[58] It is difficult to foresee the results of the international negotiations, but it seems clear that they will strongly depend on the type of decision-making instruments that are deployed. In this sense, any instrument that increases civil society participation, however limited, must constitute a step in the right direction.

9 THE PROMISE AND THE LIMITS OF A REVOLUTION IN DEMOCRACY

As I write these lines, predictions are intensifying of a second global financial meltdown sparked by a likely default by Greece on its sovereign debt, which might drag down with it Italy and Spain, creating havoc for all the economies of the Eurozone. The current global financial crisis effectively began with the collapse of the Lehman Brothers investment bank in September 2008, and continues unabated years later. Except, that is, that in a perfect example of a nationalisation of private investors' debt, what began as a financial crisis sparked by unrestrained greed and no small amount of fraudulent practices in a weakly regulated banking sector has now been transferred to the balance sheets of sovereign states. In addition to being in dire economic straits, peripheral European countries like Portugal, Ireland and Greece are having to contend with the humiliation of being dependent on International Monetary Fund (IMF) bailouts.

The IMF has changed a lot since the heights of the period in which it acted as the exporter of the neoliberal shock doctrine that was imposed on countries like Bolivia in the 1980s. Today's more modern organisation, argues Nobel laureate Joseph Stiglitz, has come to recognise that employment, equality and social justice lie at the heart of any project of economic recovery.[1] No matter, the austerity medicine being prescribed is the same as it was then, and is likely to dominate public finances for a long time to come. As a result, citizens in the affected economies of the rich world are paying for financial sector misdemeanours with falling salaries, reduced pensions, cut welfare services, and worse, unemployment.

The sources of the current financial crisis are different from the one that afflicted Latin America in the 1980s, but the results in the form of sovereign debt, and more importantly the nature of the social effects of IMF-styled 'rescue' plans, look startlingly similar. Populations have not taken the effects of ever-increasing austerity packages lying down. Instead, they have marched, protested, and called for general strikes that have brought down those governments that were seen to have failed to curb a growing dictatorship of the markets. Many citizens are realising now that venting their anger through the ballot box and replacing governments offers little that is fundamentally different in terms of the diagnosis of the problem and the solutions the alternative political parties are proposing.

For some, this only confirms that the power of markets remains unmatched by that of democracy.[2] For others, the current financial crisis in the Global North offers hope for new forms of democratic rebirth. That is why in addition to the street politics of opposition and protest, increasing numbers of citizen movements have begun the process of dreaming a different world. From Spain's *indignados* (the indignant) to Greece's *aganaktismenoi* (the outraged), to the growing numbers of the 'occupy' movement spreading around the world, spontaneous civil society movements unattached to existing political parties are starting to reclaim their role as citizens and demanding the right to play a new part in the decision-making process, which for some represents a revival of the original tenets of democracy.[3] This is where paying a little attention to countries like Bolivia, where the neoliberal revolution took hold earlier and in its most brutal form in the 1980s, can provide a sense of hope to despondent European masses and a number of useful lessons.

This book has taken an overarching look at a genuinely original process of rapid social transformation, seeking to translate its main political features for the non-specialist reader, and bringing views and interpretations of this process as they emerge. Interpretations are not always easy to find in a media that is often obsessed with the detail of the moment, with binary characterisations of the world, and with political explanations that boil down to the personality and background of individuals – in Bolivia's case, of President Morales.[4] In this book, I hope I have provided some greater understanding of a process that astonishes and confounds in equal measure, appearing to respond to a clear set of conditions one moment, only to take a detour into a complex set of self-contradictions the next. Perhaps as with the *tinku* dance of the Potosi region, which traditionally brought confrontations between men of bordering *ayllus* in the search for a union of opposites, the Bolivian process of change is difficult to understand from the outside. Perhaps, as

Boaventura de Sousa Santos has argued, only an epistemology of the South can help us in this quest of sense-making.[5] The point to be made however is that the main objective here is to learn from the recent Bolivian process of change, because it challenges received wisdom in conceptual areas that are necessary to make sense of the world around us, including the concepts of power and democracy, citizenship and well-being, and development.

A BOTTOM-UP PROCESS OF CHANGE

The story retold in this book begins at a point that is now becoming all too familiar to southern Europeans. By the end of the 1980s, Bolivia was in the midst of a dual crisis. Saddled with a creaking economy, hyperinflation and overblown levels of debt, a small Bolivian elite was persuaded to implement a new economic policy that consisted of all-out privatisation and fiscal austerity. The result was a profound crisis of the neoliberal economic model that put a stop to hyperinflation at too high a human cost. Neoliberalism came in the form of laissez-faire liberalism that promoted the primacy of the market over and above democratic forms of regulation and control. Effectively, the argument went, markets left to their own devices and free from government or other forms of interference were the best mechanism for wealth creation and a reversal of the country's economic fortunes. It was the human suffering dished out by neoliberalism that eventually led to popular discontent, sowing the seeds that led to grassroots mobilisation in favour of the current process of change.[6]

At the same time there was a crisis of what Bolivians have referred to as *partidocracy* and of political institutions mired in corruption. Party structures became unable to represent and channel social demands, including the mass discontent with neoliberal reforms that extended from the mid-1980s. This situation took the country to a political crisis where the very idea of democracy itself was called into question. Once the masses reached the conclusion that political parties were part of the problem, a new set of political actors stepped into the void created in the public democratic space. Trade unions had been the unquestioned political actors of the second half of the twentieth century, especially in their opposition to military governments. However, they had been decimated by the neoliberal revolution and especially by decree 21060. The political vacuum left by the loss of influence and power of the trade unions was filled by the social movements. In this way they became the true historic agent for the refoundation of Bolivia, acting beyond simple opposition and protest movements to present alternative visions to the existing hegemonic model of politics in the form of representative democracy; society, in the form of a society that excluded a majority of its citizens; and economy, as represented by the neoliberal order.[7]

Civil society represents the reconstitution of the collective political activity of Bolivian society. Every sector of society was incorporated to become part of a process of change that began with the emancipation of indigenous peoples and their constitution as political actors. The indigenous marches of 1990 and 2002 were key milestones in this process, and have been most clearly associated with the demand for a constitutional assembly.[8] This became most apparent at the times of the national crises and popular uprisings that had common roots in the fight against the privatisation of natural resources: water in Cochabamba in 2000, and gas in El Alto in 2003. These crises led the Bolivian population to demand a constitutional assembly: that is, a process of debate and deliberation that incorporated every sector of society, through which a new constitution could be written. Thus, during a process of national crisis brought to a head by the dual economic and political failings of neoliberalism, the constitutional assembly was presented as the mechanism that could deliver a resolution by creating a roadmap for a new Bolivia on the basis of new sets of values and purposes. In what constitutes a unique experience around the world, the constitutional assembly was duly inaugurated on Bolivian Independence Day in 2006 in a ceremony that celebrated the richest democratic experience of participation, and a representation of Bolivia's political and cultural diversity.

The new constitution promised to change the country's political sphere, by introducing a range of levels of decentralisation and a new relationship between the social movements and the state. It also aimed to redefine the relationship between the individual and the state, re-establishing the social protection role of the state and integrating excluded majorities. The constitution also proposed to regain for the state a dominant role in steering the economy, while incorporating a plurality of forms of economic practice and property ownership in a course towards a post-neoliberal paradigm. Finally, it denounced imperialism and promised to redefine international relations, bringing a new understanding that, as with people, accepts the existence of interdependencies between regions and countries and builds on these interdependencies through values of solidarity to deliver better futures for those involved.[9] While the new constitution was written and eventually approved by the Bolivian people via a referendum, the political process before, during and after the production of the constitutional document provided a glimpse of the difficulties involved in renegotiating national values and power relations in a highly divided society.

OBSTACLES ON THE PATH OF NATIONAL REBIRTH

Rather like the explorer launching into uncharted territory, leaders of Bolivia's process of change cannot have been aware of how a process of resistance to neoliberalism that began in the 1980s, was continued in the 1990s by indigenous communities, was joined by coca growers in their opposition to US-sponsored coca eradication plans, and was radicalised in 2000 and 2003 at the same time as it spread to the Bolivian masses, would prove to lead to a new political era. The time of *Pachakuti* – literally a new era that follows tumultuous events – had arrived, it seemed, when indigenous and peasant social movements, parties of the left, trade unions and urban middle classes could join in a coalition of forces under the borrowed name of MAS, headed by a leader of the coca growers, and win the 2005 elections outright. It was the culmination of what would be described as a plebeian revolutionary process.[10]

The significance of this momentous point in Bolivia's recent political history was largely lost on international news agencies, which chose to focus instead on the new president's humble origins and on his soon to be famous jumper.[11] The jumper was nonetheless symbolically significant because it represented a new beginning that left behind the politics of grey-suited men who shared the spoils of office and represented their own interests alongside those of transnational capital. Men like Gonzalo Sánchez de Lozada, like the conquistadors, governed a country with a sense of entitlement in spite of representing imported ideologies, values and policies. That was how it appeared, in any case.

It seemed that the revolutionary construction of alternatives to the neoliberal project had resulted in a new political beginning for Bolivia. And yet what the 2005 electoral victory of MAS represented was no more than the beginning of a new period of struggle in a divided society. What Bolivian vice-president García Linera would describe as a catastrophic draw emerged in 2004: on one side, the masses backing the project of change that had begun more than a decade earlier, and on the other, an economic and social elite representing the interests of agribusinesses, landowners and cattle ranchers.[12] The former were dominant in the highlands, and coalesced around the October Agenda and national rebirth based on a new constitution, the nationalisation of natural resources and a plurinational state; whereas the latter were calling for autonomous government for their regions in the east of the country, in an attempt to bypass the process of change and maintain their economic and social privileges. Thus began a new period of political and social strife, represented by a MAS-supporting highlands versus the opposition-controlled lowlands of the *media luna*; a MAS-controlled Congress versus the opposition-controlled Senate; a poor mass of indigenous peoples in rural areas versus white and *mestizo* economic elites in a number of urban centres. Business interests soon made their choice in favour of the opposition, including the vast network of private television and radio stations, and so did eventually the Catholic Church, as an institution that stood to lose high levels of power, influence and land.

Much of the account in this book retraces the steps of these conflicts as they were played out in the battlefields of the constitutional assembly, the streets of Sucre, the forests of Pando and the seat of government in La Paz during the first MAS administration (2006–10). Key to that entire period was the central role played by the process of writing the foundational text of the new Bolivia, a process that proved to be more difficult than anyone had anticipated. The obstacles created inside the assembly by the unrepresentative inflated presence of opposition parties concentrated on the mechanisms for decision making and on the nature of Bolivia. Bolivia managed to get a new constitution eventually, but not without conflict and not without a large degree of tampering with the constitutional text by Congress.[13] Conflict inside the constitutional assembly spilled out to the streets, for instance over the opposition-led calls for a transfer to Sucre of the seat of government, and when in August and September 2008 a civic-committee-inspired bout of violence led to the Pando massacre. The promise of deliberative practices in the new space for national reconciliation and consensus building of the constitutional assembly was therefore not entirely realised, or not as had been promised, at any rate.

The government responded in each case by trying to appease its critics on the one hand, and resorting to conventionally democratic methods on the other. Indeed, the MAS can count a number of electoral victories during that period. So, with the MAS government, we have the apparent contradiction of a 'revolutionary' process of change in search of social justice as part of a process to overcome colonialism and neoliberalism that was pursued entirely through liberal political institutions such as elections and political referenda. To this extent, authors like Postero have posited that Bolivia might not be moving 'beyond neoliberalism but simply vernacularising liberalism to make it more democratic and more relevant to Bolivia's indigenous peoples'.[14] Either way, what the latest presidential election seemed to have confirmed, at a time of clearly defined ideological difference between those for and against the process of change, was a way out of this catastrophic draw in the form of a decisive victory for the political project represented by MAS. Would this herald a new era of unobstructed and deepening change at last?

It had taken MAS a whole term in office and multiple crises to finally deliver on a new constitution that promises much. The clear demand from the population, as was seen after the historic victory of Morales in the elections of December 2009, was to deepen this process of change by means of 'consolidating power and initiating decolonisation'.[15] In conversation with members of government during Christmas 2009, I gained a clear sense of the historic responsibility they felt towards the new governing challenges that were heading their way. The period of catastrophic draw had been extremely difficult politically, and threatened to derail the entire MAS project at times. However, with as clear and decisive a victory as the one just gained, there was, it seemed, no longer the possibility of finding excuses that could explain further delays in implementing the deep structural changes to society that could deliver the Bolivia envisioned in the new constitutional text. The electoral victory of 2009 had inaugurated a new period of hegemonic domination, a leadership that went beyond the overwhelming political superiority over opposition parties that had delivered for the first time a majority in both chambers, and effectively extended over the moral and intellectual arenas.[16] The process of change was surely unstoppable now.

A NEW DIRECTION OF TRAVEL?

And yet the inescapable observation to be made of the last two years of MAS government is that the achievement of complete political hegemony by the MAS has done nothing to calm the conflict-ridden nature of political life in the country. If anything, the intensity and number of conflicts have increased in this period. However, there is a difference to the main political conflicts that have dominated the agenda since January 2010, and that is the origin of those conflicts. They are not with the political opposition, like those that characterised the 2004–09 period when they wanted to put the brake on the process of change, but with sections of the political grassroots that initiated the process of change in the first place and constitute Morales' strongest supporters. Problems began immediately following the electoral landslide of December 2009, which gave MAS an increased 64 per cent share of the vote. As early as May 2010 however, protests degenerated into all-out violence. In the town of Caranavi there had been weeks of tension and road blockades by local groups demanding the promised state investment in a citrus fruit processing plant that would have generated new jobs in an economically depressed area. The violence resulted in the deaths by shooting of two protesters.

A second damaging conflict in the MAS stronghold of Potosí took place in July and August 2010. The local civic committee led direct action which saw the city closed off to the outside world, and all economic activity ceased for close on three weeks. The demands from the city were mostly economic (new factories to produce cement and to smelt minerals, new roads and so on), and although the conflict was resolved peacefully, it was also highly damaging to the government. The third, widely reported period of conflict took place during Christmas 2010 as a result of a government decision to remove a long-established state subsidy on fuel prices, a move that would have resulted in increases of up to 80 per cent on diesel. Although the government had important reasons for this decision – not least breaking the incentive for contraband that cheap Bolivian prices provide – and announced economic measures to minimise the effect of these price hikes, the popular reaction was so strong that these measures had to be abandoned.[17]

The *gasolinazo* conflict over petrol price increases revealed the less-than-solid relationship between the government and the social movements, as well as the clear differences of interests that exist within the social movements themselves. Two other conflicts between the government and the indigenous social movements that have made the headlines in the last two years might become more intractable.

The first took place in June 2010, when after months of

discussions, members of the Confederación Indígena del Oriente Boliviano (CIDOB) began a march from Trinidad to protest against the lower than expected levels of direct representation for indigenous peoples in the plurinational assembly. (The figure dropped from 18 to seven in the final version of the constitution.) In addition, CIDOB members were demanding clarity over the principle of prior informed consent that indigenous peoples demand for matters that affect them in their territories. Although the conflict was patched up at the time, initial attempts by the government to delegitimise the protest by associating it with USAID highlighted the mistrust that exists between the government and some indigenous social movements. These are hardly the harmonious relations one would expect from a party that claims to belong in the social movements. In addition, the crisis highlighted the differences that exist between movements like CIDOB and CONAMAQ, and the coca growers and the peasant workers' federation, CSUTCB, which are much closer to government positions.

The principles that led to this June 2010 march were put to the test again in another period of conflict between indigenous peoples and the government in September 2011. This began with a march to La Paz of indigenous peoples from the Isiboro-Sécure National Park and Indigenous Territory (TIPNIS). Their protest was against a planned road through their territory that had been approved without their consent, something that was against both the constitution and international law in its denial of indigenous rights. What marked this conflict out from the others was the violent reaction from the government against the indigenous marchers, and the government's attempts to discredit, criminalise and prevent marchers from protesting by blocking their path with the police and pitting them against the coca growers and the *colonizadores*. Police stopped the march by arresting its members on September 25, a move that only escalated the tenseness of the political situation. Other social movements, trade unions, students and residents throughout the country came out in support of the indigenous people and against the government's actions.

In what has been described as the most serious political crisis of the MAS to date, interior minister Sacha Llorenti resigned, as did the defence minister and other key members of the cabinet in the departments of Rural Affairs and Migration.[18] Even Bolivia's ambassador to the United Nations, Pablo Solón, published an open letter to the president describing his dismay at the police actions, and arguing that the Bolivian government cannot pretend to be at the forefront of indigenous demands at the United Nations while breaking the terms of its own constitution on indigenous rights and on those of Mother Earth.[19] Construction of the road was halted by President Morales as a result, but the decline in his popularity was not reversed.

In sum, the last two years have shown the deep cleavages that lie under the surface of relations between different social movements and between the social movements and the government.[20] Thus the hegemonic domination heralded after the landslide victory in the 2009 elections might have been premature. Indeed, the MAS government did not manage to achieve the expected show of superiority during the municipal elections of 2010, in which, showing an unparalleled degree of political pragmatism, it decided to go into alliance with members of the opposition parties in areas like Santa Cruz, while distancing itself from close allies in its strongholds. Its aim was to win mayoral elections without having to share power with its allies. The strategy backfired spectacularly, and MAS did not achieve the expected result in places like La Paz, where the Movimiento Sin Miedo now holds the mayoral seat. Worst of all, it showed that MAS is not immune to the opportunistic wheeling and dealing politics of the past.[21]

The real questions are why these conflicts are arising with what is meant to be the MAS's natural support base, and why the government is using the same dirty tricks as parties of yesteryear. Vice president Garcia Linera, keen to produce an intellectual commentary on Bolivia's process of change, has named this a new period of 'creative tensions' in order to explain why the population are growing restless and conflicts are increasing in the ranks of MAS supporters. His argument is effectively that these tensions are about defining the speed and the depth of the process of change.[22]

Clearly not everybody agrees with this analysis, least of all the authors of an open letter to the government that preceded the latest crisis.[23] The critique, published widely in Bolivia in June 2011, was signed by the likes of former minister of land Alejandro Almaraz, former ambassador to the United States Gustavo Guzmán, constitutional assembly member and ex-minister Raúl Prada, along with activists such as Oscar Olivera and committed intellectuals like Pablo Regalski among others. Entitled 'For the recovery of the process of change for and by the people', the letter condemned a number of policies of the Morales government, and described in detail a series of tensions between formal political positions and the reality of the changes taking place in Bolivian politics, society and economy.[24] In many ways, the contents of this document chime with the overall assessment of progress in the process of change that has been made in previous chapters. The discursive elements of the process have been able to enthuse the Bolivian masses and many of the army of foreign observers, who see in the new constitution and in the political process of change the seeds of a radically new society that is more just, inclusive and sustainable. However, it is important to remember that the discursive element by no means represents anything more than an avowed aspiration to change. The reality, as we have seen, is more complex, nuanced and limited in its achievements.

Bolivia has a history of lofty aspirations crystallized in progressive legislation that makes little difference in reality because it is not implemented. It is the argument of the signatories of this document that the reality of the changes being implemented since the December 2009 landslide are contrary to the spirit and the letter of the constitutional text and the expectations of MAS supporters. One of the tensions between discourse and reality discussed at the political level confirms the observation made in Chapter 3: it condemned the editing of the constitutional text by Congress that took place before it was put to the Bolivian people. Congress had had no authority to do this. The letter also criticised a nascent authoritarianism in the government, which did not reflect the principle of deepened forms of democracy that was the hallmark of the process of change. As was argued in Chapter 4, this letter echoed the complaint that the so-called 'structures of social control' only served the purpose of rubber-stamping decisions that are increasingly being taken by a cabal of individuals close to the very top of the political hierarchy.

The signatories also cited the ill-feeling created by the role played by MAS in shortlisting candidates for the elections to the judiciary in October 2011, and accused the government of effectively vetting candidates to ensure political control of the judiciary. The document accused the government of having abandoned the plurinational construction of the country by producing an electoral law that minimised the possibilities for direct representation of indigenous nations in the plurinational assembly, and passing legislation on indigenous rights that is contrary to the new constitution as well as to the ILO Convention 169 on the Rights of Indigenous Peoples and to the 2007 UN declaration on the same issue.

In economics, the letter condemned the government for the continual support it provided to the domination of the economy by transnational corporations (TNCs) in the hydrocarbons and mining sectors, in spite of the rhetoric about regaining control of natural resources. It also criticised the extent to which the Bolivian treasury supports the same capitalist system decried in international fora by investing in foreign government bonds, while the communitarian and social sectors of the economy that the government pretends to support cannot be developed for lack of investment. The letter carried an implicit condemnation of the government's reliance on a model of development built on the extractive industries, when this model is internationally questioned, and has been blamed by President Morales for being responsible for Bolivia's poverty and submission to a global hegemonic system that prevents its people from 'living well'. This includes the system of land exploitation and distribution since some recent legislation has gone counter to aspirations in this field. Recent legislation approved the use of GM seeds in spite of widespread opposition among social movements, and the constitution legalised the maintenance of *latifundia* (large estates) on condition that they serve an economic purpose and land is not used for speculative purposes.[25]

Overall then, a powerful critique of the MAS government's role has emerged since the electoral landslide of 2009. It concentrates on the double discourse that presents Bolivia at the forefront of international progressive forces in favour of the rights of indigenous peoples, new forms of democracy, and environmental sustainability, while practising increasingly authoritarian politics, supporting TNCs and irreparably damaging Mother Nature at home. Signatories of the letter proposed nine points that would help the government to return to and apply the spirit and the letter of the constitutional text. They included revising the legislation approved by MAS since December 2009, developing a new economic agenda that allows the country to move away from the model of natural resource exploitation while taking steps to make a reality of a model of development based on food security, respect for Mother Earth, and deepening democracy so that the full participation of all sectors of society can take place.[26]

CONCLUSION

At the time of writing, the MAS has reached yet another crossroads. This is not in itself new for a country in which political instability and a tradition of struggle have brought Bolivia to the brink on numerous occasions. What is different about the political crisis following the TIPNIS debacle is that it has highlighted the policies and actions of the government that are less than consistent with radical indigenous, communitarian, participatory and environmentalist discourses. Perhaps more worryingly, the crisis of September and October 2011 brought to the streets MAS voters in the tens of thousands who shouted for the first time 'Evo decía que todo cambiaría: mentira, mentira, la misma porquería' (Evo said everything would change: lies, lies, this is the same old shit). This sent a warning shot to a party that thought of itself as hegemonic. These spontaneous street demonstrations of opposition were further reinforced by the results of the October 2011 judicial elections, in which a majority of voters spoiled their ballot, many by writing the word TIPNIS on it. At the same time, the eighth indigenous march eventually arrived to La Paz to a multitudinous welcome from the city, in spite of the government's refusal to discuss their demands.

The fact is that a number of commentators have for some time identified weaknesses in the organisational structure and the operations of MAS. These might explain the latest realisation that, in spite of the claim that this is a party of the social movements, there is a lack of connection between the masses and the current government. Regalsky has argued that indigenous forms of direct participation and of democracy have been marginalised under the MAS government by a series of strategies that control the selection of candidates, maintaining a party-based system of political representation and co-opting many of these leaders into the structure of the MAS.[27] For his part, Hervé do Alto's critique explains the lack of democracy at the heart of the MAS through the fact that, in bringing together disparate movements with their own membership and demands, the MAS has only been able to maintain organisational cohesion through the distribution of *pegas* (political jobs and goods) in a system of corporate democracy in which political clientelism persists.[28] It seems then that not everything is as new in Bolivia as was claimed, making more credible recent critiques that, in spite of the rhetoric about a new postneoliberal paradigm, only a thin veneer covers what is a reformist agenda squarely set within a reconstituted version of neoliberalism.[29]

What is then left of Bolivia as a 'resistance movement and counterhegemonic project' in the Latin American region?[30] The jury is still out on the long-term potential of the current constitution to deliver its promise in the context of long-established social cleavages. However Bolivia has often come to the brink of social and economic collapse. And just as everyone is expecting the worst, it somehow manages to retreat, negotiate, reorganise and move forward, as was the case in the previous 'worst crisis' in August and September 2008. The strength of the process of change will be measured by its ability to yet again step back from the brink and continue this perilous and imperfect process towards a more inclusive, just society. On this road, the TIPNIS crisis closes a circle that began in 1990 with the first march of lowland indigenous peoples to La Paz. A baby was born during that march, and 21 years later, that same Anahí Dignidad Líder led the latest march to La Paz. She did so as a spokesperson from the Sirionó nation, but more symbolically, as a symbol of the opposition to the government that emerged from the insertion of indigenous peoples into the political process of change.[31] She symbolises Bolivia's ability to deliver political renewal and new leaderships through a healthy civil society, perhaps the best guarantee that the process of change will not become stagnant in the near future.

NOTES

ACKNOWLEDGEMENTS

1   My thanks go to Ceri Davies and Marian Barnes for introducing me to the concept of cognitive justice. See M. Van der Velden (2004) 'From communities of practice to communities of resistance: civil society and cognitive justice', *Development* 47(1), 73–81.

INTRODUCTION

1   Asamblea Constituyente (2008) *Nueva Constitución política del estado. Versión oficial*. La Paz: Representación presidencial para la asamblea constituyente (REPAC).
2   *El Tiempo Latino* (2008) 'Luz verde al referéndum', October 24. Available on <www.eltiempolatino.com/edic_Ant./08oct/4/Americas/morales.html> (accessed on October 12, 2009).
3   A. García Linera (2010) *La potencia plebeya: Acción colectiva e identidades indígenas, obreras y populares en Bolivia*. La Paz: CLACSO.
4   C. Hay (2007) *Why We Hate Politics*. London: Polity.
5   M. Kenny (1995) *The First New Left: British intellectuals after Stalin*. London: Lawrence & Wishart.
6   X. Albó, personal interview, June 18, 2009.
7   J. Crabtree and L. Whitehead (2008) *Unresolved Tensions: Bolivia past and present*. Pittsburgh, Pa.: University of Pittsburgh Press.
8   K. Artaraz (2009) *Cuba and Western Intellectuals since 1959*. New York: Palgrave Macmillan.
9   B. De Sousa Santos (2010) *Refundación del estado en América Latina: Perspectivas desde una epistemología del sur*. La Paz: Plural.

1   THE ECONOMIC BIRTH PAINS OF POOR COUNTRIES

1   Open Democracy (2006) 'Evo Morales sworn in as Bolivia's first indigenous president hails election as "end of colonial and neo-liberal

era".' Interview by Open Democracy with James Petras, January 23, 2006. Available on <www.democracynow.org/2006/1/23/evo_morales_ sworn_in_as_bolivias> (accessed February 23, 2011).

2   E. Galeano (1973) *Open Veins of Latin America: Five centuries of the pillage of a continent.* New York: Monthly Review Press, p. 31.

3   S. Eckstein and F. Hagopian (1983) 'The limits of industrialization in the less developed world: Bolivia', *Economic Development and Cultural Change* 32(1), 63–95.

4   L. Oporto Ordóñez (2007) *Uncía y Llallagua: Empresa minera capitalista y estrategias de apropiación real del espacio (1900–1935).* La Paz: Plural.

5   Ordóñez (2007), p. 38.

6   B. Keen and M. Wasserman (1988) *A History of Latin America.* Boston, Mass.: Houghton Mifflin.

7   U. Reye (1967) 'Agricultural reform and economic development: the Bolivian example', *Intereconomics* 2(6–7), 174–7.

8   R. Prebisch (1950) *The Economic Development of Latin America and its Principal Problems.* New York: United Nations.

9   Key publications include F. H. Cardoso (1979) *Dependencia y desarrollo en América Latina*, Mexico City: Siglo XXI; and O. Sunkel and P. Paz (1970) *El subdesarrollo latinoamericano y la teoría del desarrollo*, Mexico City: Siglo XXI.

10   A. G. Frank (1967) *Capitalism and Underdevelopment in Latin America*, New York: Monthly Review Press; S. Amin (1976) *Unequal Development: An essay on the social formations of peripheral capitalism*, New York: Monthly Review Press; I. Wallerstein, (1979) *The Capitalist World Economy*, Cambridge: Cambridge University Press.

11   P. O'Brien (1984) 'Dependency revisited', Latin American Studies occasional paper no. 40, University of Glasgow.

12   P. Pacheco (2006) 'Agricultural expansion and deforestation in lowland Bolivia: the import substitution versus the structural adjustment model', *Land Use Policy* 23(3), 205–25.

13   A. Mayorga (1978) 'National-popular state, state capitalism and military dictatorship in Bolivia 1952–1975', *Latin American Perspectives* 5(2), 89–119.

14   Keen and Wasserman (1988).

15   R. Albro (2005) 'The indigenous in the plural in Bolivian oppositional politics', *Bulletin of Latin American Research* 24(4), 433–53.

16   J. D. Sachs, J. Bulow and K. Rogoff (1988) 'Comprehensive debt retirement: the Bolivian example', *Brookings Papers on Economic Activity*, No. 2: 705–15.

17   D. Green (1995) *Silent Revolution: The rise of market economics in Latin America.* London: Latin American Bureau.

18   J. Painter (1994) *Bolivia and Coca: A study in dependency.* Boulder, Colo.: Lynne Rienner.

19   N. Klein (2007) *The Shock Doctrine: The rise of disaster capitalism.* London: Allen Lane.

20 J. L. Cariaga (1990) 'Three policy experiments: Bolivia', pp. 41–53 in J. Williamson (ed.), *Latin American Adjustment: How much has happened?* Washington DC: Institute for International Economics.

21 J. Sachs (1987) 'The Bolivian hyperinflation and stabilisation', *American Economic Review* 77(2), 211–37.

22 J. Dunkerley (1990) 'Political transition and economic stabilisation: Bolivia, 1982–1989', research paper no. 22, Institute of Latin American Studies, University of London.

23 J. Crabtree, G. Buffy and J. Pearce (1988) 'The great tin crash: Bolivia and the world tin market', *Bulletin of Latin American Research* 7(1), 174–5.

24 Klein (2007).

25 Green (1995).

26 M. Peirce (ed.) (1997) *Capitalization: The Bolivian model of social and economic reform.* Miami, Fla.: Woodrow Wilson Center and North South Center.

27 F. Molina (2007) 'Biografía del Bonosol', pp. 21–38 in G. Aponte, J-C. Jemio, R. Laserna, F. Martínez, F. Molina and E. Skinner (eds), *La Inversión Prudente: Impacto del Bonosol sobre la familia, la equidad social y el crecimiento económico.* La Paz: Fundación Milenio,.

28 K. Müller (2008) 'Contested universalism: from Bonosol to Renta Dignidad in Bolivia', *International Journal of Social Welfare* 18(2), 163–72.

29 J. A. Morales (1996) 'Economic policy in Bolivia after the transition to democracy', pp. 30-48 in J. A. Morales and G. McMahon (eds), *Economic Policy and the Transition to Democracy: The Latin American experience.* London: Macmillan.

30 J. A. Morales and J. Sachs (1990) 'Bolivia's economic crisis', pp. 157-268 in J. Sachs (ed.), *Developing Country Debt and Economic Performance. Vol. 2, The Country Studies: Argentina Bolivia, Brazil, Mexico.* Chicago, Ill.: University of Chicago Press,

31 M. Pastor (1991) 'Bolivia: hyperinflation, stabilisation and beyond', *Journal of Development Studies* 27(2), 211–37.

32 B. Kohl (2004) 'Privatization Bolivia style: a cautionary tale', *International Journal of Urban and Regional Research* 28(4), 893–908.

33 D. Kaimowitz, G. Thiele and P. Pacheco (1999) 'The effects of structural adjustment on deforestation and forest degradation in lowland Bolivia', *World Development* 27(3), 505–20.

34 M. Pastor (1993) 'Managing the Latin American debt crisis: the International Monetary Fund and beyond', pp. 289–313 in G. A. Epstein, J. Graham and J. G. Nembhard (eds), *Creating a New World Economy: Forces of change and plans for action.* Philadelphia, Pa.: Temple University Press.

35 B. Kohl and L. Farthing (2009) 'Less than fully satisfactory development outcomes: international financial institutions and social unrest in Bolivia', *Latin American Perspectives* 36(3), 59–78.

36   R. Thiele (2003) 'The social impact of structural adjustment in Bolivia', *Journal of International Development* 15(3), 299–319.

37   P. Van Dijck (1999) *The Bolivian Experiment: Structural Adjustment and Poverty Alleviation.* La Paz: Centro de Estudios para el Desarrollo Laboral y Agrario (CEDLA).

38   UNDP (2010) *Human Development in the Department of Potosi.* La Paz: UNDP.

39   M. Frost, R. Forster and D. Haas (2005) 'Maternal education and child nutritional status in Bolivia: finding the links', *Social Science and Medicine* 60(2), 395–407.

40   Instituto Nacional de Estadística (INE) (2005) *Anuario estadístico.* La Paz: INE.

41   C. Larrea and W. Freire (2002) 'Social inequality and child malnutrition in four Andean countries', *Revista Panamericana de Salud Publica* 11(5). Available on <www.scielosp.org/scielo.php?script=sci_arttext&pid=S1020-49892002000500010> (accessed March 15, 2011).

42   R. Jenkins (1997) 'Trade liberalisation in Latin America: the Bolivian case', *Bulletin of Latin American Research* 16(3), 307–26.

43   Morales (1996), p. 37.

44   L. A. Echazú Alvarado (1997) *Los nuevos dueños de Bolivia: Inversiones extranjeras en Bolivia.* La Paz: Universidad nacional Siglo XX.

45   R. Fernández Terán (2004) *FMI, Banco Mundial y Estado Neocolonial: Poder Supranacional en Bolivia.* Cochabamba: Plural Editores.

46   J. E. Stiglitz (2003) *Globalization and its Discontents.* New York: W.W. Norton.

47   J. Shultz (2009) 'Lessons in blood and fire: the deadly consequences of IMF economics', pp. 117–44 in J. Shultz and M. Crane Draper (eds), *Dignity and Defiance: Stories from Bolivia's challenge to globalisation.* Berkeley, Calif.: University of California Press.

48   Klein (2007).

49   Painter (1994).

50   D. L. Van Cott (1994) 'Indigenous peoples and democracy: issues for policy-makers', pp. 1–27 in D. L. Van Cott (ed.), *Indigenous Peoples and Democracy in Latin America.* New York: St Martin's Press.

51   D. Perreault, J. M. Roper and P. Wilson (2003) 'Introduction: indigenous transformational movements in contemporary Latin America', *Latin American Perspectives* 30(1), 5–22.

52   World Bank (2006) *Poverty Reduction and Growth: Virtuous and vicious circles.* Available on <http://siteresources.worldbank.org/EXTLACOFFICEOFCE/Resources/870892-11139877599088/virtuous_circles1_complete.pdf> (accessed March 22, 2010).

53   X. de la Barra (2006) 'Who owes and who pays? The accumulated debt of neoliberalism', *Critical Sociology* 32(1), 125–61.

54 A. Hall and J. Midgely (2004) *Social Policy for Development*. London:
    Sage.
55 M. T. Zegada, Y. Tórrez and G. Cámara (2008) *Movimientos socia-
    les en tiempos de poder: articulaciones y campos de conflicto en el
    gobierno del MAS*. La Paz: Centro Cuarto Intermedio.
56 J. Crabtree and L. Whitehead (2008) *Unresolved Tensions: Bolivia past
    and present*. Pittsburgh, Pa.: University of Pittsburgh Press.
57 B. Kohl (2001) 'Stabilizing neoliberalism in Bolivia: popular
    participation and privatization', *Political Geography* 21(4), 449–72.

2 POLITICAL FAILURES AND POLITICAL REVIVAL

1   Indeed, the literature is testament to this. See W. Q. Morales (1992)
    Bolivia, Land of Struggle, Boulder, Colo: Westview Press; J. Dunkerley
    (1984) *Rebellion in the Veins: Political struggle in Bolivia 1952–1982*,
    London: Verso; J. R. Webber (2011) *From Rebellion to Reform in
    Bolivia*, Chicago, Ill.: Haymarket; J. Crabtree (2005) *Patterns of
    Protest: Politics and Social Movements in Bolivia*, London: Latin
    American Bureau.
2   W. Robinson (2008) *Latin America and Global Capitalism: A critical
    globalization perspective*. Baltimore, Md.: Johns Hopkins University
    Press., ch. 6.
3   L. Gill (2004) *The School of the Americas: Military training and
    political violence in the Americas*. Durham, N.C.: Duke University
    Press.
4   M. Alcántara (1999) *Sistemas políticos de América Latina*. Madrid:
    Tecnos.
5   E. A. Gamarra and J. M. Malloy (1995) 'The patrimonial dynamics
    of party politics in Bolivia', pp. 399-433 in S. Mainwaring and T. R.
    Scully (eds), *Building Democratic Institutions. Party politics in Latin
    America*. Stanford, Calif.: Stanford University Press.
6   Civic committees were particularly visible during the first MAS admin-
    istration (2006–10) as the main opposition to the MAS project. They
    were concentrated in the east of the country and led by cattle ranchers
    and soya producers, exercising their power through regional prefects.
7   Many parties came and went during the neoliberal period, including
    Movimiento Bolivia Libre (MBL), Condepa, UCS and NFR.
8   S. Lazar (2004) 'Personalist politics, clientelism and citizenship: local
    elections in el Alto, Bolivia', *Bulletin of Latin America Research* 23(2),
    228–43.
9   E. Gamarra (1997) 'Hybrid presidentialism in Bolivia', pp. 109–41
    in H. Von Mettenheim (ed.) *Presidential Institutions and Democratic
    Politics: Comparing regional and national contexts*. Baltimore, Md.
    and London: Johns Hopkins University Press,
10 R. Martínez (2004) 'La atípica elección presidencial boliviana',

Cuestiones Constitucionales 10 (Jan.–June). Available on <www.ejournal.unam.mx/cuc/cconst10/CUC1002.pdf> (accessed April 12, 2011).

11 J. L. Exeni (2007) 'Democracia pactada', pp. 34–50 in D. Ayo (ed.) *Democracia Boliviana: un modelo para des armar*. La Paz: FES-ILDIS.

12 M. Zuazo (2009) *¿Cómo nació el MAS? La ruralización de la política en Bolivia*. La Paz: Friedrich Ebert Stiftung.

13 M. Seligson et al. (2003) *Auditoria de la democracia: Bolivia 2002*, La Paz: UCD; M. Seligson et al. (2005) *Auditoria de la democracia: Bolivia 2004*, La Paz: UCD.

14 J. Prats (2005) 'Bolivia tras el fracaso de la democracia pactada', *Corte Nacional Electoral. Revista Agora* 3 (Sept.), 4–5.

15 According to the IMF, GDP growth in Bolivia collapsed from 5 per cent in 1998 to 0.4 per cent in 1999. IMF (2010) *World Economic Outlook*, Washington DC: IMF.

16 In 1950, British sociologist T. H. Marshall wrote a seminal work on the concept of citizenship. In it, he claimed that the effective exercise of citizenship had to be accompanied of three sets of rights, including the civil, political, and crucially, social rights associated with the welfare state. See T. H. Marshall (1950) *Citizenship and Social Class and Other Essays*. Cambridge: Cambridge University Press.

17 L. Whitehead (2001) 'Bolivia and the viability of democracy', *Journal of Democracy* 12(2), 6–16.

18 Along with the agrarian reform and the nationalisations of the mines, the national revolution of 1952 led by the MNR introduced universal suffrage for the first time in history. See J. De Mesa, T. Gisbert and C. Mesa (1999) *Historia de Bolivia*, La Paz: Editorial Gisbert.

19 Morales (1992).

20 PNUD (2007) *Informe Nacional sobre Desarrollo Humano. El estado del estado en Bolivia*. La Paz: PNUD.

21 J. Linz and A. Stepan (1996) *Problems of Democratic Transition and Consolidation: Southern Europe, South America and post-communist Europe*. Baltimore, Md.: Johns Hopkins University Press.

22 G. O'Donnell, P. Schmitter and L. Whitehead (1999) *Counterpoints: Selected essays on authoritarianism and democratization*. Notre Dame, Ind.: University of Notre Dame Press.

23 Crabtree (2005).

24 B. Munoz-Pogossian (2008) *Electoral Rules and the Transformation of Bolivian Politics*. New York: Palgrave Macmillan.

25 Whitehead (2001).

26 See J. Mahoney (2003) 'Long-run development and the legacy of colonialism in Spanish America', *American Journal of Sociology* 109(1), 50–106.

27 N. Klein (2007) *The Shock Doctrine: The rise of disaster capitalism*. London: Allen Lane.

28 S. Orozco Ramírez, A. García Linera and P. Stefanoni (2006) 'No somos juguete de nadie...', Análisis de la relación de movimientos sociales, recursos naturales, estado y descentralización. La Paz: Plural.

29 The link between Bolivia's social movements and access to natural resources has been most vividly recounted by B. Dangl (2007) in The Price of Fire: Resource wars and social movements in Bolivia. Oakland: A K Press.

30 G. O'Donnell, P. Schmitter and L. Whitehead (1988) Transitions from Authoritarian Rule: Prospects for democracy, Vols 2, 3 and 4. Baltimore, Md. and London: Johns Hopkins University Press.

31 See I. Wallerstein (1974) The Modern World-System. New York: Academic Press.

32 W. Robinson (1996) Promoting Polyarchy: Globalization, US intervention and hegemony. Cambridge: Cambridge University Press.

33 Robinson (1996).

34 Robinson (2008).

35 A. Rossi (2009) 'Militarizacion y 'cooperacion' militar', Le Monde Diplomatique, edición boliviana (Sept.), 10–12.

36 P. Stefanoni, and H. Do Alto (2007) 'The emergence of indigenous nationalism in Bolivia', pp. 9–35 in F. Polet (ed.) The State of Resistance: Popular struggles in the Global South. London and New York: Zed.

37 CSUTCB (1995) VI congreso. Documentos y resoluciones. La Paz: CEDOIN, p. 31.

38 Zuazo (2009).

39 M. Sivak (2008) Jefazo: retrato íntimo de Evo Morales, Buenos Aires: Debate; P. Stefanoni and H. do Alto (2006) Evo Morales, de la coca al palacio, La Paz: Malatesta; S. Harten (2011) The Rise of Evo Morales and the MAS, London: Zed.

40 MIP challenged MAS for the indigenous vote in the 2002 elections but eventually disappeared after 2005, partly as a result of the way in which it represented only Aymara demands.

41 B. Kohl and L. Farthing (2006) Impasse in Bolivia: Neoliberal hegemony and popular resistance. London: Zed, p. 140.

42 See T. Campbell, (2003) The Quiet Revolution: Decentralization and the rise of political participation in Latin American Cities (Pitt Latin American Series), Pittsburgh, Pa.: University of Pittsburgh Press; L. Avritzer (2006) 'New public spheres in Brazil: Local democracy and deliberative politics', International Journal of Urban and Regional Research 30(3), 623–37; G. Baiocchi (2005) Militants and Citizens: The politics of participatory democracy in Porto Alegre, Palo Alto, Calif.: Stanford University Press.

43 See B. Kohl (2003) 'Democratizing decentralisation in Bolivia: the Law of Popular Participation', Journal of Planning Education and Research 23, 153–64.

44 P. Pacheco (2004) 'What lies behind decentralisation? Forest, powers

and actors in lowland Bolivia', *European Journal of Development Research* 16(1), 90–109.

45 B. Kohl (2001) 'Stabilizing neoliberalism in Bolivia: popular participation and privatization', *Political Geography* 21(4), 449–72.

46 S. R. Arnstein (1969) 'A ladder of citizen participation', *Journal of the American Institute of Planners* 35(4), 216–24.

47 J.-A. Mcneish (2006) 'Stones on the road: the politics of participation and the generation of crisis in Bolivia', *Bulletin of Latin American Research* 25(2), 220–40.

48 I. A. Goudsmit and J. Blackburn (2001) 'Participatory municipal planning in Bolivia: an ambiguous experience', *Development in Practice* 11(5), 587–96.

49 C. Medeiros (2001) 'Civilizing the popular? The law of popular participation and the design of a new civil society in 1990s Bolivia', *Critique of Anthropology* 21(4), 401–25.

50 Stefanoni and Do Alto (2007).

51 Whitehead (2001).

52 M. Barlow (2008) *Blue Covenant: The global water crisis and the coming battle for the right to water.* New York: New Press.

53 O. Olivera and T. Lewis (2004) *Cochabamba! Water war in Bolivia.* Cambridge, Mass.: South End Press.

54 W. Assies (2001) 'David vs. Goliat en Cochabamba: los derechos del agua, el neoliberalismo y la renovación de la propuesta social en Bolivia', *T'inkazos* 4(8), 106–34.

55 D. L. Van Cott (2003) 'From exclusion to inclusion: Bolivia's 2002 elections', *Journal of Latin American Studies* 35(4), 751–75.

56 Kohl and Farthing (2006).

57 H. Klein (2011) 'The historical background to the rise of the MAS, 1952–2005', pp. 27–63 in A. Pearce (ed.), *Evo Morales and the Movimiento al Socialismo in Bolivia: The first term in context, 2006–2010.* London: Institute for the Study of the Americas and Bolivia Information Forum.

58 B. Kohl and L. Farthing (2009) 'Less than fully satisfactory outcomes: international financial institutions and social unrest in Bolivia', *Latin American Perspectives* 36(3), 59–78.

59 D. L. Van Cott (2005) *From Movements to Parties in Latin America: The evolution of ethnic politics.* New York: Cambridge University Press.

60 H. Do Alto (2007) 'El MAS-IPSP boliviano entre la protesta callejera y la política institucional', pp. 71–110 in K. Monasterios, P. Stefanoni and H. Do Alto (eds), *Reinventando la nación en Bolivia: Movimientos sociales, estado y poscolonialidad.* La Paz: Plural.

61 A. García Linera (2008) 'Empate catastrófico y punto de bifurcación', *Crítica y emancipación* 1(1), 23–33. Available on <http://bibliotecavirtual.clacso.org.ar/ar/libros/secret/CyE/cye2S1a.pdf> (accessed June 20, 2010).

62 T. Salman (2007) 'Bolivia and the paradoxes of democratic consolidation', *Latin American Perspectives* 34(6), 111–30.

3 REVOLUTION IN DEMOCRACY?

1   R. Martínez Dalmau (2008) *El proceso constituyente boliviano en el marco del nuevo constitucionalismo latinoamericano (2006–2008)*. La Paz: Oxfam GB.

2   N. Correa, N. Pacari and F. Barrios (2005) *Asamblea constituyente. Aprendiendo de otras experiencias: Colombia, Ecuador, Venezuela*. La Paz: Plural and Ildis.

3   A. García Linera (2010) *La potencia plebeya: Acción colectiva e identidades indígenas, obreras y populares en Bolivia*. La Paz: Comuna y CLACSO.

4   C. Romero (2005) *El proceso constituyente boliviano: EL hito de la cuarta marcha de tierras bajas*. Santa Cruz: CEJIS.

5   N. A. Robins (2002) *Genocide and Millennialism in Upper Peru: The Great Rebellion of 1780–1782*. Westport, Conn.: Praeger.

6   A. García Linera, M. Chávez León and P. Costas Monje (2005) *Sociología de los movimientos sociales en Bolivia: Estructuras de movilización, repertorios culturales y acción política*. La Paz: Plural, pp. 501–40.

7   Z. Lehm (1999) *Milenarismo y movimientos sociales en la Amazonia Boliviana: La busqueda de la Loma Santa y la Marcha por el Territorio y la Dignidad*. Santa Cruz: APCOB-CIDEB BENI-OXFAM.

8   P. Wilson and M. Stewart (2008) *Global Indigenous Media: Culture, poetics and politics*. Durham, N.C.: Duke University Press.

9   A. Brysk (2000) *From Tribal Village to Global Village: Indian rights and international relations in Latin America*. Stanford, Calif.: Stanford University Press.

10 United Nations (2002) *International Decade of the World's Indigenous People: Final Report*. Available on <www.un.org/rights/indigenous/mediaadv.html> (accessed August 25, 2010).

11 Brysk (2000).

12 N. Fraser (1997) *Justice Interruptus*. London: Routledge.

13 *Ayllu* is the term used to refer to semi-independent Aymara and Quechua communities in the Bolivian highlands. In the Bolivian highlands, the *ayllus* became the source of indigenous rebellion once their land became coveted by successive governments after independence.

14 See article 8.1 in Asamblea Constituyente (2008) Nueva Constitución política del estado. Versión oficial. La Paz: REPAC, p. 6.

15 X. Albó (2008) *Movimientos y poder indígena en Bolivia, Ecuador y Perú*. La Paz: CIPCA.

16 The Confederación Sindical de Colonizadores de Bolivia (CSCB), founded in 1971 and affiliated to the Central Obrera Boliviana (COB), grouped rural communities of landless peasants settled in new subtropical areas. The term *colonizador* (settler) is now rejected by the organisation, which has been renamed the Confederación Sindical de Comunidades Interculturales de Bolivia (CSCIB) to take account of its plurinational composition.

17 A. Almaraz, I. Rodríguez and M. Torres (2005) *Pacto de Unidad: Propuestas de nuevo país desde los sectores mayoritarios. Constituyente soberana.* Available on <www.constituyentesoberana.org/info/?q=node/355> (accessed July 22, 2010).

18 F. Garcés et al. (2010) *El pacto de unidad y el proceso de construcción de una propuesta de constitución política del estado.* La Paz: Pacto de Unidad.

19 *Criollo* (creole) was the term used for Spaniards born in the colony, whom the hierarchical society of the time placed below the *peninsulares*, the term for those born in Spain.

20 The forms of limited recognition that characterised the 1990s have been referred to as 'neoliberal multiculturalism' by authors like Willem Assies. See W. Assies (2011) 'Bolivia's new constitution and its implications', pp. 93–116 in A. J. Pearce (ed.), *Evo Morales and the Movimiento al Socialismo in Bolivia: The first term in context, 2006–2010.* London: Institute for the Study of the Americas.

21 H. Moldiz (2010) 'Una prueba de fuego para el Pacto de Unidad. Rebelión, 30 June 2010', available on <www.rebelion.org/noticia.php?id=108838> (accessed September 7, 2010). See also the ILO Convention 169 on the Rights of Indigenous Peoples (Defensor del pueblo (2008) Convenio No. 169 de la O.I.T sobre pueblos indígenas y tribales en paises independientes aprobado en 1989). Geneva: ILO.

22 The indigenous component is not hegemonic within the MAS although it is represented in the figure of foreign secretary David Choquehuanca. Authors have noted that the party represents a further two ideological currents: an orthodox, 'old' left statist one represented by vice-president Linera and a populist one represented by Morales himself. See R. Laserna (2010) 'Mire, la democracia boliviana en los hechos ...', *Latin American Research Review*, special issue 'Living in actually existing democracies', pp. 27–58.

23 J. Gaventa (2006) 'Triumph, déficit or contestation? Deepening the 'deepening democracy' debate', IDS working paper no. 264, University of Sussex.

24 Albó (2008), p. 89.

25 I M. Young (2000) *Inclusion and Democracy.* Oxford: Oxford University Press.

26 R. Zabaleta Mercado (1986) *Lo nacional popular en Bolivia,* Mexico: Siglo XXI; L. Antezana (1991) *La diversidad social en Zabaleta Mercado,* La Paz: CEBEM.

27 A. García Linera (2008) 'Empate catastrófico y punto de bifurcación', *Crítica y emancipación* 1(1), 23–33. Available on <http://biblioteca virtual.clacso.org.ar/ar/libros/secret/CyE/cye2S1a.pdf> (accessed June 20, 2010).

28 F. Gamboa (2009) *Dilemas y conflictos sobre la constitución en Bolivia: Historia Político de la Asamblea Constituyente.* La Paz: Konrad Adenauer Stiftung.

29 Corte Nacional Electoral (2007) *Compendio Electoral*. La Paz: Corte Nacional Electoral.

30 F. Gamboa (2007) 'El trabajo de la asamblea constituyente', *Opiniones y análisis* 88, 11–46.

31 The figure of 55.8 per cent is lower than the 62 per cent of the Bolivian population who, according to the 2001 census, consider themselves to belong to an indigenous community. See X. Albó (2008) 'El perfil de los constituyentes', *T'inkazos* 11(23–4), 49–64.

32 The violence towards indigenous Bolivians that took place on May 24, 2008 in Sucre was documented by Cesar Brie, who borrowed the title of Dovstoyevski's 1861 novel *The Insulted and Injured* for his documentary. See C. Brie (2008) *Ofendidos y humillados*, independent documentary. Sucre. Available on <http://video.google.com/videoplay? docid=4622053352668424213#> (accessed June 28, 2010).

33 Apostamos por Bolivia (2006) *Construyendo: El álbum de los constituyentes*, 28 (August), 1–24.

34 S. Doria Medina, G. Richter and C. Romero (2008) 'Asamblea Constituyente: Un balance a varias voces', *T'inkazos* 11(23–24), 15–34.

35 Rosalia del Villar, constitutional assembly member, personal interview, February 12, 2009.

36 Gamboa (2009).

37 I am grateful to Loyola Cultural Action (ACLO) in Sucre for sharing with me multiple hours of radio recordings about the constitutional assembly.

38 The 21 commissions were: Understanding of Bolivia; nationalities and citizenship; rights and responsibilities; plurinational and political structure; legislative structure; executive structure; judiciary; other organs of the state; decentralisation and autonomy; education, culture and sport; human development; health, work and social security; hydrocarbons; mining; water; forestry; land and territory; rural development; coca; economy and finance; national security and international relations. Their role was to produce up to two versions of the proposed articles for the final constitutional document that would have to be approved in the main assembly.

39 Loyola Guzmán, constitutional assembly member, personal interview, May 18, 2009.

40 For some this process classified assembly members according to different political cultures, including those so-called 'professional politicians' who were less willing to take this aspect of their role seriously. Raquel Romero, Colectivo Cabildeo, personal interview, June 10, 2009.

41 Angélica Siles, constitutional assembly member, personal interview, June 23, 2009.

42 The literature on the possibilities of deliberation has been dominated by views that assume that conflict and self-interest cannot be reconciled with a deliberative process that must always be driven by the 'common good'. More recently authors have put forward theories that

incorporate conflict and self-interest into deliberative processes. See Young (2000).

43 Ana Maria Ruiz, constitutional assembly member, personal interview, February 11, 2009.

44 J. De Mesa, T. Gisbert and C. Mesa (1999) *Historia de Bolivia*. La Paz: Editorial Gisbert.

45 Loyola Guzmán, interview.

46 La Prensa (2008) 'El número de muertos en los hechos de septiembre podría ser mayor a 18', *Red UNITAS*, Boletín virtual, November 5. Available on <www.redunitas.org/boletin/11noviembre08/05unasur1 8muertos.php?PHPSESSID=d54a9046576ac118226798d54f359430> (accessed September 23, 2010).

47 BBC (2008) 'Bolivia tells US envoy to leave', BBC news, September 11. Available on <http://news.bbc.co.uk/1/hi/7609487.stm> (accessed September 23, 2010).

48 His full speech is available at the official UN website, available on <www.un.org/en/ga/63/generaldebate/bolivia.shtml> (accessed September 23, 2010).

49 P. Regalsky (2009) *Las paradojas del proceso constituyente boliviano*. Cochabamba: CENDA.

50 Pacto de Unidad (2007) 'Propuesta consensuada del Pacto de Unidad: Constitución Política del Estado Boliviano', May 23. La Paz.

51 Asamblea Constituyente (2007) Constitución política del estado (Aprobada en grande). Sucre: Representación presidencial para la asamblea constituyente (REPAC).

52 Asamblea Constituyente (2008) *Nueva Constitución política*.

53 Asamblea Constituyente (2008), p. 5.

54 R. Prada Alcoreza (2008) 'Análisis de la nueva Constitución Política del Estado. Crítica y emancipación', *Revista latinoamericana de Ciencias Sociale*s 1(1), 35–50.

55 Assies (2011), p. 93.

56 The Centro de Estudios Políticos y Sociales (CEPS) has provided technical and legal advice to constitutional processes and development plans in Venezuela, Ecuador, Bolivia, Paraguay and El Salvador.

57 Asamblea Constituyente (2008), pp. 10–11.

58 Asamblea Constituyente (2008), pp. 50–1.

59 Asamblea Constituyente (2008), pp. 55–70.

60 A. García Linera (2008) *Los tres pilares de la nueva Constitución Política del Estado*. La Paz: Vicepresidencia de la República, p. 15.

61 A. García Linera (2008) 'Del neoliberalismo al modelo nacional productivo: los ciclos de la economía Boliviana', *Revista de Análisis* (June 22).

62 X. Albó (2008) 'Para leer la nueva constitución', *Constituyente Soberana*. Available on <www.constituyentesoberana.org/3/noticias/ac/112008/171108_2.html> (accessed August 24, 2010).

63 R. Paz Ballivián (2007) 'Impacto de la asamblea constituyente en la coyuntura política boliviana 2006–2008', *Opiniones y análisis* 88, 47–70.

4 NEW POLITICS: IN SEARCH OF A WORKING RELATIONSHIP
BETWEEN THE STATE AND CIVIL SOCIETY

1   L. Whitehead (2001) 'Bolivia and the viability of democracy', *Journal of Democracy* 12(2), 6–16.

2   J. S. Dryzek (1990) *Discursive Democracy: Politics, policy and political science*. Cambridge: Cambridge University Press.

3   During this period MAS has won a number of other elections, including the nomination of constitutional assembly members in July 2006, the recall referendum of August 2008, approval of the new constitution in January 2009, the presidential election of December 2009, and local elections in April 2010.

4   The pains of a growing statehood and national identities are inextricably linked in a country like Bolivia, as are historical events such as the War of the Pacific (1879–80) and the Chaco War (1931–36). The collective national identity brought about by this experience explains the 1952 revolution that delivered, amongst other things universal suffrage, land reform and state-hegemonic forms of production. See J. de Mesa, T. Gisbert and C. Mesa (1999) *Historia de Bolivia*. La Paz: Editorial Gisbert.

5   D. Della Porta and M. Diani (1999) *Social Movements: An introduction*, Oxford: Blackwell; E. Jelin (2003) *Más allá de la nación: Las escalas múltiples de los movimientos sociales*, Buenos Aires: Libros del Zorzal; I. Rauber (2006) *Movimientos sociales y representación política*, La Paz: Fundación Boliviana para la democracia multipartidaria.

6   J. Crabtree (2005) *Patterns of Protest: Politics and social movements in Bolivia*. London: Latin American Bureau.

7   J. Gaventa (2006) 'Triumph, deficit or contestation? Deepening the 'deepening democracy' debate', IDS working paper no. 264, University of Sussex.

8   A. Chaplin (2010) 'Social movements in Bolivia: from strength to power', *Community Development Journal* 45(3), 346–55.

9   D. Green (1995) *Silent Revolution: The rise of market economics in Latin America*. London: Latin American Bureau.

10 R. Zibechi (2010) *América Latina: Contrainsurgencia y pobreza*. Bogotá: Desdeabajo. Zibechi argues that social movements are different in Latin America from the political category described by the same term in the Global North because in Latin America, social movements tend to have a territorial base and to practise non-capitalist social relations. Zibechi cites the case of the *ayllu* in the Bolivian highlands as an example of a type of community in which decision-making processes take place in counterhegemonic ways.

11 A. García Linera (2010) *La potencia plebeya: Acciones colectivas e identidades indígenas, obreras y populares en Bolivia*. La Paz: CLACSO.

12 M. Zuazo (2010) 'Los movimientos sociales en el poder? El gobierno del MAS en Bolivia', *Nueva Sociedad* 227 (May–June), 120–35.

13 M. Glasius (2010) 'Dissecting global civil society: values, actors, organisational forms', *Open Democracy*. Available on <www.open-democracy.net/5050/marlies-glasius/dissecting-global-civil-society-values-actors-organisational-forms> (accessed November 21, 2010).

14 M. Kaldor (2003) 'The idea of global civil society', *International Affairs* 79(3), 583–93.

15 M. Edwards and J. Gaventa (2001) *Global Citizen Action*. London: Earthscan.

16 M. Glasius, D. Lewis and H. Seckinelgin (eds) (2004) *Exploring Civil Society: Political and cultural contexts*. London: Routledge.

17 M. Mayo (2005) *Global Citizens, Social Movements and the Challenge of Globalisation*. London: Zed.

18 The literature on social movements is extensive. A quick survey includes D. Della Porta, H. Kriesi and D. Rucht (2009) *Social Movements in a Globalising World*, New York: Palgrave; J. Holst (2002) *Social Movements and Radical Education*, Westport, Conn.: Bergin & Garvey.

19 M. Barnes, J. Newman and H. Sullivan (2007) *Power, Participation and Political Renewal: Case studies in Public Participation*. Bristol: Policy Press.

20 The working definition offered in what has now become a Bolivian classic study of the country's social movements is indeed very similar. See A. García Linera, M. Chávez León and P. Costas Monje (2005) *Sociología de los movimientos sociales en Bolivia: Estructuras de movilización, repertorios culturales y acción política*. La Paz: Plural.

21 See for example C. D. Deere and M. León (2001) 'Institutional reform of agriculture under neoliberalism: the impact of women's and indigenous movements', *Latin American Research Review* 36(2), 31–63; W. Assies (2000) 'Land, territories, and indigenous peoples' rights', pp. 93–110 in A. Zoomers and G. van der Haar (eds), *Current Land Policy in Latin America: Regulating land tenure under neo-liberalism*, Amsterdam: KIT; A. Brysk (2000) *From Tribal Village to Global Village: Indian rights and international relations in Latin America*, Stanford, Calif.: Stanford University Press.

22 ILO (1989) *Convenio 169 de la O.I.T sobre pueblos indígenas y tribales en países independientes*. La Paz: Defensor del Pueblo. The ILO convention was ratified by Bolivia in 1991.

23 A. Escobar and S. Alvarez (1992) 'Theory and protest in Latin America today', pp. 1–18 in A. Escobar and S. Alvarez (eds) *The Making of Social Movements in Latin America: Identity, strategy and democracy*. Oxford: Westview.

24 See R. Albró (2005) 'The indigenous in the plural in Bolivia oppositional politics', *Bulletin of Latin American Research* 24(4), 433–53. See also X. Albó (2008) 'The "long memory" of ethnicity and some temporary oscillations', pp. 13–34 in J. Crabtree and L. Whitehead (eds) *Unresolved Tensions: Bolivia past and present*. Pittsburgh, Pa.: University of Pittsburgh Press.

25 The potential of the peasant as a revolutionary class became a promi-
    nent debate for a time in the 1960s during the Cuban Revolution and
    inspired Che Guevara's own attempts to spark revolutionary struggle
    in Bolivia.

26 See S. Rivera Cusicanqui (1990) 'Liberal democracy and ayllu democ-
    racy in Bolivia: the case of Northern Potosí', *Journal of Development
    Studies* 26(4), 97–121. On the other hand, García Linera is at pains
    to stress that often, the indigenous use of the term *sindicato* does not
    denote practices that are in any way dissimilar to traditional, solidarity-
    based forms of decision making, working the land and community life.
    See Linera et al. (2005).

27 X. Albó (2002) *Pueblos Indios en la Política.* La Paz: Plural Editores.

28 N. Fraser (1997) *Justice Interruptus. Critical reflections on the 'post-
    socialist' condition.* London and New York: Routledge. See also N.
    Fraser and A. Honneth (eds) (2003) *Redistribution or Recognition? A
    political-philosophical exchange.* New York: Verso.

29 Linera et al. (2005).

30 The militarisation of the tropics of Cochabamba that followed brought
    about the anti-imperialist and anti-US discourse that survives in MAS.
    See N. Lupu (2004) 'Towards a new articulation of alternative devel-
    opment: lessons from coca supply reduction in Bolivia', *Development
    Policy Review* 22(4), 405–21.

31 C. Espósito Guevara and W. Arteaga Aguilar (2007) *Movimientos
    sociales urbano-populares en Bolivia: Una lucha contra la exclusión
    social, económica y política.* La Paz: UNITAS.

32 G. Arrighi, T. Hopkins and I. Wallerstein (1997) *Antisystemic
    Movements.* London: Verso

33 CSUTCB is the oldest, having been created with the 1952 revolution.
    CONAMAQ was created in 1997 and CIDOB is the most recent.
    Indigenous peasant women are part of CNMCIOB 'BS', created in
    1980. Finally, the CSCIB represents a range of indigenous communities
    that have migrated within Bolivia.

34 P. Stefanoni and H. Do Alto (2007) 'The emergence of indigenous
    nationalism in Bolivia', pp. 29–35 in F. Polet (ed.), *The State of Resist-
    ance: Popular struggles in the Global South.* London and New York:
    Zed.

35 Whitehead (2001).

36 See R. O'Brien, A. M. Goetz, J. A. Scholte and M. Williams (2002)
    *Contesting Global Governance: Multilateral economic institutions
    and global social movements.* Cambridge: Cambridge University Press.
    Other examples of the way in which global civil society engages with,
    in this case, the United Nations system, include N. McKeon (2009)
    *The United Nations and Civil Society: Legitimating global governance
    – whose voice?* London: Zed.

37 J. Petras (1997) 'Imperialism and NGOs in Latin America', *Monthly
    Review* 49(7). Available on <www.monthlyreview.org/1297petr.htm>

(accessed December 3, 2010). See also G. Sandoval, J. Cordova, B. Ascarrunz, A. Balbóa, G. Gonzales and G. Velásquez (1998) 'Grass-roots organizations and local development in Bolivia: a study of the municipalities of Tiahuanacu, Mizque, Villa Serrano, and Charagua', Local Level Institutions working paper no. 4. Washington DC: World Bank.

38 B. Kohl (2003) 'Democratizing decentralization in Bolivia: the Law of Popular Participation', *Journal of Planning Education and Research*, 23, 153–64.

39 Kaldor (2003).

40 J. Petras and H. Veltmeyer (2005) *Social Movements and State Power: Argentina, Brazil, Bolivia, Ecuador*. London: Pluto, p. 4.

41 I. Farah (2008) 'Proceso político boliviano y rol de las ONG', pp. 55–74 in A. Chaplin and I. Farah (eds) *Fortalecimiento de la sociedad civil: Metodología para la medición de impacto*. La Paz: OXFAM-NOVIB.

42 C. Boulding and C. Gibson (2009) 'Supporters of challengers? The effects of non-governmental organisations in local politics in Bolivia', *Comparative Political Studies* 42(4), 479–500.

43 A. Main (2010) 'USAID: the bone of contention in US–Bolivia relations', Center for Economic and Policy Research. Available on <www.cepr.net/index.php/blogs/cepr-blog/usaid-bone-of-contention-in-us-bolivia-relations> (accessed December 14, 2010).

44 Ministerio de planificación de Bolivia (2006) Plan nacional de desarrollo 2006–2010. Available on <www.planificacion.gov.bo/BANNER/PARA%20PAG%20WEB/pnd1.html> (accessed December 9, 2010).

45 M. T. Zegada, Y. F. Torrez and G. Cámara (2008) *Movimientos sociales en tiempos de poder: Articulaciones y campos de conflicto en el gobierno del MAS*. La Paz: Centro Cuarto Intermedio.

46 A similar concern occupies the work of Hervé do Alto who has argued that 'The so-called "government of social movements" has more complex and pragmatic political origins than the official discourse would suggest; a power transfer has taken place from the plurinational assembly (with a strong indigenous presence) to an executive that coalesces around the figure of Morales; and fellow-travellers in the form of Bolivian NGO members constitute since 2005 a large percentage of the executive.' H. Do Alto (2011) 'Un partido campesino en el poder. Una mirada sociológica del MAS boliviano', *Nueva Sociedad* 234, 95–111.

47 Andean Information Network (2010) 'Potosí protest: resolved or postponed?', August 24. Available on <http://ain-bolivia.org/2010/08/potosi-protest-resolved-or-postponed> (accessed December 10, 2010).

48 R. Zibechi (2010) 'Bolivia and Ecuador: the state against the indigenous people', *Indigenous Policy Journal* 21(3). Available on <www.indigenouspolicy.org/ipjblog/post/Bolivia-and-Ecuador-The-State-Against-the-Indigenous-People.aspx> (accessed December 15, 2010).

49 Asamblea Constituyente (2008) Nueva Constitución política del estado. Versión oficial. La Paz: REPAC, p. 11.

50 CIDOB (2011) 'Carta de agradecimiento de la VIII marcha de los pueblos indígenas de tierras bajas del oriente, chaco, amazonia y CONAMQ', September 16. Available on <www.constituyentesober-ana.org/3/pronunciamientos/indic-pronun.html> (accessed September 17, 2011).

51 The Bolivian climate change platform was created in March 2009. It brings together representatives from Bolivia's social movements, national, and international NGOs to put forward legislative proposals for the implementation of the environmental principles of the Bolivian constitution. See Plataforma de Cambio Climático (2009) 'Declaración de la plataforma sobre cambio climático', March 18, La Paz. Available on <www.cambioclimatico.org.bo/hist/declaracion_plataforma.pdf> (accessed May 12, 2011).

52 Then again, as a 'government of the social movements', the Bolivian government ought to feel comfortable with the contribution of transnational civil society. The events of April 2010 in Cochabamba suggest that the Bolivian government was in fact rather displeased about the independently organised 'Table 18' to consider the country's challenges regarding climate change. See J. C. Aguirre and E. S. Cooper (n.d.) 'Evo Morales, climate change and the paradoxes of a social movement presidency.' Available on <www.latinamericanperspectives.com/exclu-sives_Aguirre%20and%20Cooper.html> (accessed June 25, 2011).

53 Associated Press (2011) 'Critics say environmentalist rhetoric of Bolivian president Evo Morales rings hollow', *Washington Post*, August 14. Available on <www.washingtonpost.com/world/americas/critics-say-environmentalist-rhetoric-of-bolivian-president-evo-morales-rings-hollow/2011/08/14/gIQAwmVFFJ_story.html> (accessed August 21, 2011).

54 Do Alto (2011), p. 106.

55 P. Regalsky (2010) 'Political processes and the reconfiguration of the state in Bolivia', *Latin American Perspectives* 37(3), 35–50.

56 Asamblea Constituyente (2008) Nueva Constitución, p. 29.

57 Glasius (2010).

58 J. Petras and H. Veltmeyer (2006) 'Social movements and the state: political power dynamics in Latin America', *Critical Sociology* 32(1), 83–104.

59 A. Garcia Linera (2011) *El 'Oenegismo', enfermedad infantil del derechismo*. La Paz: Vicepresidencia del estado plurinacional, pp. 11 and 12.

60 See S. Harten (2011) 'Towards a "traditional party"? Internal organisation and change in the MAS in Bolivia,' pp. 63–92 in A. J. Pearce (ed.), *Evo Morales and the Movimiento al Socialismo in Bolivia: The first term in context, 2006–2010*. London: Institute for the Study of the Americas. Focusing more on the ideological content of the MAS,

Webber has also argued that MAS has betrayed its indigenous ideo-logical origins to become a reformist party. See J. Webber (2011) *From Rebellion to Reform in Bolivia: Class struggle, indigenous liberation and the politics of Evo Morales.* Chicago: Haymarket.

5 NEW CITIZENS, WELFARE AND WELL-BEING

1 G. Hall and H. A. Patrinos (eds) (2006) *Indigenous Peoples, Poverty and Human Development in Latin America.* New York: Palgrave Macmillan.
2 Asamblea Constituyente (2008) Nueva Constitución política del estado. Versión oficial. La Paz: REPAC, p. 6.
3 The so-called 'Indian question' considered indigenous peoples an obstacle to modernity, a view reinforced by the 1952 revolution. See R. Stavenha-gen (2002) 'Indigenous peoples and the state in Latin America: an ongoing debate', pp. 22–44 in R. Siede (ed.), *Multiculturalism in Latin America: Indigenous rights, diversity and democracy.* New York: Palgrave.
4 C. Romero (2005) *El proceso constituyente boliviano: el hito de la cuarta marcha de tierras bajas.* Santa Cruz: CEJIS.
5 This violent episode could be seen as the last-ditch attempt against growing indigenous mobilisation in Bolivia and its demands for recog-nition of collective rights and self-determination. See N. Postero and L. Zamosc (2004) *The Struggle for Indigenous Rights in Latin America.* Eastbourne: Sussex Academic Press.
6 The thesis belongs to anthropologist Rivera Cusicanqui but has been recently discussed by other authors. See C. Hale and R. Millamán (2004) 'Rethinking indigenous politics in the era of the "indio permitido"', *NACLA Report on the Americas* 38(2), 16–21; J. McNeish (2008) 'Beyond the permitted Indian? Bolivia and Guate-mala in an era of neoliberal developmentalism', *Latin American and Caribbean Ethnic Studies* 3(1) (March), 33–59.
7 X. Albó (2008) 'The "long memory" of ethnicity in Bolivia and some temporary oscillations', pp. 13–34 in J. Crabtree and L. Whitehead (eds) *Unresolved Tensions: Bolivia past and present.* Pittsburgh, Pa.: University of Pittsburgh Press.
8 Interestingly, attempts to physically bar indigenous people from city centres were a dominant note of a number of conflicts in Cochabamba, Sucre and Santa Cruz during 2006–8.
9 N. Postero (2007) *Now We Are Citizens: Indigenous politics in post-multicultural Bolivia.* Stanford, Calif.: Stanford University Press.
10 Postero (2007), pp. 216–32.
11 C. Toranzo (2008) 'Let the mestizos stand up and be counted', pp. 35–50 in Crabtree and Whitehead.
12 See S. Roccas and M. B. Brewer (2002) 'Social identity complexity', *Personality and Social Psychology Review* 6, 88–106.

13   D. Zabaleta (2008) 'Oversimplifying identities: the debate over what is *indígena* and what is *mestizo*', pp. 51–60 in Crabtree and Whitehead.

14   See C. Armstrong (2002) 'Complex equality: beyond equality and difference', *Feminist Theory* 3(67), 67–81; M. Waltzer (1983) *Spheres of Justice: A defence of pluralism and equality*, Oxford: Robertson.

15   Asamblea Constituyente (2008) Nueva Constitución, pp.10–11.

16   Mainstream social policy concerns have traditionally focused solely in the relationship between the state and the market. Since the 1990s and in the development literature, a new paradigm that embraces civil society as a key sphere in the relationship has become widely accepted. See J. Howell and J. Pearce (2001) *Civil Society and Development: A critical exploration*. Boulder, Colo.: Lynne Rienner.

17   S. Lazar (2004) 'Education for credit: development as citizenship project in Bolivia', *Critique of Anthropology* 24(3), 301–319 (see p. 301).

18   T. Salman (2008) 'Reinventing democracy in Bolivia and Latin America', *European Review of Latin American and Caribbean Studies* 84(1), 87–99.

19   J. S. Tulchin and M. Ruthenburg (2006) *Citizenship in Latin America*. Boulder, Colo./London: Lynne Rienner. See also G. Gray Molina (2007) *El estado del Estado en Bolivia – Informe Nacional sobre Desarrollo Humano*, La Paz: UNDP / PNUD.

20   A resolution recognising drinking water and sanitation as a basic human right was adopted by the United Nations as a result of a Bolivian proposal on July 28, 2010. See United Nations (2010) 'General Assembly Adopts Resolution Recognizing Access to Clean Water, Sanitation as Human Right, by recorded vote of 122 in favour, none against, 41 abstentions'. Available on <www.un.org/News/Press/docs/2010/gal10967.doc.htm> (accessed October 1, 2010).

21   I refer to *suma qamaña* as a generic term that reflects indigenous conceptions of the good life. Article 8.1 of the Bolivian constitution recognises a number of those relevant to the country, including *ñandereko* (harmonious life), *teko kavi* (good life), *ivi maraei* (land without evil) and *qhapaj ñan* (noble life). Asamblea Constituyente (2008) Nueva Constitución, p. 6.

22   The reduction of 'well-feeling' rather than well-being to utility and the inbuilt assumption that economic success is a measure of utility has been roundly criticised for confusing utility with being well-off rather than well. See A. Sen (1985) *Commodities and Capabilities*. Cambridge: Cambridge University Press.

23   M. Max-Neef (1992) 'Development and human needs', pp. 197–214 in P. Ekins and M. Max-Neef (eds) *Real Life Economics: Understanding wealth creation*. London: Routledge.

24   See C. Gilligan (1982) *In a Different Voice: Psychological theory and women's development*. Cambridge, Mass.: Harvard University Press.

25   D. Temple (2001) 'La reciprocidad y el nacimiento de los valores

humanos', pp. 101–9 in J. Medina (ed.), *La comprensión indígena de la buena vida*. La Paz: Garza Azul.

26 F. Huanacuni Mamani (2010) *Vivir bien/Buen vivir: Filosofía, políticas, estrategias y experiencias regionales*. La Paz: Instituto internacional de integración-Convenio Andrés Bello.

27 Associated Press (2011) 'Critics say environmentalist rhetoric of Bolivian president Evo Morales rings hollow', *Washington Post*, August 14. Available on <www.washingtonpost.com/world/americas/critics-say-environmentalist-rhetoric-of-bolivian-president-evo-morales-rings-hollow/2011/08/14/gIQAwmVFFJ_story.html> (accessed August 21, 2011).

28 Of course there is a danger of romanticising an idealised form of indigenous practice, leading to recycled versions of the 'noble savage' thesis, as we are warned by K. Luyckx (2004) *Land, Livelihoods and Politics in Rural Lowland Bolivia: A comparative case study of two indigenous communities*, unpublished PhD thesis, University of Leeds. Whereas it is true that the afro Bolivian communities of Yungas received a collective land title in 2011 and the Ayoreo nation await theirs, some authors have explored the dominant tension between a discursive collectivism and the highly individualistic desires that dominate inside the Bolivian landless peasant movement. See N. Fabricant (2010) 'Between the romance of collectivism and the reality of individualism: *ayllu* rhetoric in Bolivia's landless peasant movement', *Latin American Perspectives* 37(4), 88–107.

29 K. Luyckx (2010) *Bolivia: Living well together*. London: CAFOD. Available on <http://blog.cafod.org.uk/2010/01/12/bolivia-living-well-together/> (accessed September 1, 2011).

30 J. Medina (2001) *La comprensión indígena de la buena vida*. La Paz: Garza Azul.

31 Ministerio de Planificación y Desarrollo de Bolivia (2006) Plan Nacional de Desarrollo 'Bolivia digna, soberana, productiva y democrática para Vivir Bien'. *Lineamientos estratégicos 2006–2011*. La Paz, pp. 1–7.

32 Article 8.1 of the new constitution establishes that the Bolivian state upholds the ethical and moral principles of *suma qamaña* and of the 'good life' enshrined in the knowledge of other indigenous nations. Article 8.2 commits the state to pursue values of social justice based on equality, inclusion, dignity, solidarity and redistribution in order to achieve the aim of 'living well'. Asamblea Constituyente (2008) Nueva Constitución, p. 6.

33 J.-P. Faguett (2004) 'Does decentralization increase government responsiveness to local needs? Evidence from Bolivia', *Journal of Public Economics* 88(3), 867–93.

34 C. Espósito and W. Arteaga (2006) *Movimientos sociales urbano-populares en Bolivia: una lucha contra la exclusión social, económica y política*. La Paz: UNITAS.

35 I. A. Goudsmit and J. Blackburn (2001) 'Participatory municipal planning in Bolivia: an ambiguous experience', *Development in Practice* 11(5), 587–96; J. A. McNeish (2006) 'Stones on the road: the politics of participation and the generation of crisis in Bolivia', *Bulletin of Latin American Research* 25(2), 220–40.

36 A. Zoomers (2006) 'Pro-indigenous reforms in Bolivia: is there an Andean way to escape poverty?' *Development and Change* 37(5), 1023–46.

37 Instituto Nacional de Estadística (INE) (2005) *Anuario estadístico*. La Paz: INE.

38 DFID (2005) 'Social transfers and chronic poverty: emerging evidence and challenges ahead', practice paper, October. London: DFID.

39 A. Barrientos et al. (2003) *Non-contributory Pensions and Poverty Prevention: A comparative study of Brazil and South Africa.* Manchester: IDPM and DFID.

40 Ministerio de Educación (2009) 'Bono Juancito Pinto: Para Universalizar la educación de los niños.' Available on <www.presidencia.gob.bo/documentos/bono%juancito%20pinto.pdf> (accessed August 12, 2011).

41 The maximum of Bvs1,820 can be reached if women attend four checks during pregnancy (Bvs 200), give birth in hospital (Bvs120) and take the child for bi-monthly checks and vaccinations for their first two years of life (Bvs1,250).

42 M. Bolivia Rothe (2009) 'Salud gratuita: El desafío del proceso', *Le Monde Diplomatique, edición boliviana* (Nov.), p. 6.

43 F. Chávez (2011) 'Bolivia: cash for checkups to slash maternal deaths'. *IPS News*, March 10. Available on <http://ipsnews.net/news.asp?idnews=50509> (accessed July 12, 2011).

44 A. Barrientos (2006) 'Pensions for development and poverty reduction', pp. 781–98 in G. L. Clark, A. H. Munnell and M. Orszag (eds) *Oxford Handbook of Pensions and Retirement Income.* Oxford: Oxford University Press,.

45 Servicios de Información y análisis de la Gestión Municipal (SIAM) (2008) *Boletín Informativo No. 3,* March. Federación de asociaciones municipales de Bolivia.

46 Ministerio de Hacienda (2007) 'IDH, Renta Dignidad y Bonosol: entrevista con el ministro de Hacienda Luis Arce', *Economía Al Día* 701 (October 23). Available on <www.hacienda.gov.bo/prensa/ecodia/Al_dia_701.pdf> (accessed August 12, 2009).

47 P. Lloyd-Sherlock and K. Artaraz (forthcoming 2012) 'Pension reform in Bolivia: two models of income security in old age', in K. Hudjo (ed.), *Reforming Pensions in Developing and Transition Countries.* Geneva: United Nations Research Institute for Social Development (UNRISD).

48 Carlos Arze, CEDLA, personal interview, August 4, 2010.

49 X. Mejia Bastos and C. Dusseau, C. (2008) 'Protección social para todos: por el derecho de las personas mayores a una pensión social, salud y trabajo dignos.' La Paz: HelpAge Internacional.

50   K. Müller (2008) 'Contested universalism: from Bonosol to Renta
     Dignidad in Bolivia', *International Journal of Social Welfare* 18(2),
     163–72.
51   F. Molina (2007) 'Biografía del Bonosol', pp. 21–38 in G. Aponte,
     J-C. Jemio, R. Laserna, F. Martínez, F. Molina and E. Skinner (eds) *La
     Inversión Prudente: Impacto del Bonosol sobre la familia, la equidad
     social y el crecimiento económico,* La Paz: Fundación Milenio,.
52   M. Ticona, vice-minister of pensions, personal interview, July 28,
     2010.
53   Asamblea Constituyente (2008) Nueva Constitución, p. 16.
54   Ministerio de Economía y Finanzas Públicas (2011) 'Beneficiarios de la
     Renta Dignidad, Bono Juancito pinto y Bono Juana Azurduy.' Avail-
     able on <www.economiayfinanzas.gob.bo/index.php?opcio=com_indic
     adores&ver=indicadores&idc=573> (accessed July 14, 2011).
55   L. Willmore (2007) 'Universal pensions for developing countries',
     World Development 35(1), 24-51.
56   E. Skinner (2007) 'Proteger y mejorar los medios de subsistencia de los
     adultos mayores: el rol del Bonosol en La Paz', pp. 145–76 in Aponte
     et al.
57   Fundación Jubileo (2008) 'La pobreza extrema afecta al 64% de
     la población rural', *Revista Jubileo* 13 (Nov.-Dec.), 2–3. Available
     on <www.jubileobolivia.org.bo/recursos/files/pdfs/Revista_Jubileo_13.
     pdf> (accessed July 1, 2011).
58   These figures have been quoted by vice-president García Linera citing
     UDAPE. See A. Garcia Linera (2011) 'El "Oenegismo", enfermedad
     infantil del derechismo', La Paz: Vicepresidencia del estado plurinacio-
     nal, pp. 14–24.
59   UDAPE (2010) *Dosier de estadísticas sociales y económicas 2010.* Vol.
     20 (Dec.) La Paz: UDAPE. Available on <www.udape.gob.bo/portales_
     html/dossierweb2010/dossier20.htm> (accessed July 12, 2011).
60   P. Riggirozzi (2010) 'Social policy in post-neo-liberal Latin America:
     the cases of Argentina, Venezuela and Bolivia', *Development* 53(1),
     70–7.
61   J. Medina (2000) 'Repensar la pobreza en una sociedad no occidental',
     La Paz: Ministerio de Hacienda, p. 12.

6 NEW ECONOMICS: THE PROMISE AND THE LIMITS OF POST-NEOLIBERAL DEVELOPMENT

1   J. Martí (2001) *Obras completas,* Vol. 6, p. 154. *La Habana* : Centro
     de Estudios Martinianos (CEM).
2   A. Buick, J. Crump and J. O'Neill (1988) 'State capitalism: the wages
     system under new management', *Political Quarterly* 59(3), 398–9.
3   This figure includes external debt to international creditors, as well as
     internal debt and the cost of servicing that debt. See G. Hurley (n.d.)

'Bolivia update on debt issue', Eurodad Secretariat. Available on <www.choike.org/documentos/gail_report.pdf> (accessed June 29, 2011). Bolivia is a heavily indebted poor country (HIPC) as classified by the IMF and the World Bank. In 2005 these institutions began a process of debt relief for HIPC countries with the objective of contributing to their development and achievement of the Millennium Development Goals (MDGs) by 2015. A new initiative by a number of countries, the Multilateral Debt Relief Initiative (MDRI), aimed to further reduce the debt burden. See J. Fajgenbaum and A. MacArthur (2008) *External and Public Debt Sustainability Analysis*, International Monetary Fund Bolivia. Available on <www.imf.org/external/pubs/ft/dsa/pdf/dsacr0927.pdf> (accessed June 29, 2011); N. Buxton (2008) 'Economic strings: the politics of foreign debt', pp. 145–80 in J. Shultz and M. Crane Draper (eds), *Dignity and Defiance: Stories from Bolivia's challenge to globalisation*, Berkeley, Calif.: University of California Press.

4   The Human Development Index is a composite measure of a number of human well-being indicators that includes measures of health, income and education. See UNDP (2010) *International Human Development Indicators*. Available on <http://hdrstats.undp.org/en/countries/profiles/BOL.html> (accessed July 12, 2011).

5   In 2005 the levels of poverty were by no means the highest during the neoliberal period. These peaked in 1986 and again in 2000. In addition, the headline figure of 38 per cent hides the enormous inequalities in distribution between the rural areas, where 62 per cent of the population lived in extreme poverty, and the urban ones where 'only' a quarter of the population did so. See Fundación Jubileo (2010) 'La pobreza alcanza su nivel más bajo en una década pero existe el riesgo de que los logros no sean sostenibles', *Fundación Jubileo?* 16 (Jan–Feb), 3.

6   Ministerio de Planificación y Desarrollo (2010) Plan Vida para la erradicación de la extrema pobreza. La Paz.

7   See UNDP (2010) *Human Development Report 2010*. Available on <http://hdr.undp.org/en/media/HDR_2010_EN_Table13_reprint.pdf> (accessed June 12, 2011).

8   Instituto Nacional de Estadística (INE) (2010) *Bolivia: Indicadores de Pobreza*. Available on <www.ine.gov.bo/indice/visualizador.aspx?ah=PC3060101.htm> (accessed August 20, 2010).

9   Ministerio de planificación de Bolivia (2006) *Plan nacional de desarrollo 2006–2010*. Available on <www.planificacion.gov.bo/BANNER/PARA%20PAG%20WEB/pnd1.html> (accessed October 14, 2010).

10   A. García Linera (2008) 'Los tres pilares de la nueva constitución política del estado. Discursos y ponencias del ciudadano vicepresidente Álvaro García Linera.' Discurso en la sede del CSUTCB, 4 Nov. La Paz: Vicepresidencia de la República.

11   K. Weyland (2009) 'The rise of Latin America's two lefts: insights from rentier state theory', *Comparative Politics* 41(2), 145–64.

12   Asamblea Constituyente (2008) Nueva Constitución política del estado. Versión oficial. La Paz: REPAC.

13   A. García Linera (2008) 'El Nuevo Modelo Nacional Productivo.' *Revista de Análisis: Reflexiones sobre la coyuntura* 2, 3–18.

14   EFE (2011) 'Bolivia creates company to industrialise natural gas', *Latin American Herald Tribune*, Caracas, July 4. Available on <www.laht.com/article.asp?CategoryId=14919&ArticleId=348019> (accessed July 12, 2011).

15   R. Carroll and A. Schipani (2009) 'Multinationals eye up lithium reserves beneath Bolivia's salt flats', *Guardian,* June 17. Available on <www.guardian.co.uk/world/2009/jun/17/bolivia-lithium-reserves-electric-cars> (accessed June 12, 2011).

16   Asamblea Constituyente (2008) Nueva Constitución.

17   T. Mkandawire (2001) *Social Policy in a Development Context.* Geneva: UNRISD.

18   R. Thiele (2001) 'The social impact of structural adjustment in Bolivia', Kiel working paper no. 1056. Kiel: Kiel Institute of World Economics.

19   IMF (2011) 'Bolivia', IMF country report no. 11/124, June 2. Washington DC: IMF. Available on <www.imf.org/external/pubs/ft/scr/2011/cr11124.pdf> (accessed July 14, 2011).

20   L. Sykes (2007) 'Resolving the Bolivian gas crisis: lessons from Bolivia's brush with international arbitration', *George Washington International Law Review* 39, 947.

21   It is important to note that whereas the language of nationalisation has been consistently used by the Bolivian state, this was no nationalisation in the strict sense of the word, but a buyout at market prices that included compensation to the TNCs for their losses. As a result, no TNCs have stopped operating in the country since the arrival of MAS in power. See B. Z. Kaup (2010) 'A neoliberal nationalisation? The constraints on natural-gas-led development in Bolivia', *Latin American Perspectives* 37(3), 123–38.

22   Fundación Jubileo (2011) 'Análisis del presupuesto general del estado 2011', Reporte de coyuntura no. 13. Fundación Jubileo. Available on <www.jubileobolivia.org.bo/recursos/files/pdfs/AC13Analisis_PGN_2011.pdf> (accessed July 1, 2011).

23   R. Rojas (2008) 'Nacionaliza Bolivia la telefónica Entel y recupera control de los hidrocarburos', May 2. Available on <www.jornada.unam.mx/2008/05/02/index.php?section=economia&article=022n1ec o> (accessed June 12, 2011).

24   I. Mansfield (2010) 'Telecom Italia compensated for Bolivian expropriation', November 10. Available on <www.cellular-news.com/story/46381.php> (accessed July 15, 2011).

25   D. Ore and E. Garcia (2010) 'Bolivia nationalizes four power companies', *Washington Post*, May 2. Available on <www.washingtonpost.com/wp-dyn/content/article/2010/05/01/AR2010050102858.html> (accessed July 12, 2011). In the case of the British Rurelec plc and its

British subsidiary Guaracachi America Inc (GAI), the forced nationalisation of a controlling state of its shares led to the company launching a claim for compensation at the international arbitration court which continues unresolved.

26 S. Romig (2011) 'Bolivia's plan to nationalise mines hits a snag', *Inter American Security Watch*, April 21. Available on <http://interameri­cansecuritywatch.com/bolivias-plan-to-nationalize-mines-hits-snag/> (accessed July 12, 2011). In the case of Glencore's Vinto tin smelter, the company and the government of Bolivia have been embroiled in a bitter dispute since 2007.

27 W. Vásquez (2011) 'Planta Urea-Carrasco exportará 90% de su producción desde el 2015', *La Razón*, July 10, p. 12.

28 R. Hollender and J. Shultz (2010) 'Bolivia and its lithium: can the 'gold of the 21st century' help lift a nation out of poverty?' Democracy Centre Special Report. Available on <http://democracyctr.org/pdf/DClithiumenglishexecutivesummary.pdf> (accessed July 15, 2011).

29 Comibol (2011) 'Inspección presidencial de la planta piloto de industrialización de los recursos evaporíticos', April 19. Available on <www.evaporiticosbolivia.org/> (accessed June 12, 2011).

30 IMF (2011), p. 2.

31 See E. Morales (2008) '42 days? Try 18 months', *Guardian*, June 16. Available on <www.guardian.co.uk/commentisfree/2008/jun/16/eu.immigration> (accessed July 14, 2011). Others have put this figure as high as 7.4 per cent of GDP at its highest in 2007, having fallen to as low as 5 per cent in 2009. See M. Weisbrot, R. Ray and J. Johnston (2009) 'Bolivia: the economy during the Morales administration', December, p. 29. Washington DC: Center for Economic and Policy Research (CEPR). Available on <www.cepr.net/documents/publications/bolivia-2009-12.pdf> (accessed June 30, 2011).

32 IMF (2011), p. 8.

33 F. Chavez (2010) 'Bolivia: private sector gives way under government's public sector push', *Bolivia Rising*, October 8. Available on <http://boliviarising.blogspot.com/search/label/economy> (accessed July 12, 2011).

34 América Economía (2011) 'INE: exportaciones bolivianas cierran con ventas por US$6.956M en 2010', *America Economía*, January 27. Available on <www.americaeconomia.com/economia-mercados/finan­zas/ine-exportaciones-bolivianas-cierran-con-ventas-por-us6956m-en-2010> (accessed June 12, 2011).

35 The increase in prices was argued by the government to be necessary because the current subsidy is so great that the gap between the international price of oil and Bolivian prices act as a disincentive to increased production for internal consumption and encourages contraband. See Information Forum (2011) 'To the brink, and back again', BIF Special Briefing, January. Available on <www.boliviainfoforum.org.uk/documents/71858759_BIF%20Briefing%20January%202011.pdf> (accessed July 12, 2011).

36   Ministerio de Economía y Finanzas Públicas (2011) 'Superávit fiscal del sistema público no financiero.' Available on <www.economiayfinanzas. gob.bo/index.php?opcion=com_indicadores&ver=indicadores&idc=56 7> (accessed July 14, 2011).

37   Weisbrot et al. (2009).

38   Ministerio de Economía y Finanzas Públicas (2011) 'Reservas Internacionales netas del BCB.' Available from <www.economiayfinanzas. gob.bo/index.php?opcion=com_indicadores&ver=indicadores&idc=56 1> (accessed July 12, 2011).

39   IMF (2005) 'IMF to extend 100 per cent debt relief for 19 countries under the multilateral debt relief initiative', press release no. 05/286, December 21. Available on <www.imf.org/external/np/sec/pr/2005/ pr05286.htm> (accessed June 12, 2011).

40   Fundación Jubileo (2010) 'Estado de la deuda externa de Bolivia', Reporte de coyuntura no. 11, Fundación Jubileo. Available on <www.jubile-obolivia.org.bo/recursos/files/pdfs/REPORTE_COYUNTURA_N_11_ DEUDA_EXTERNA.pdf> (accessed July 1, 2011).

41   A. García Linera (2008) 'Del liberalismo al Modelo Nacional Productivo: Los ciclos de la economía boliviana', *Revista de Análisis: Reflexiones sobre la coyuntura* 3, 5–21.

42   Kaup (2010).

43   J. Colloque and P. Poveda (2010) 'Hegemonía transnacional en la minería boliviana', *Le Monde Diplomatique*, no. 28 (August), 4–7.

44   R. Jordan (2010) *La generación, distribución del excedente y renta en la minería mediana y determinantes del crecimiento minero 2000– 2009*. La Paz: PIEB.

45   F. Wanderley (2005) 'La construcción de ciudadanía económica. El desafío del nuevo modelo de desarrollo económico', *T'inkazos* 18, 31–52.

46   F. Wanderley (2008) 'Beyond gas: between the narrow-based and broad-based economy', pp.194–212 (see p. 209) in J. Crabtree and L. Whitehead (eds) *Unresolved Tensions: Bolivia past and present.* Pittsburgh, Pa.: University of Pittsburgh Press.

47   C. Miranda (2008) 'Gas and its importance to the Bolivian economy', pp. 177–93 in Crabtree and Whitehead.

48   Kaup (2010).

49   Santos Ramirez was a close political ally of President Morales and head of YPFB. In January 2009 he was accused of receiving bribes from a company that had been awarded a multimillion-dollar deal by YPFB. The affair was politically costly to MAS. On a broader level, it shows the difficulties that resource-rich countries have in dealing with corruption. See C. Leite and J. Weidmann (1999) 'Does Mother Nature corrupt? Natural resources, corruption and economic growth', working paper no. WP/99/85. Washington DC: IMF.

50   E. Cerutti and M. Mansilla (2008) 'Bolivia: the hydrocarbons boom and the risk of Dutch disease', working paper no. 08/154. Washington DC: IMF.

51 J. Vidal (2009) 'Evo Morales stunts Copenhagen with demand to limit temperature rise to 1C', *Guardian*, December 16. Available on <www.guardian.co.uk/environment/2009/dec/16/evo-morales-hugo-chavez> (accessed May 19, 2011).

52 Associated Press (2011) 'Critics say environmentalist rhetoric of Bolivian president Evo Morales rings hollow', *Washington Post*, August 14. Available on <www.washingtonpost.com/world/americas/criticssay-environmen talist-rhetoric-of-bolivian-president-evo-morales-rings-hollow/2011/08/14/gIQAwmVFFJ_story.html> (accessed August 21, 2011).

53 See R. Moran (2008) 'Minando el Agua: La mina San Cristóbal, Bolivia', FRUTCAS. Available on <www.constituyentesoberana.org/3/destacados/122009/181209_1.pdf> (accessed July 12, 2011). Other social and environmental costs have been denounced by those opposing the construction of a mega hydroelectric project, Cachuela Esperanza, whose main objective would be to sell electricity to Brazil. See also X. Albó (2011) 'Carreteras, indígenas y vivir bien', *Bolivia Rural*. Available on <www.boliviarural.org/index.php?option=com_content&view=article&id=1050&catid=56&Itemid=67> (accessed July 12, 2011).

54 A. Goodman (2010) 'UN declares water a fundamental human right – US abstains from voting on resolution', Alternet, August 1. Available on <www.alternet.org/water/147704/un_declares_water_a_funda mental_human_right_--_u.s._abstains_from_voting_on_resolution/> (accessed July 12, 2011).

55 See Albó (2011).

56 Kaup (2010).

57 J. Webber (2011) *From Rebellion to Reform in Bolivia: Class struggle, indigenous liberation and the politics of Evo Morales*. Chicago, Ill.: Haymarket.

7 BOLIVIAN–US RELATIONS: BREAKING THE STRANGLEHOLD

1 P. McDonnell (2008) 'Bolivia orders US envoy's expulsion', *Los Angeles Times,* September 11. Available on <http://articles.latimes.com/2008/sep/11/world/fg-bolivia11> (accessed July 12, 2011).

2 J. Borger (2002) 'War on terror may extend to Cuba', *Guardian*, May 7. Available on <www.guardian.co.uk/world/2002/may/07/cuba.usa> (accessed July 15, 2011).

3 N. Davis (1985) *The Last Two Years of Salvador Allende*. Ithaca, N.Y.: Cornell University Press.

4 G. C. Herring (2008) *From Colony to Superpower: U.S. foreign relations since 1776*. Oxford: Oxford University Press.

5 J. Sexton (2011) *The Monroe Doctrine: Empire and nation in nineteenth-century America*. New York: Hill & Wang.

6 P. Turton (1986) *José Martí: architect of Cuba's freedom*. London: Zed.

7   V. I. Lenin (1966) *Imperialism: The highest stage of capitalism*, 13th edn. Moscow: Progress.

8   P. Jalee (1968) *The Pillage of the Third World*. New York: Monthly Review Press.

9   W. Robinson (2008) *Latin America and Global Capitalism: A critical globalization perspective*. Baltimore, Md.: Johns Hopkins University Press.

10   J. Domínguez (1999) 'U.S.–Latin American relations during the cold war and its aftermath', working paper 99–01, Weatherhead Centre for International Affairs, Harvard University.

11   The quote was published by the *New York Times* on June 1, 1969. It has been widely reproduced since.

12   N. Chomsky (2004) *Hegemony or Survival: America's quest for global dominance*. London and New York: Penguin.

13   K. Lehman (1999) *Bolivia and the United States: A limited partnership*. Athens, Ga.: University of Georgia Press.

14   G. Smith (1994) *The Last Years of the Monroe Doctrine, 1945–1993*. New York: Hill & Wang.

15   S. Lukes (1974) *Power: A radical view*. London: Macmillan. In this classic study, Lukes outlines a third dimension through which to theorise power, exploring as a prelude to the work of Foucault the ways in which unconscious thought, actions and values can represent the ultimate exercise in power. In very different contexts, the work of Ariel Dorfman and Edward Said has also explored power relations at the level of ideas, values and cultural products that could apply to the case of the United States and Latin America. See A. Dorfman and A. Mattelard (1971) *Para leer al pato Donald*, Valparaiso: Ediciones universitarias de Valparaiso; E. Said (1978) *Orientalism*, New York: Random House.

16   J. Shultz (2008) 'Lessons in blood and fire: the deadly consequences of IMF economics', pp. 117–44 in J. Shultz and M. Crane Draper (eds) (2009) *Dignity and Defiance: Stories from Bolivia's challenge to globalisation*. Berkeley, Calif.: University of California Press.

17   B. Kohl and L. Farthing (2009) '"Less than fully satisfactory development outcomes": international financial institutions and social unrest in Bolivia', *Latin American Perspectives* 36(3), 59–78.

18   W. Robinson (1996) *Promoting Polyarchy: Globalization, US intervention and hegemony*. Cambridge: Cambridge University Press.

19   P. H. Smith (1999) *Talons of the Eagle: Dynamics of U.S.–Latin American relations*. Oxford: Oxford University Press.

20   Modernisation theory effectively assumed that economic growth would act as an antidote to communism in the region. Its policy embodiment, the Alliance for Progress, has been compared to a Marshall Plan for Latin America although it never had the same degree of economic or political backing. See W. Rostow (1991) *The Stages of Economic Growth: A non-communist manifesto*, 3rd edn. Cambridge: Cambridge University Press.

21 J. Taffet (2007) *Foreign Aid as Foreign Policy: The Alliance for Progress in Latin America.* London: Routledge.

22 J. Siekmeier (2011) *The Bolivian Revolution and the United States, 1952 to the Present.* University Park, Pa.: Penn State Press.

23 J. Dunkerley (1984) *Rebellion in the Veins: Political struggle in Bolivia 1952–1982.* London: Verso.

24 L. Gill (2004) *The School of the Americas: Military training and political violence in the Americas.* Durham, N.C.: Duke University Press.

25 R. Debray (1968) *Revolution in the Revolution? Armed struggle and political struggle in Latin America.* Harmondsworth: Penguin.

26 J. L. Anderson (1997) *Che Guevara: A revolutionary life.* London: Quality Paperbacks Direct, pp. 701–39.

27 J. De Mesa, T. Gisbert and C. Mesa Gisbert (1999) *Historia de Bolivia.* La Paz: Editorial Gisbert.

28 C. A. Youngers and E. Rosin (2005) *Drugs and Democracy in Latin America: The impact of US policy.* Boulder, Colo.: Lynne Rienner.

29 Luis García Meza went into exile but was eventually extradited from Brazil in 1995 and sentenced to 30 years imprisonment, which he is currently still serving in Bolivia.

30 W. L. Rensselaer (1989) *The White Labyrinth: Cocaine and political power.* New Brunswick: Transaction, p. 119.

31 A. Canelas Orellana and J. C. Canelas Zannier (1983) *Bolivia, Coca, Cocaína: Subdesarrollo y poder político.* Cochabamba: Los amigos del libro.

32 C. Conzelman, C. Youngers, J. Shultz, C. Esch, L. Olivera and L. Farthing (2008) 'Coca: the leaf at the center of the War on Drugs', pp. 181–212 in Shultz and Draper (2009).

33 *El tio* is the name given to a spiritual dweller in a mine, and is associated with the Christian devil. A small statue representing *el tio* is normally placed in work areas inside Bolivian mines where ritual offerings of alcohol, tobacco and coca leaves are made. See R. Godoy (1985) 'Mining: anthropological perspectives', *Annual Review of Anthropology* 14, 199–217.

34 F. Hylton and S. Thompson (2007) *Revolutionary Horizons: Past and present in Bolivian politics.* London and New York: Verso.

35 J. Painter (1994) *Bolivia and Coca: A study in dependency.* Boulder, Colo.: Lynne Rienner.

36 A. Rossi (2009) 'Militarizacion y 'cooperacion' militar', *Le Monde Diplomatique, edición boliviana* (Sept.), 10–12.

37 The revolutionary cycle that culminated in 2003 with the so called Gas War essentially erupted in opposition to government plans to export Bolivian gas through Chile. See R. Salazar Pérez (2002) 'Los avatares del plan Colombia, plan dignidad y el plan Puebla Panamá', *Convergencia* 30(3), 97–120. Available on <http://redalyc.uaemex.mx/src/inicio/ArtPdfRed.jsp?iCve=10503006> (accessed June 12, 2011).

38   R. Boucher (2000) 'The United States supports Bolivia's *Plan Digni-dad*', US State Department, September 29. Available on <www.fas.org/irp/news/2000/09/irp-000929-bolivia.htm> (accessed June 12, 2011).

39   P. Stefanoni and H. do Alto (2006) *Evo Morales, de la coca al palacio*. La Paz: Malatesta.

40   E. Gamarra (2007) 'Bolivia on the brink', report no. 24, February. New York Council on Foreign Relations, Centre for Preventive Action.

41   M. Sivak (2011) 'The Bolivianisation of Washington-La Paz relations: Evo Morales's foreign policy agenda in historical context', pp.143–74 in A. J. Pearce (ed.) *Evo Morales and the Movimiento al Socialismo in Bolivia: The first term in context 2006–2010*. London: Institute for the Study of the Americas and Bolivian Information Forum.

42   The timely intervention from UNASUR which expressed its full support for the democratic process was credited at the time by the Bolivian government for preventing the escalation of the insurrec-tion. See Reuters (2008) 'Boliviano Morales critica EEUU', September 23. Available on <http://lta.reuters.com/article/domesticNews/idLTAS-IE48N06820080924> (accessed August 12, 2011).

43   P. Worsnip (2008) 'Bolivia's Morales seeks better ties with Obama', Reuters, November 17. Available on <www.reuters.com/article/2008/11/17/us-bolivia-morales-un-idUS TRE4AG7ET20081117> (accessed June 30, 2011).

44   B. Obama (2009) 'Official remarks by US President Barack Obama at the opening of the fifth Summit of the Americas', April 18. Avail-able on <http://fifthsummitoftheamericas.org/official_statements.htm> (accessed August 17, 2011).

45   Asamblea Constituyente (2008) Nueva Constitución política del estado. Versión oficial. La Paz: REPAC, p. 7.

46   Nueva Constitución, p. 66.

47   A. Howard (2009) 'Bolivia: Hillary Clinton and James Steinberg talk tough on Latin America', Council on Hemispheric Affairs, Febru-ary 4. Available on <www.coha.org/bolivia-hillary-clinton-and-james-steinberg-%E2%80%9Ctalk-tough%E2%80%9D-on-latin-america/> (accessed August 12, 2011).

48   The report on Human Rights in Bolivia can be found on the La Paz US embassy website. See <http://spanish.bolivia.usembassy.gov/inf2009.html> (accessed August 12, 2011).

49   J. Walsh (2009) *U.S. Decertification of Bolivia: A blast from the past*, p. 1. Washington DC: Washington Office on Latin America (WOLA), September 17. Available on <www.wola.org/news/us_decertification_of_bolivia_a_blast_from_the_past> (accessed July 14, 2011).

50   L. Skeen (2010) 'Dubious progress in Bolivia-U.S. reconciliation', North American Congress on Latin America (NACLA), July 19. Avail-able on <https://nacla.org/node/6668> (accessed July 12, 2011).

51   C. Youngers (2011) 'U.S. renews anachronistic campaign to stamp out coca leaf chewing', *Foreign Policy in Focus*, January 14. Available on <www.

fpif.org/blog/us_renews_anachronistic_campaign_to_stamp_out_coca_
leaf_chewing?utm_source=feedburner&utm_medium=feed&utm_cam
paign=Feed%3A+FPIF+%28Foreign+Policy+In+Focus+%28All+News
%29%29> (accessed August 17, 2011).

52 M. Jelsma (2011) 'Bolivia's denunciation of the 1961 Single Conven-
    tion on Narcotic Drugs', Transnational Institute, June 30. Available
    on <www.druglawreform.info/en/issues/unscheduling-the-coca-leaf/
    item/2596-bolivias-denunciation-of-the-1961-single-convention-on-
    narcotic-drugs-> (accessed July 1, 2011).

53 C. Torrens (2011) 'Morales: Actitud impositiva de EEUU impide
    acuerdo con Bolivia', El Nuevo Herald, August 1. Available on <www.
    elnuevoherald.com/2011/07/27/991770/actitud-impositiva-de-eeuu-
    impide.html> (accessed August 2, 2011).

54 Sivak (2011), p. 147.

55 The argument has been put by Jorge Castañeda in relation to the appar-
    ent failure of the United States to act in the Honduran crisis of 2009.
    See J. Castañeda (2009) 'Adios Monroe Doctrine: when the Yanquis go
    home', The New Republic, December 28. Available on <www.tnr.com/
    article/world/adios-monroe-doctrine> (accessed August 7, 2011).

56 M. Weisbrot (2011) 'Latin America shakes off the US yoke. The current
    spat with Ecuador is symptomatic of Washington's failure to grasp that
    it no longer exercises regional hegemony', Guardian, April 8. Avail-
    able on <www.guardian.co.uk/commentisfree/cifamerica/2011/apr/08/
    venezuela-ecuador> (accessed June 29, 2011).

8 BOLIVIA'S PLACE IN LATIN AMERICA

1 J. Vidal (2009) 'We are fighting for our lives and our dignity',
   Guardian, June 13. Available on <www.guardian.co.uk/environment/
   2009/jun/13/forests-environment-oil-companies (accessed May 6,
   2010).

2 J. Triana (2006) 'La crisis de la Comunidad Andina de Naciones',
   Divergencia, no. 5. Available on<http://portal.uexternado.edu.co/irj/
   go/km/docs/doc ... ero5/jennyTriana.pdf> (accessed May 8, 2010).

3 Asamblea Constituyente (2008) Nueva Constitución política del
   estado. Versión oficial. La Paz: Representación presidencial para la
   asamblea constituyente (REPAC).

4 E. Menéndez del Valle (2008) 'Bolivia: el ejemplo positivo de UNASUR',
   El País, October 15. Available on <www.comunidadandina.org/prensa/
   articulos/elpais15-10-08.htm> (accessed May 6, 2010).

5 F. Kaltenthaler and F. Mora (2002) 'Explaining Latin American
   economic integration: the case of Mercosur', Review of International
   Political Economy 9(1), 72–97.

6 R. Álvarez Valdés (2009) 'UNASUR: Desde la perspectiva subregional
   a la regional', Programa Seguridad y ciudadanía. FLACSO, Santiago

de Chile. Available on <www.comunidadandina.org/unasur/unasur_rodrigo_alvarez%28flacso%29.pdf> (accessed May 6, 2010).

7   UNASUR (2008) 'Tratado constitutivo de la unión de naciones suramericanas.' Available on <www.comunidadandina.org/unasur/tratado_constitutivo.htm> (accessed May 18, 2010).

8   Cumbre social de los pueblos (2006) 'Comunidad Sudamericana de Naciones: Para "Vivir Bien" Sin Neoliberalismo. Llamamiento y propuestas desde la visión de los pueblos indígenas y naciones originarias. Cochabamba.' Available on<www.comunidadandina.org/unasur/llamamiento_cochabamba.htm> (accessed May 14, 2010).

9   Amnesty International (2009) 'Bolivia: Victims of the Pando massacre still await justice.' Available on <www.amnesty.org/en/for-media/press-releases/bolivia-victims-pando-massacre-still-await-justice-20090909> (accessed May 23, 2010).

10 B. Fernández (2010) 'Honduras one year later', *Upside Down World* (June 27). Available on <http://upsidedownworld.org/main/honduras-archives-46/2562-honduras-one-year-later-> (accessed September 12, 2011).

11 F. Fukuyama (1992) *The End of History and the Last Man*. London: Penguin.

12 J. Partlow (2008) 'Ecuador giving US air base the boot', *Washington Post*, September 4. Available on <www.washingtonpost.com/wp-dyn/content/article/2008/09/03/AR2008090303289.htm> (accessed May 23, 2010).

13 F. Solanas (2004) *Memoria del saqueo* (Social Genocide). Argentina: Cinesur.

14 T. Benner, W. H. Reinicke and J. M. Witte (2004) 'Multisectoral networks in global governance: towards a pluralistic system of accountability', *Government and Opposition* 1, 191–210.

15 J. Smith (2009) 'Solidarity networks: what are they and why should we care', *The Learning Organisation* 16(6):, 460–8. Available on <www.emeraldinsight.com/Insight/viewContentItem.do;jsessionid=3F0962E30A1D12F33E9ED88F263EBEF6?contentType=Article&contentId=1812399> (accessed November 28, 2009).

16 G. Palast (2003) 'Chavez versus the free trade zombies of the Americas.' Available on <www.venezuelanalysis.com/analysis/251> (accessed March 2010).

17 J. Holloway and E. Peláez (1998) *Zapatista! Reinventing revolution in Mexico*. London: Pluto.

18 M. I. Saguier (2007) 'The Hemispheric Social Alliance and the Free Trade Area of the Americas Process: the challenges and opportunities of transnational coalitions against neo-liberalism', *Globalizations* 4(2), 251–65.

19 K. Janicke (2008) 'Summit of the Bolivarian Alternative (ALBA) concludes in Venezuela', *Global Research*. Available on <www.globalresearch.ca/index.php?context=va&aid=7935> (accessed March 2010).

20 Saguier (2007).

21 B. Brennan and C. Olivet (2007) 'Regionalism's futures: the challenges for civil society', *Global Social Policy* 7(3), 267–70.

22 X. de la Barra and R. A. Dello Buono (2009) *Latin America after the Neoliberal Debacle: Another region is possible*. Lanham, Md.: Rowman & Littlefield.

23 Smith (2009).

24 C. Katz (2006) *The Redesign of Latin America: FTAA, MERCOSUR and ALBA*. Buenos Aires: Ediciones Luxemburgo.

25 R. Munck (2006) 'Global civil society: royal road or slippery path?', *Voluntas* 17, 325–32 (see p. 331).

26 J. Briceño Ruiz (2007) 'Strategic regionalism and regional social policy in the FTAA process', *Global Social Policy* 7(3), 294–315.

27 Ministerio de planificación de Bolivia (2006) *Plan nacional de desarrollo 2006–2010*. Available on <www.planificacion.gov.bo/BANNER/PARA%20PAG%20WEB/pnd1.html> (accessed October 14, 2007).

28 R. Bossi (2009) 'Que es el ALBA? Construyendo el ALBA desde los pueblos.' Available on <www.alianzabolivariana.org/modules.php?name=News&file=article&sid=470> (accessed March 2010).

29 This section draws from research that has been published in K. Artaraz (2011) 'New Latin American networks of solidarity?' *Global Social Policy* 11(1), 88–105.

30 S. Van Gelder (2007) 'Por qué Cuba exporta asistencia medica a los pobres del mundo?' ALBA. Available on <www.alternativabolivariana.org/modules.php?name=News&file=article&sid=2041> (accessed October 2007).

31 J. Kirk and M. Erisman (2009) *Cuban Medical Internationalism: Origins, evolution and goals*. New York: Palgrave Macmillan.

32 J. Feinsilver (1993) *Healing the Masses: Cuban health politics at home and abroad*. Berkeley, Calif.: University of California Press.

33 J. Nye (2004) *Soft Power: The means to success in world politics*. New York: Public Affairs. Nye's concept has been applied to the Cuban case in S. Clemons (2009) 'Cuba's soft power. Exporting doctors rather than revolution', *Huffington Post*. Available on <www.huffingtonpost.com/steve-clemons/cubas-soft-power-exportin_b_355373.html> (accessed January 12, 2011).

34 N. Heredia, Bolivian health minister, personal interview, July 7, 2009.

35 Telesur (2010) 'Operación Milagro realizó medio millón de cirugías oftalmológicas en Bolivia', March 19. Available on <www.telesurtv.net/noticias/secciones/nota/68719/operacion-milagro-realizo-medio-millon-de-cirugias-oftalmologicas-en-bolivia/> (accessed March 30, 2010).

36 Bolpress (2007) 'Bolivia: Cubanos brindan 6 millones de consultas gratuitas en un año y medio', ALBA . Available on <www.alternativabolivariana.org/modules.php?name=News&file=article&sid=2269> (accessed October 2007).

37   Kirk and Erisman (2009).

38   Pan American Health Organisation (PAHO) (n.d.) *Bolivia: Health situation analysis and trends summary.* Available on <www.paho.org/English/DD/AIS/cp_068.htm> (accessed March 23, 2010).

39   M. Bolivia Rothe (2009) 'Salud gratuita: el desafío del proceso', *Le Monde Diplomatique, edición boliviana* (Nov.), 6.

40   H. Tejerina Silva, P. De Paepe, W. Soors, O. V. Lanza, M. C. Closon, P. Van Dessel and J. P. Unger, (2011) 'Revisiting health policy and the World Bank in Bolivia', *Global Social Policy* 11(1), 22–44.

41   La Prensa (2008) 'La UNESCO avala que Bolivia está libre de analfabetismo', *La Prensa*, December 21.

42   G. Guzmán (2007) 'Aproximaciones hacia una explicación de la "revolución democrática y cultural" en Bolivia', speech at the University of Pittsburgh. Available on <www.ucis.pitt.edu/clas/events/gap_conference/AproximacionesHaciaUnaExplicacion-Guzman.pdf> (accessed September 12, 2011).

43   A. Avila, Cuban head of literacy campaign, personal interview, June 16, 2009.

44   H. Bhola (1984) *The Cuban mass literacy campaign, 1961.* Paris: UNESCO.

45   Ministerio de Educación y Culturas (2008) 'Bolivia se declara libre de analfabetismo este sábado en la ciudad de Cochabamba.' Available on <www.minedu.gov.bo/minedu/showNews.do?newsId=1203> (accessed March 30, 2010).

46   Ministerio de Educación y Culturas (2006) 'Ya puedo leer. Yo sí puedo más', Cartilla de lectura. La Paz: Ministerio de Educación y Culturas, pp. 7, 16, 23.

47   M. Zuazo (2010) 'Los movimientos sociales en el poder? El gobierno del MAS en Bolivia', *Nueva Sociedad* 227 (May–June), 120–35.

48   B. Ayma, director, Bolivian literacy campaign, interview, August 1, 2009.

49   R. Dello Buono (2007) 'The redesign of Latin America: FTAA, MERCOSUR and ALBA', *Critical Sociology* 33(4), 767–74.

50   P. Bond (2006) 'Civil society on global governance: divergent analysis, strategy and tactics', *Voluntas* 17, 359–71.

51   N. Klein (2007) *The Shock Doctrine: The rise of disaster capitalism.* London: Allen Lane.

52   L. Henry, G. Mohan and H. Yanacopulos (2004) 'Networks as transnational agents of development', *Third World Quarterly* 25(5), 839–55.

53   Smith (2009).

54   A. Avila, Cuban head of literacy campaign, interview, June 16, 2009.

55   Government of Bolivia (2010) *World People's Conference on Climate Change and the Rights of Mother Earth.* Available on <http://cmpcc.org/> (accessed May 15, 2010).

56   Limited experience of this degree of civil society involvement exists at

the United Nations. See N. MacKeon (2009) *The United Nations and Civil Society: Legitimating global governance – whose voice?* London: Zed.

57 See N. Klein (2010) 'Bolivia's fight for survival can help save democracy too', *Guardian,* April 22. Available on <www.guardian.co.uk/commentisfree/cifamerica/2010/apr/22/how-bolivia-transformation-could-change-world> (accessed May 18, 2010).

58 N. Buxton (2010) 'People's conference model of inclusion offers only path forward on climate change', Transnational Institute. Available on <www.tni.org/article/peoples-conference-model-inclusion-offers-only-path-forward-climate-change> (accessed May 18, 2010).

9 THE PROMISE AND THE LIMITS OF A REVOLUTION IN DEMOCRACY

1 J. Stiglitz (2011) 'The IMF's change of heart', *Al Jazeera,* May 7. Available on <http://english.aljazeera.net/indepth/opinion/2011/05/2011571 2428956842.html> (accessed May 19, 2011).

2 G. Younge (2001) 'Democracy is no match for market power', *Guardian Weekly,* July 8, p. 19.

3 C. Douzinas (2011) 'In Greece, democracy is born', *Guardian Weekly,* June 24, p. 20. See also M. Carrión (2011) 'Camp Sol: Spain's 'indignant' give lessons in true democracy.' Available on <www.naomiklein.org/articles/2011/06/camp-sol-spains-indignant-give-lessons-true-democracy> (accessed June 4, 2011).

4 The mainstream media's role in the presentation of political processes of change is limited in that it often concentrates its efforts on the personality of Evo Morales himself, repeating clichés about his poor background.

5 B. de Sousa Santos (2010) *Refundación del estado en América Latina.* La Paz: Plural.

6 C. Arze and T. Kruse (2004) 'The consequences of neoliberal reform', *NACLA Report on the Americas* 38(3), 23–8.

7 From Y. Torrez, D. Ayo and J.-C. Velásquez (2007) 'Agenda de la Asamblea Constituyente', *Cuadernos de Diálogo y Deliberación.* La Paz: Corte Nacional Electoral.

8 J. de la Fuente Jeria (2010) 'El difícil parto de otra democracia: la asamblea constituyente de Bolivia', *Latin American Research Review,* special issue 'Living in actually existing democracies', pp. 5–26 (see p. 8).

9 In the field of international relations, care ethics is forcing authors to question the morality of what is in the 'national interest' and reconsider their obligations in search of global justice. See F. Robinson (1997) 'Globalizing care: ethics, feminist theory and international relations', *Alternatives* 22(1), 113–33.

10 J. Dunkerley (2007) 'Evo Morales, the "two Bolivias" and the

third Bolivian revolution', *Journal of Latin American Studies* 39(1), 133–66.

11 *Economist* (2006) 'Bolivia: enter the man in the stripy jumper', January 19. Available on <www.economist.com/node/5418173> (accessed August 25, 2011).

12 A. García Linera (2008) 'Empate catastrófico y punto de bifurcación', *Crítica y emancipación* 1(1), 23–33. Available on< http://bibliotecavirtual.clacso.org.ar/ar/libros/secret/CyE/cye2S1a.pdf> (accessed June 20, 2010).

13 P. Regalsky (2009) *Las paradojas del proceso constituyente boliviano.* Cochabamba: CENDA.

14 N. Postero (2011) 'The struggle to create a radical democracy in Bolivia', *Latin American Research Review*, special issue 'Living in actually existing democracies', pp. 59–78 (see p. 63).

15 B. Kohl and R. Bresnahan 2010) 'Bolivia under Morales: consolidating power, initiating decolonization', *Latin American Perspectives* 37(3), 5–17.

16 P. Stefanoni (2009) 'Reelección… ¿y después?' *Le Monde Diplomatique*, *edición boliviana* 20 (November), 3–4.

17 Bolivia Information Forum (BIF) (2011) 'To the brink, and back again', BIF Special Briefing. Available on <www.boliviainfoforum.org.uk/documents/71858759_BIF%20Briefing%20January%202011.pdf> (accessed August 12, 2011).

18 Associated Press (2011) 'Bolivia: Otro ministro renuncia por represión a indígenas', *El Nuevo Herald*, September 27.

19 P. Solón (2011) 'Carta de Pablo Solón al Presidente Evo Morales', September 28. Available on <www.cambioclimatico.org.bo/negint/092011/300911_1.pdf/> (accessed September 30, 2011).

20 So for example, coca growers and colonizadores support the road through TIPNIS precisely because it will allow them – as well as logging and hydrocarbons sector companies – to access new land.

21 H. Do Alto (2011) 'Un partido campesino en el poder. Una mirada sociológica del MAS boliviano', *Nueva Sociedad* 234, 95–111.

22 The vice-president's periodisation includes five main phases to the process of change explored in this book. See A. García Linera (2011) 'Las tensiones creativas de la revolución. La quinta fase del proceso de cambio', La Paz: Vice presidencia del estado.

23 K. Arkonada (2011) 'Tensiones y contradicciones del Proceso de Cambio en Bolivia', *Kaos en la Red*, July 3. Available on <www.kaosenlared.net/noticia/tensiones-contradicciones-proceso-cambio-bolivia> (accessed July 5, 2011).

24 A. Almaraz et al. (2011) 'Por la recuperación del proceso de cambio para el pueblo y con el pueblo', *Bolpress*, June 22. Available on <www.bolpress.com/art.php?Cod=2011062207> (accessed August 21, 2011).

25 Servicio de noticias ambientales (SENA) (2011) 'Estado del saneamiento de tierras', entrevista al ex-director de tierras Juan Carlos

Rojas. Bolpress, May 5. Available on <www.bolpress.com/art. php?Cod=2011050512> (accessed September 5, 2011).

26 Almaraz et al. (2011).

27 P. Regalsky (2011) 'Political process and the reconfiguration of the state in Bolivia', *Latin American Perspectives* 37(3), 35–50.

28 H. Do Alto and P. Stefanoni (2010) 'El MAS: las ambivalencias de la democracia corporativa', pp. 305–24 in L. A. García Orellana and F. L. García Yapur (eds) *Mutaciones del campo político en Bolivia*. La Paz: UNDP.

29 J. R. Webber, 2011) *From Rebellion to Reform in Bolivia*. Chicago, Ill.: Haymarket.

30 William Robinson has used this term to refer to a wide range of political manifestations of resistance such as the transnational indigenous movement, the immigrant rights movement in the United States, and the Bolivarian revolution in Venezuela, but the Bolivian process of change could well be part of his category. See W. Robinson (2008) *Latin America and Global Capitalism*. Baltimore, Md.: Johns Hopkins University Press, chs 5 and 6.

31 B. Miranda Espinoza (2011) 'La generación de 1990 guía a los indígenas en la caminata', *Página Siete,* August 17. Available on <www. paginasiete.bo/2011-08-17/Nacional/Destacados/3Esp00117.aspx> (accessed August 21, 2011).

INDEX